MW01200517

The Great Depression— How We Coped, Worked and Played

The Great Depression —
How We Coped,
Worked and Played

Life-Experience Stories
From the Carolinas' Piedmont

Edited by
Margaret G. Bigger

Illustrated by
Lexie Little Hill

ABB   A. Borough Books

ISBN 1-893597-04-0

Library of Congress Control Number: 2001132524

Printed in the United States of America

Illustrations by Lexie Little Hill

COVER PHOTO: The crowd at President Franklin D. Roosevelt's Green Pastures Rally in the new WPA-built Memorial Stadium in Charlotte, North Carolina, September 10, 1936. See pages 258-259. Photo by Jerre Caldwell Whitsett. From the H. Haywood Robbins Papers, Special Collections, UNC Charlotte Library.

ABB

A. Borough Books
P.O. Box 15391
Charlotte NC 28211

FOREWORD

The Great Depression tiptoed into the Carolina Piedmont well before the Stock Market crash of 1929. Cotton and tobacco farmers were growing more than the world market, still reeling from World War I, could consume; farm prices fell. Textiles, as well, grappled with eroding profits. Mill owners imposed "stretch-outs" that forced workers to tend more machines for less pay. Twenty-five textile mills across the Carolinas erupted in strikes in early 1929.

After the crash on October 24, 1929, things only got worse. Banks failed; 190 in NC alone during 1930 - 1933. Charlotte's First National Bank, which had just built the city's tallest skyscraper (it still stands in the first block of South Tryon Street), shut its doors never to reopen. Unemployment hit 25% nationally by 1932, with much worse figures in some sectors; nearly half of the 209,000 industrial workers in North Carolina lost their jobs.

Ironically, it seemed the poorer you were, the less you felt the Depression. "Modern" Carolinians had tended to look down on country folk who still hunted and grew all the food for their table. But now mill workers and white-collar city residents often sent their children to live with cousins back on the farm, knowing that they would at least have food to eat.

Carolinians voted overwhelmingly for Franklin Delano Roosevelt for President in 1932 over conservative Republican Herbert Hoover. Roosevelt won the election with only vague promises of change, but once in office, he moved quickly to shake up the US economy.

Roosevelt's New Deal stopped America's economic slide. Unemployment began to inch downward, farm prices stabilized. But the country's economy did not fully recover until World War II, when a hungry war machine primed by massive deficit spending put Americans back to work.

When Roosevelt died in April 1945 at his winter home in Warm Springs, Georgia, Carolinians turned out by the thousands to watch his funeral train chug up the Southern Railway mainline toward Washington. "Somber throngs jammed every crossing for blocks down the track. Women—and a few men—were sobbing," *The Charlotte Observer* reported.

In this book you'll hear some of that emotion. You'll meet Carolinians who weathered the Great Depression, feel the fear and the hard times, and share the triumph that came with just getting by. Read on!

Dr. Tom Hanchett, Historian
Levine Museum of the New South

Acknowledgements

In 1992, when Sally D. Robinson, the founding chairman of the Museum of the New South, requested me to ask senior citizens in my Shepherd's Center class to do an oral history project, I declined. I was teaching a Recalling Memories for Posterity writing course, and knew nothing about oral history. The fledgling museum at that time had no building, just an office, where they were collecting oral history. Sally Robinson persisted, and within a short time, we were doing a joint project sponsored by The University of North Carolina's Special Collections Department, the Museum of the New South, Shepherd's Center of Charlotte, and Central Piedmont Community College's Continuing Education Department. The Museum's curator of education and programs, Amy Swisher, taught class members to interview one another on audio tapes, during the same six weeks that they were writing their stories for a photocopied booklet, *The Great Depression: We Survived*. Although the authors lived in the Charlotte area, many of them had grown up in other states.

Because the Museum focuses on the Piedmont of the Carolinas, we began again in 1999, seeking stories only from people who spent the Depression in this region. We held taping sessions and writing workshops and did numerous interviews. A few authors had Depression memories in our original booklet or other publications. Through word-of-mouth, others found us and submitted their stories.

I am especially grateful to Dr. Tom Hanchett, Historian, Dr. Brenden Martin, past Historian, and Heath Lee, past Director of Education, as well as Emily F. Zimmern, Executive Director, and the Board of Directors of the new Levine Museum of the New South.

Although too young to have Great Depression stories of their own, these people introduced me to men and women who did: Dot Siler, Thereasea Clark Elder, Adele and Tom Pope, Dorothy Vaughn, Sharon Ward, Nina Gosnell, Dennis Fowler, Mary Ann Aiken, Sue Brown, W.G. (Tony) Teachey, Judy Dodge, Meredith Galvin, Ann Ross Liles, Ann Kugler, Kathy Moss, Fann Montague, Dan Morill, Nancy Blood, Becky Derrick, Judy Brown, Beth Klosky, Josephine Jennings, Dorothea Critz, Molly Rawls and Jane Pyle.

And a hearty "thank you" to those who helped gather facts and photos: W. Hugh Harkey, Jr., local historian, Rosemary Lands, and Valerie Burnie, Carolina Room, Public Library of Charlotte and Mecklenburg County, Holt Kornegay, Franklin County Library, Robin Copp, South Caroliniana Library, University of South Carolina, Steve Tuttle, South Carolina Department of Archives and History, Eddie Stubbs, WSM Radio, Nashville, Robin Brabham and Marilyn Schuster, Special Collections Department, University of North Carolina at Charlotte, John Williams, Emery Wister, Eva Torrence Whitsett, Barbara W. Edwards, Elizabeth W. Bridges and Jerre W. Snider.

To the many others who told brief anecdotes or helped with background information, I extend my deep appreciation.

CONTENTS

HOW WE COPED

HOW OTHERS COPED

HOW WE WORKED

HOW OTHERS WORKED

HOW WE PLAYED

HOW OTHERS PLAYED

WHEN PROHIBITION AND THE
DEPRESSION COINCIDED

WHAT WAS *REALLY* IMPORTANT

APPENDIX

HOW WE COPED

Family, friends and faith were the ties that bound people together and gave them hope in those desperate times, according to these Carolinians who record history from their own experience.

NORTH CAROLINA

An Apple a Day Didn't Keep the Pain Away
by
Julia Neal Sykes
Co-Author with Oscar DePriest Hand, Sr. of
Footprints on the Rough Side of the Mountain

What's a 10-year-old girl to do? My stomach is massaging my backbone; intestines growling from being caught in the middle. Hunger pains are so overwhelming, I blot out the sound of my mom's voice saying, "Don't go near the Brown's orchard." But those golden apples seem to be beckoning me: "Come! Taste! Enjoy!"

It was 1933, and we were poor black sharecroppers—eight children, Mom and Dad. Victims of a trickle-down effect of the Depression, we, the Clarence Neal family, had just moved to the Brown farm in the Steele Creek area of Mecklenburg County. And although I was too young to realize why things had gone sour, we had been introduced to hard times.

This farm was owned by a bachelor son, old-maid daughter and their mother. Everything was different from our life on Ben Weathers' farm a few miles away. I guess Mr. Brown had to tighten the screws on what his tenants could do in order to make up for his losses because of the economy. I mean he was such a tightwad he squeaked when he walked.

No longer did we have the freedom to grow and raise things and live off the land. Everything went to the Brown family. We learned what it meant to be hungry. Mostly, we ate what we called "chunk-up" (cornbread/buttermilk) and mush made from cornmeal, leaves from cabbages (we couldn't wait for the heads to form), creasy greens (which grew wild) and, at times, some pole beans, corn or even a chicken, pilfered by my sisters from the Browns.

I believe all of us would have become thieves had we stayed there longer. However, I learned my lesson about stealing the hard way, a very *painful* way.

The trees in the Browns' orchard were always laden with fruit during the season. But he'd given orders for us not to set foot over there. We had to go to the "big house" to pump water from their well, which was near the orchard.

On that fateful day when Mom sent me to get water, it just seemed impossible for me to resist those beautiful, delicious golden apples. When I stared at a tree so full that the limbs were almost touching the ground, I had a tug-of-war with my conscience: "I'll get caught. Mom will kill me! Girl, you can't do it. But I'm so hungry! I can hide out in the barn and eat them. They'll never miss a few apples."

Temptation possessed me. I gave in to it. Surely, I could crawl under the tree without anyone seeing me.

I got on my stomach and slithered inch by inch up under the tree, heart pounding so loud it was deafening. When I reached up and wrapped my fingers around an apple, I was so nervous I lost my balance—crashing down on a small bush. It broke from the impact, causing splinters to go from the inside fat part of my hand all the way through to the outside. Oh, holy cow! The pain was so excruciating, I forgot about the apples and hightailed it out of there, forgetting the water bucket.

I felt like running past our house. But where? Tears were burning my face. I needed my mom to make the pain go away, so I had to tell her the truth. Lying was no option. I ran inside.

"What happened? What on earth went wrong at the well? Where is the water bucket?" she rattled off in rapid succession.

I had to confess, although I was afraid she was going to add to my suffering by using her switch on my behind for disobeying her. Thank God she didn't!

Her only concern was getting the splinters out of my hand. She started probing with a needle. I couldn't bear it, so Mom used one of her old home remedies. She wrapped a piece of fatback meat on it and let it stay overnight. The next morning, pus was in the wound. Mom began squeezing my hand until the splinters floated out. I nearly passed out.

After that painful ordeal, I vowed to myself that I would never steal anything else, no matter how hungry I got.

The Brown clan made it extremely difficult to keep that vow, as the years on their farm rolled by and we barely existed.

From her window, Mother Brown would patrol the big walnut tree out front. One day, my innocent baby sister, Lovie, picked up some walnuts and was caught red-handed. Old lady Brown waddled to the door and yelled, "Honey, if you hull the walnuts, you can have half, and I'll keep half."

Lovie dropped those walnuts and kept walking, never looking back.

Bravo for her!

Potatoes and Tears
by
Julia Neal Sykes
Co-Author with Oscar DePriest Hand, Sr. of
Footprints on the Rough Side of the Mountain

Acres and acres of sweet potatoes! It seemed as though there was no end of the fields or the potatoes, and we had to pick them all! I would pick up a potato and drop a tear. I didn't want to do this the rest of my life, and I didn't want to miss school.

Neither of my parents had a formal education. But my father, Clarence Neal, had learned to read in Sunday school. He had the potential of being a great man, if he had been given the opportunity to receive formal training. But, in spite of that, he knew how to use his hands to build things. When I was knee high to a duck, he cut strips from a white oak tree to make chair bottoms and baskets for cotton and for catching fish. A self-taught carpenter and painter, he could well have been called "Mr. Fix It." In short, Dad was very resourceful in making our lives—and those of our neighbors—better than circumstances predicted.

A homemaker, my mother Mary, did all the house chores of a woman of her day, made our clothes and managed what little money and resources we had. She could really stretch a dollar! And she bore 11 children, eight of whom survived: David, Annie Lee, Clarence, Jr., Blandina, Carrie Bell, me and then John and Lovie.

While we were sharecropping in Mecklenburg County, those of us old enough attended the three-room Grier School in the Steele Creek area. Three teachers ran the school, including our principal, Mr. G.E. McKeithan. They did their best to teach us the three Rs with few books or supplies, and we got a good foundation. Mr.

McKeithan, who lived in Charlotte, would bring his saxophone and some individual reeds (mouthpieces) so he could teach some older students to play the instrument. Everyone could see extreme pride on the faces of the ones he allowed to accompany the Glee Club.

We had to walk to school in all kinds of weather and carried our lunch in a lard bucket. Our favorite treat was a sweet pastry Mom made that we called a "sticky." In the summertime, we went barefoot, but we needed shoes for school.

One time, while on the Brown farm, I had to stay home because I had none. Though devastated, I was brave enough to write a letter to Mr. McKeithan telling him of my plight. I knew he had brought shoes to some other children, and sure enough, he found some for me. He brought several pairs of shoes that he'd gotten from people in Charlotte. I squeezed my foot into a pair of little-old-lady's medium heel shoes. I could hardly walk in those tight shoes, but I had no choice.

At Glee Club practice one day, my feet hurt so badly, I started sweating profusely, but I didn't dare ask to sit down. As usual, Mr. McKeithan had us standing for hours. I really began to feel sick and finally slumped over. He let me sit down. I eased my aching free out of those shoes as fast as I could. But I never let anybody know those ugly toe-crushers were "killing" my feet

I was about 12 when we moved to North Belmont in 1937. For the first time in our lives, Carrie Bell, John and I rode a school bus. Students were bused in from Mt. Holly, Lowell, Cramerton, McAdenville, Neely's Grove, Belmont and South Gastonia to the only black high school in the area, Reid School in the Booger Town community.

Although the parents were not educated, they always tried to create a climate wherein education became a priority. That certainly was true of my mother and father, who were supportive and encouraging. With the prevailing separate but unequal situation in the county-wide school system, teachers and parents found ways to raise funds for what few materials they had. They sold a lot of candy and had fish fries on Saturday nights. By the time we were enrolled, they had the use of buses that were worn out after being used by the white schools. Those buses broke down frequently and were unheated.

Carrie Bell was the first in our family to finish high school. I was next. That set a precedent for the Neal family. From then on, the rest of the children, grandchildren, great-grandchildren and so on, went to college or furthered their education in some training institution.

Our dad was proud of his family. He always told us, "Be your best, no matter what the endeavor." He sang his praise for every one of us, especially when he lost his sight. He would sit for hours talking about each one of us being the best at whatever he or she was doing.

The genes of Mary and Clarence Neal produced a nurse, doctor, lawyer, teachers, artists, craftspeople, a mortician, system analyst manager, hotel manager, educational consultant, lab technician, recreational manager, social worker, counselor, computer technologist, astronaut trainee, political scientist, and client support specialist as well as government workers, business managers, banking personnel, entrepreneurs, great cooks like Mom and, yes, builders, like Dad. The Neal legacy is like the Energizer Bunny, it goes on and on.

When I was in that sweet potato field dropping a tear for every potato I picked up, I had a dream of being a teacher. After four years at Fayetteville State, I realized that dream.

Handouts? Never!
by
Harvey Michael

Bags and bags of greens! And we were each given a bag to take home. After the dismissal bell had run at Belmont Central that day, our teacher had asked some of us to follow her to another room on a lower level of the building. That's where they doled out the greens — kale, I think.

I couldn't comprehend why someone was giving food to us, but I took it and hurried off with my friends back to the Eagle Mill village.

At home, my dad asked where it came from. When I told him, I was surprised at his reaction. He snatched that bag of greens, took it across the yard to the chicken lot and dumped it over the fence! "We'll not take handouts from the government!" he shouted. "As long as I can work, I'll feed my family!"

I didn't understand his actions then, but I do now. Some have said such an attitude is stupid. After all, that's why government exists: to take care of us, especially when we are in need. True. But my father, George Michael, saw beyond that and stubbornly asserted his own priorities. Hard work would put food on the table and leave intact our self respect and dignity.

The Great Depression was the medium of my childhood. In my developing awareness while growing up on the red clay hillside above the Eagle Mill in Belmont, I assumed that the conditions of my life were universal.

I was never hungry for very long. We grew our food in our garden or in the fields surrounding the mill village which was my universe. Penny, our Jersey cow, provided milk and butter; our chickens, eggs, and our pigs grew into hogs on "shorts" and slop.

Thrift and hard work made it possible for us to make ends meet. We were sheltered in a mill house, clothed in hand-me-downs, scrubbed clean with Octagon soap and marched to church on Sundays. It was an exhilarating world full of things to be discovered and enjoyed.

At the end of my father's life, he demonstrated those qualities that made him and my mother survivors.

In his 80s, he was confined to the hospital. In pain and restricted by the tubes that were part of his treatment, he was the "good patient." He did not want to "bother the nurses" with his needs. I fought back tears as I sat with him one day.

"Everything will be all right, Son," he said. He then clenched his teeth and repeated what I had heard often in those early years: "We just have to tough it out."

He did.

We all did.

My Saving Grace: Cooking
by
Alberta Black Harris

"Nobody knows the trouble I've seen..." our school glee club sang with trained blended voices. As I was singing, I was excited about graduating from the seventh grade at Huntersville's Rosenwald School. I was 18 years old that year, 1929, and none of the white folks in our town could possibly know the trouble I and my classmates had seen even before the Great Depression.

Some of the others had taken as long as I did to graduate, but not because we were dumb. Whenever we had to work in the fields or had no shoes or if the creek overflowed along the bottom land, we couldn't get there. And, for my race, public school in Huntersville ended at seventh grade. A few of my classmates would

18

be going on to Second Ward High School in Charlotte or to Barber-Scotia in Concord, but that took money. I cried and Mama cried. "If I could send you, I would," she said through her tears. For me, formal education would have to wait until Central Piedmont Community College offered a high school completion program. It was a struggle, but I persevered to complete those five years as a mature adult.

We were tenant farmers, and our troubles started when my father, Jake Black had a stroke and died in 1921. My oldest brother was 19. I was 10 and the only girl of seven children. My mother, Mattie Park Black, was carrying my baby brother, who was born a month after Daddy died.

Soon after we buried him, a man from a store in Huntersville came and took our cows, mules and pigs. Daddy's coffin had come from his store. I never knew how much we owed, but that man left us with no source of food or livelihood.

At that time, we were living in the Black Jack area near Concord. All we could do was pick up the gleanings after the corn had been harvested. The cost of grinding it at the mill was a portion of the cornmeal. That was all we had. Literally. Even after an aunt moved us to an empty shack on the Bradford farm near Huntersville, we had little more than cornbread that first year. Because we had no cow, we went from neighbor to neighbor to "borrow" enough milk to make the bread. People helped out with what they had. Sometimes, they gave us some liver mush or some sausage or a few vegetables. We took cornbread patties to school for lunch, and I was embarrassed to let the others see that was all I had. Yet, even in those hard times, no one was stealing—except a watermelon now and then. Everybody did that.

That spring, we moved to the Beatty farm off the Huntersville Poplar Tent Road to sharecrop. Gus Sherrill, a friend of Papa's, showed my brothers how to work a farm and the younger boys how to cut wood for cooking. Trees were plentiful then, and we could have all the wood we needed. All of us old enough to walk learned how to pick cotton. Mama helped Mrs. Beatty at the house and whenever the washing was done.

Usually, we went to church only in the summer, after getting new clothes. That year, we didn't get to go. By harvest, there was cash from only two bales that was not owed. With that, Mama bought us all shoes. We needed coats, but couldn't afford them.

Often, those shoes didn't last until the next harvest. One March was particularly cold, and my shoes had worn out. Still, I was out barefooted, carrying fertilizer and cotton seed to my brothers in the field.

Mrs. Beatty had prissy little girls. One of them had the prettiest dress with colorful appliques. My mother got some un-bleached domestic cloth and asked her to make me one for church. That was my favorite dress. I wore it every Sunday. It was washed so many times, it bleached out white. Later, Mama learned to cut patterns out of newspapers and make all our clothes. She became a good seamstress and made my panties and slips out of feed sacks. The next summer, she made two dresses for me.

Another devastating year was the one when cotton was three cents a pound and weather conditions caused the cotton to be late opening. We had to pull the bolls off the plant and sit around at night to crack them open. We couldn't get enough to fill a wagon to take to market. And one-third of next-to-nothing earned us a pathetic amount to get through the next year.

When I was a little older, I picked berries to sell by the quart (strawberries at ten cents; blackberries, five cents). Finally, I had enough to buy a dress and pretty little hat I had seen upstairs at the general store.

At 11, I started cooking. At first, my brothers teased me, but then they admitted that they liked what I fixed. Little by little, we had more foods to prepare after we had raised a garden. Mother did a lot of canning, too, in half-gallon jars. Every year, we picked two tin tubs full of blackberries in one day for her to can.

Each fall, Mother would tear the pages from every old book she could find and paste them on the walls over the cracks to keep winter winds out. I would go around the room, looking for recipes and trying those with the ingredients we could get. There were many days when we had only one. That is, if we had turnip greens or a pot of peas, that's all we had.

Eventually, Mother let me stay home to fix the midday meal, while she and the boys worked in the fields. Of course, I had to clean up and do other household chores, so I'd usually get out to help them about 4:30 p.m.

We moved every couple of years to share crop at a different farm in the area. Again and again, we were disappointed to find that, somehow, we owed the landowner most of what we earned, when it came time to "settle up."

Before I finished the seventh grade, I was cooking in people's homes on the mill hill for $2.50 a week. From time to time, I'd go to help do a big wash on a washboard for 75 cents. Mother and my brothers did odd jobs, too—whatever we could find. Our family actually fared better during the Depression than in the eight years before it began.

After graduation, I continued working in homes. Later, I joined other girls and women who rode the train every Monday to Mooresville, where we could earn $2.50 plus room and board. On Fridays, we'd come back home.

About the only entertainment then was baseball. Huntersville had a black team and a white one, which occasionally played one another. If a game was in town on a Saturday, stores would close so everybody could go. The black team's star was Isaac Harris. Although Ike was the regular catcher, he could pitch, too, and people would come from miles around to see him. If things had been as they are today, he probably would have played for a major league team. He was so good that other teams would hire him when he didn't have a Huntersville game.

One Saturday, Ike was having terrible cramps. He said it was from the food his brother's girlfriend had cooked. Ike called me over and handed me some money. "Would you go buy a steak and cook it for me?"

I said I would. I fixed him a good meal with hot homemade biscuits and gravy. That night, he began to talk of marriage.

On September 21, 1933, we were married at the court house. Both of Ike's parents were dead, so we would share a house and kitchen with another couple. But both of us were bringing in income and could save to fix up his dad's house when the estate was settled. At the time, he was helping out on a farm for 50 cents a day.

I laughed and told Ike that all he wanted was someone to keep him fed, and he got a cook very cheap. He didn't pay but $2.50 for me.

He really did get a bargain. I'm still cooking for that kind man.

His Date, My Fate
by
Alberta Black Harris

"How many children did you have?" a lady asked me recently.

"I don't know," I said.

She gave me a strange look and laughed nervously.

It's not easy to explain. But when I was pregnant with my first child in 1934, Dr. Tom Craven, our family doctor, was in the Army Reserves and had to leave for a while that summer. His substitute worked at the Huntersville TB sanatorium.

After a normal pregnancy, I went into labor on a Saturday.

My husband Ike had a baseball game to play that day. He was winding up for a pitch when his friend tapped him on the shoulder to tell him I was ready to deliver. Ike dropped the ball and sprinted more than a mile down the road to be with me.

The doctor came and gave me a shot to slow the pain and left. He seemed to be in a hurry. He came back later that night, gave me another shot and rushed out to his automobile, where his girlfriend was waiting.

Ike went to get an older woman, Ola Ross, who said she would help me when I was ready to give birth. Ola stayed all night, but I slept like a log. "Something's wrong," she said the next morning and started giving me hot tea.

She had responsibilities at her church and had to leave, but the young blond-haired doctor came again. He was still courting, for his date was in the car. He saw that I was not ready and left.

At nightfall, he came back to check on me. My pains were not yet five minutes apart, but he started giving me something to make them come hard. He didn't give me anything to open me up. He just started pulling me, pulling me across the bed. I was hurting so bad I could hardly stand it. He pulled so hard, my back just gave away. "I'd just rather die," I cried.

The doctor started taking the baby, without giving me time to open up. "I'm not trying to save her," he said. "I'm trying to save you."

Meanwhile his girlfriend was waiting in his car.

That man scraped me all the way to my rectum and tore me up inside. He didn't put a stitch in me. Meanwhile, he had Ola pulling me under the arms, and another friend pouring ether onto a gauze.

The ether was supposed to go over my nose, but it was spilling into my left eye and burned the skin around it. It was burning like hot grease. My eye felt afire.

My daughter's head was a ball of blood, and that doctor nearly broke her neck pulling her out.

A month after Dorothy Lee was born, I ended up in the hospital. Dr. Kennedy, who treated me, said, "The doctor you had should be sued for the condition he left you in."

22

Dr. Kennedy told me that the only reason he didn't perform a hysterectomy was because I was so young and would want to have more children.

I was so weak and run down, my mother took me home. I still couldn't see out of my left eye, which was very sore. Dorothy Lee's head was so bruised that it still looked like a ball of blood. Her neck showed an injury from the instrument the doctor had used.

Alberta and Dorothy Lee Harris
1943

Much later, I got pregnant again. I kept him five months. Every two or three months after that I got pregnant. After a while I lost count, as I lost child after child.

They told me I had tumors in the mouth of the womb and those would swell, causing miscarriages. More than once, I nearly bled to death. All the while, I was praying to have another healthy baby.

For years, that went on until another doctor, a specialist, began giving me treatments. Just before the last treatment, I became pregnant and had another miscarriage. The next time, I was able to go to full term, but I was in pain all the time.

After nine years of trauma and nine months of misery, Spencer Isaac Harris was my gift from God.

Bum Leg, Bad Breaks — Some Good Ones, Too!
by
Marvin R. Sechler

If I hadn't messed my leg up when I was playing ball, we may never have known what was wrong with my dad. I was about 9 years old when he took me to Landis to let a colored doctor look at me.

Dr. Levi Gibson, who was well respected in the community,

recommended that I go to Charlotte to see a specialist, but he was interested in my father's ailment, too. Dad told him he had been treated for Bright's disease for five years.

"Man, you don't have Bright's disease," the kindly doctor said. "I can look at you and tell you have a kidney stone."

He told my father to go to Charlotte to get an x-ray.

We lived in the Atwell Township in Rowan County, five miles from China Grove and five miles from Landis, with no hard-surface roads in any direction and no electricity.

Not long after that, my father cranked his 1917 Model T and headed for Charlotte, a long drive back then. Sure enough, the x-rays showed large kidney stones in both kidneys. He was told, "You might live one or two days—or five years."

Five years later, after awful suffering, he died on June 15, 1929.

Calvin Burgess Sechler left eleven living children: three daughters by his first wife and eight children by my mother, Carrie Melissa Sechler. Almost 14, I was the oldest son. Our baby brother, Hugh, was nine months old.

Neighbors helped out when they could, and somehow our family kept up the farm. Dad had no insurance, but at least the farm was paid for.

At first, I was still going to Deaton School. I had to get up at 4:30 a.m. to milk the cows and run the milk through a separator. Then I walked two miles to school, rain or shine. If it was my turn to start the fire in the pot-bellied stove, I'd have to be there earlier. After school, we'd all help in the fields. During cotton season, everyone got a break to get the crop in.

Our family grew some cotton, but wheat was the biggest crop in Rowan County. We raised wheat and also corn, oats, barley, hay, sweet potatoes and everything we ate. And we had cows, hogs and chickens.

Among my jobs was to crank the old Fordson tractor. It could kick hard enough to break a man's arm, but we needed it for plowing and hauling, although we also had four mules. Kerosene for the tractor cost eight-to-ten cents a gallon.

When it was time to take the cotton to the gin, we'd get up at 2 a.m. to ride the wagon pulled by mules to the gin in Landis. It was only five miles, but on that unpaved road, it felt like your whole insides were coming out. We'd get there by daylight, but the line would be so long it might be dinner time before it was our turn. Not many people had trucks then, just wagons. The gin would run 100 to 110 bales a day.

Uncle Charlie Simpson, my mother's sister's husband, usually drove the wagon. Several years he worked shares on our farm. One year, he could get only $28 for a 500-pound bale, if he sold the seeds separately.

Washday was also a long day. We had no running water, so we would have to get up early to draw from the two wells and haul buckets of water to the three washpots and build fires under them. The females did most of the washing, but everybody helped out.

At hog-killing time, neighbors came to help. We, in turn, would go help them. That's how we survived, by helping one another. Neighbors assisted with the threshing, too.

We ate a lot of rabbits and squirrels. My brothers and I killed them with shotguns. That was good eating—better than chickens, when chickens tasted better than they do now.

A couple of stores bought eggs from Mother, but they went to 7 cents a dozen, and she had to trade it out in groceries or feed.

To make ends meet, Mother sold the biggest cow for only $18. The meat market man came out and took it to the woods, where he killed, hung and dressed it.

Some time after I finished school, I was having so much trouble with my leg that I had to have an operation. My leg got so twisted at the ankle that I couldn't walk on it. I wore a brace, which was very expensive, according to our mother ($12 to $15, which was a lot then). At the Eye, Ear, Nose and Throat Hospital in Charlotte, a doctor cut under my ankle on each side, stood my foot up on edge and put a cast on it. Had I not had crutches, I would have been walking on the side of my foot. When the cast came off six weeks later, my foot started flopping, but it eventually got better. The leg never grew or fully developed after that. Dr. Alonzo Myers, who operated, said, "Better get a good education. You'll never be able to lift anything."

Deaton School, with two teachers, had only seven grades, and I was needed on the farm. But I wish that doctor could have seen how much I've lifted over time.

I was in my early 20s, when Ed Johnson at Cannon Mills in Cabarrus County hired 60 of us for two weeks before Christmas. We were put to work washing windows and blowing off looms. Then we were all laid off.

My friend Mitch Garver and I went back and reapplied. Mitch worked in the harness department, tying up harnesses for looms. I was hired to shellac the harnesses to make them strong. I couldn't take the odor and the mess and asked for another task.

"If you'll go on second shift," Mr. Johnson said, "You'll learn how to weave."

I worked there ten years on and off — ran every loom in the #6 Weave Room, making towels, bath mats and sheets.

Twelve days after Japan bombed Pearl Harbor, I married Elizabeth Walkup, who was my wife for 58 years.

The Army turned me down because of my leg injury, but I helped the war effort by working in the Newport News shipyard.

Like I said, I wish that doctor could have seen me work.

Mooing In the Night
by
Lois Moore Yandle
Author of *Spirit of a Proud People*

One of the most treasured animals at our house was Daddy's cow. Yes, we had chickens and a goat (for a little while), too. The chickens provided eggs and meat. The goat, trouble. He was forever getting loose. One time he ran away and was headed up the railroad tracks far from our house when someone caught him. Another time, he ate some of the laundry hanging on the line. Mama was relieved to see him sold.

But the cow, during the Depression, not only furnished milk for the Joe and Madeline Moore family, she was a source of income. My mother's butter and buttermilk were sought after by many of our neighbors from the Highland #3 mill village in North Charlotte. If money were not available, they would use the barter system.

Caring for the cow was a family job. My job was to help mix the feed and then fan the flies that gathered around as Daddy or Mama would milk. I preferred feeding the chickens and gathering eggs, for the cow barn was always dirty, smelly and full of all kinds of creatures that girls do not care for.

Mama took charge over the milk. It had to be strained through a very clean and fine cloth to be stored in the ice box. We drank whatever we wanted, but the remainder was left in the box until there was enough to partially fill the churn, which Mama set on the hearth so the milk would clabber (turn sour and thicken). When it was ready, we all took turns at churning. It seemed to take forever for the butter to form on the top, but it finally did and Mama took over.

26

She would scoop out the butter, then begin to knead out the milk, adding a little salt along the way. She had no recipe; it just came naturally to her. When she was satisfied with the look and taste of it, the butter was put into wooden molds with a flower print.

Bedtime came early in our village, so we were all asleep one night when about 11 p.m. there came a pounding at our front door that would wake up the dead. Ever been aroused from a sound sleep, then tried to get clothes on in a great hurry? Well, everyone in the house was really scared, not knowing who was banging.

Finally Daddy got to the door and found his brother John ready to start pounding again. "Joe," he said, almost breathless, "Your cow has broken out of the cow lot and is under our house bawling her head off!"

Daddy's mouth dropped open.

"How she got so far under the house is a mystery to me. She is so far under the floor that she's wedged in too tight to help herself." John said as they took off in the direction of the pathetic animal.

You can imagine what a stir this caused in the neighborhood. Lights came on and close friends began to come outside to see what the commotion was about and lend a hand. Daddy rushed to the barn for a rope. Some of our cousins crawled under the house with Daddy to help pull her out. This took some doing, because the poor old cow was so scared, mooing and bawling, no doubt wondering what was happening to her.

Uncle John's house had high pillars in the front with no underpinning. The farther back they all struggled, the lower the flooring was until the back of the house was almost on the ground. It took quite some time to get the cow close enough to the front that she could help herself.

Of course, this was the talk of the neighborhood for the next week, and I am sure Daddy and Uncle John took some ribbing by their friends. It was exciting to all of us, even though we felt sorry for the poor animal.

Meanwhile, our cow was extremely happy to be back in her barn. And I didn't even mind fixing her feed and swatting the flies—for the next few days.

Raised by the Community
by
William Harold Montgomery

My brother died before I knew him. My mother passed in 1930 when I was 5. My dad, Allen Montgomery, became mother and father to me and my younger sisters Emma and Catherine. They called me "Jake."

Daddy worked long hours in the Myers Park section of Charlotte doing yard work or whatever he could. Then he had to walk the five to six miles back to the Biddleville section, where we lived in one rental house after another (on Cemetery Street, Fairmont Avenue, Solomon Street and Booker Avenue). Sometimes, he'd bring meals home from the families he worked for. Other times, he would cook for us.

All three of us learned early how to do the wash, clean house and cook simple things.

Some evenings when we lived on Cemetery Street, I could walk down the block and hear what people were having for supper. Boiling black-eyed peas would have their pan tops jumping. Johnson C. Smith University had a field of black-eyed peas nearby.

One of the houses we rented was so old and dilapidated that I could look through the roof and count the stars.

Rent was usually collected on Monday morning. If a family couldn't pay, their furniture would be put out on the street the next day. The landlords were more lenient in the winter. They knew that, if a house were left empty, people would come at night and cut it into firewood to keep warm. The next morning, there might be only a chimney standing.

Near Biddleville Elementary, there was a Seaboard Railroad bridge. When a train with coal cars came by, we could see people —old and young—out there, climbing on top of those cars, pitching coal out to women with sacks or their kids with wheelbarrows and wagons.

But I didn't know we were poor. When everybody was poor, it didn't matter that much. Sadness was not in play then. People seemed happier—and kinder. So many people helped raise me. I ate at everybody's house in the neighborhood at one time or another. Even the bootleggers were nice to me. A lady and her husband who had no kids took a liking to my sister Emma and often had her to spend the night, just about adopted her. A younger widow did the same for my little sister Catherine.

I often stayed at the Gormley's house in the evening until Daddy could stop by to get me on his way home. I really liked being there, as I was friends with several of their children. They had good food, electric lights and a radio!

Not many people had electricity in our area. They used kerosene lanterns. Those who lived "down under the hill," as we referred to a certain section, used springs, pumps, outhouses and ice boxes, because they had no running water either. The ice boxes usually sat on their back porches. We could tell when someone had wrapped fish in a newspaper and stuck them in the ice box, because cats would come meowing, meowing.

Different relatives took me in from time to time. Occasionally we visited my grandparents, who lived a long walking distance away, but they had so many grandchildren (Daddy's brother had 13 children; his sister, 7) that we were only three among the many. Sometimes, I stayed with my aunt in a house owned by a relative by marriage, whom we called Grandpa K. He also lived there with his son, his grandson and great-grandson.

The family of one of my friends had a large piece of land just outside of Biddleville with pigs and chickens. He and I worked together at Five Points Soda Shop and the grocery store across the street. When I helped them pick cotton, his mother would fry me some chicken.

I worked lots of different jobs: delivered newspapers and made deliveries for a drug store and later a shoe shop. Usually, I walked wherever I needed to go until a friend, J.C. Williams, and I found some bicycle parts and built a bike. We rode each other across town to the Camp Greene section where we cleaned up a drive-in's curb lot and a barber shop. I also shined shoes there part-time.

We had fun, too.

On Fridays, Biddleville Elementary gave out bargain tickets to the Grand Theater. That plus a nickel more would get us in, and we could stay until it closed. If my friends and I had sold fruit jars, milk bottles or scrap iron that week, we would have enough for drinks and popcorn for a really good time. But if the movie had been a really scary one and I had to walk home alone down our unlighted street after dark, the neighbors would hear me yell, "Hey, this Jake. If I stop talking, come see about me!"

Daddy had been a good baseball player, so everybody encouraged me to play, too. Sometimes we made a ball out of a rock wound with twine. We'd hit it with a broomstick until the twine wore off. If we didn't have a ball, we would use a tin can until it bent out of shape or went too far under a house to retrieve.

At West Charlotte High, I enjoyed playing football and basketball, too. When Johnson C. Smith was playing football, we would do anything to get in to watch, even crawl under the fence.

On Sundays, a friend and I liked to walk out to Mount Holly (a good ten miles or so). In a particular patch of woods, there were pipe-covered cables. We would climb a nearby tree, hop onto the pipe, slide along the slope and jump down running.

We street kids didn't go to church much, but one day when we were playing in a field, a fine Christian woman, Ms. Ionia Shute, rounded us all up and took us to a Bible study at Biddleville Presbyterian Church. We went frequently to learn about Jesus and the books of the Bible.

When I was in my mid-teens, Daddy took off for Washington. We called it "going up the road" or "going North," where there were better job opportunities. Back then, when children's mothers died, fathers often put the kids in an orphanage. Daddy never did that. But when he left, I was completely on my own. Of course, I worked wherever I could, but my aunt couldn't afford to keep me up and I was embarrassed by my raggedy clothes, so I quit school my sophomore year and worked at the air base.

It was no big deal. In our neighborhood, if you finished high school, that was great, but unusual. Only the children of those who "lived high on the hog" (preachers, brickmasons, undertakers, teachers) went to college.

One of my former teachers, Ms. Cecilia Jackson, saw me hanging around the school yard talking to girls the last day of that school year. "Do me a favor," she said. "If I see that you get promoted, will you promise me that you will stay in school and graduate?"

We both made good on that bargain.

After World II, I attended Johnson C. Smith University on the G.I. Bill. When I crawled under the fence years before, I certainly did not imagine that I would ever be enrolled there.

Unfortunately, I didn't stay. Not long after that, I was working as a "red cap" at the bus station, when Ms. Shute walked up to me. "You can do better than this," she said in a motherly tone. "You were smart in school."

I knew some people who worked there, so I walked across the street to Charlotte's Main Post Office and took the postal exam. I was surprised that I wasn't called immediately, but some years later, they did hire me.

Thanks to Ms. Jackson and Ms. Shute and the community that raised me, I finally had a satisfying career as a postal worker.

Hard Times Come Again No More
From This Red Clay Hillside
The Eagle 1924 - 1950
by
Bruce Graham

Jim Lane was the first black man hired by the Eagle Mill in 1924. At that time, blacks were not hired to work inside the mill. Jim Lane was hired only to deliver coal and cord wood to the homes of the employees. His son, Alan, helped him deliver in his two-horse wagon. They lived in Lane Hollow, a short distance northeast of the Eagle Village in Belmont.

The coal was brought to the coal chute at the mill by train, nine or ten carloads at a time. Uncle Jim, as he was referred to by the white people at the Eagle, and Alan would shovel tons of coal from the chute to deliver to families who heated with coal.

Some families cooked on wood stoves, and Uncle Jim and Alan would deliver wood in the wagon. It was brought to a cord wood pile at the top of the hill by farmers in the surrounding countryside who had cut trees from their property with a cross-cut saw and cut them in four-foot pieces with an ax.

31

My brothers, Jake and Albert Graham, Charlie McClain and A.C. Stowe were the next blacks hired at the mill. They worked in maintenance. It was their job to go over to the village and clean out septic tanks that were full or giving trouble. There were no sewage lines. They would come, wearing knee-high rubber boots, with shovel and a wheelbarrow and dispose of the waste by burying it.

All of these men also unloaded the cotton bales from the boxcars that brought it up the switch track to the mill. When I first went to work in 1925 at the mill, I was put to scrubbing floors in the mill. I was later promoted to cotton opener. By 1928, I was making a little over eleven dollars a week.

Mr. Jim Stowe, owner of the mill, would come to work around nine o'clock and stay until noon, weighing his own cotton. He did this for some time before hiring someone else to take over the job.

I was finally required to run three machines in the warehouse: waste feeder, waste beater, and opener. I was paid less than thirty cents an hour, even though I worked inside.

I filed a complaint with the NRA on January 5, 1934. My wages had not been raised from thirty cents an hour from July 17, 1933. I never aggressively pursued the claim, but I quit my job at the Eagle and went to work at the Chronicle. I worked there only a few months when Mr. Jim sent word by Charlie McClain that he would give me the five cents raise on the hour for which I had asked if I would come back to the Eagle.

The cotton was stored in the warehouse. I opened the cotton bales, put the cotton in the machine that would tear the cotton up for the picker hands to pick up, and make a lap out of it. I would open between twenty-five and thirty bales a day. That procedure was changed eventually, and I brought the cotton up and it would come out a finished lap.

I worked at the Eagle forty years before retiring. During that time, when Mr. Jim's health was good, he would come down to my country home on Ratchford Road, and we would go bird hunting.

My nephew, Scoffield Graham, was the first black man hired to run drawing in the cardroom during the John F. Kennedy administration. It was then that the mills began hiring blacks to work inside.

At the time of this writing, I am 87 years old. Yesterday, I picked four gallons of blackberries. Mr. Jim's sons still come by to see me once in awhile.

NATIONAL RECOVERY ADMINISTRATION

COMPLAINT OF VIOLATION OF CODE OF FAIR COMPETITION
FOR THE ___Textile_____ TRADE/INDUSTRY
(TYPE OR PRINT INFORMATION REQUESTED)

JANUARY - 5 1934
(Date)

Name and address of person or establishment complained against (Respondent) ....
__EAGLE YARN MILLS Co., BELMONT, N.C.__

Business of Respondent ......___COTTON MANUFACTUREING___

(a) Principal product (produced, processed, or sold)___COMBED YARNS___ or

(b) Principal service performed ....

(c) State such other details as will clearly indicate the nature of the Respondent's business:

Name of Complainant __BRUCE GRAHAM__

Address of Complainant __ROUTE № 3 GASTONIA N.C.__

Nature of complaint (state sufficient facts to indicate a clear violation of some definite provision of the Code to

which the Respondent is subject).

_____I AM AN INSIDE EMPLOYEE____

1- REQUIRED TO WORK MORE THAN 40 HOURS
A WEEK
2- OPERATIVE OF THREE(3) MACHINES,
WASTE FEEDER, WASTE BEATER, AND OPENER
AND AM PAID LESS THAN 30 CENTS FOR HOURS
WORK
3- MY EMPLOYER DUE ME EXTRA COMPENSATION
FROM JULY 17-1933 UP TO PRESENT DATE

The above statements are true to the best of my knowledge and belief.

_____
(Signature of complainant)

(Space for notarization or witnesses)
Charlie McClain

May we use your name if necessary? __YES__

NOTE.—If possible, this complaint should be sworn to before a Notary or signed by at least one witness familiar with the facts.
f this is done it will lead to quicker results.

ILL IN AND MAIL TO THE DISTRICT NRA COMPLIANCE DIRECTOR AT YOUR DISTRICT OFFICE
OF THE DEPARTMENT OF COMMERCE   16—1399

33

"New" School Clothes
by
Mary Huffman

The late summer of 1931, I kept wondering when Mama would take me fabric shopping. All my clothes and my four brothers' shirts were tailored by Mama. The Singer pedal sewing machine stayed busy much of the time, but she hadn't bought any new fabric lately.

Getting more anxious with school starting soon, I questioned her, "When are we going to buy school clothes?"

"We'll see," was Mama's answer.

Our family lived in rural Catawba County on a small farm, but we occasionally took a shopping trip into Hickory, about 15 miles away. Although my parents, Arthur and Isma Huffman, raised chickens, pigs, cows and vegetables, Dad had a job in town at Hickory Furniture Company.

Early one morning, Mama took her blue serge winter dress, her church dress, out of the closet. She started opening seams and, with a flat iron heated on kitchen stove, pressed the seams open. She brought out a jumper pattern and used the large kitchen table as a cutting board. Soon a blue serge jumper was ready for sewing.

The next garment she made was a blue-striped shirt, also Mama's, cut down to my size. Then she did the same with a pretty printed silk blouse. My leftover clothes from the previous year and these three garments were my winter wardrobe.

My feelings about the project were mixed. The jumper was beautifully tailored. But Mama told me, "Dad lost his job at the furniture plant." She explained that we would have no income, but we would make do until the plant reopened.

Grateful for such a giving parent, I realized that the Depression was upon us. It was my first feeling that we must be poor.

Our situation, I learned, was similar to that of many families in the community. All furniture factories closed, and most of the hosiery plants. I know of only two that worked something like two days a week to help families keep food on the table. The cotton mills never completely closed but ran short hours.

We were low on cash, but we had plenty of food. Thinking back, I recalled how often we had company, people knowing they would be given something from the garden to take with them.

And then there was my friend who came home from church

with me. At lunch, she ate and ate. And when we returned to the church in town for the evening service, she raved to the others about what delicious food we had "...and cake with real whipped cream!" she had added.

When I went home with her one Sunday, they had to search around for a snack. Her mother broke a cookie in two and gave them to her and a sibling. I was the only person to get a whole one.

That fall, when I returned to Hickory High for my senior year, I got a big surprise. A Barker girl, whose family purchased all their clothes at the finest stores, asked me, "Where do you buy your clothes? I haven't seen anything like that beautiful outfit where I shop."

Our Greatest Asset
by
Alex R. Josephs

Before the Depression, my father, L.M. Josephs, was fairly wealthy. We were riding high; we had a Dodge automobile with a chauffeur and lived in a good section on Morehead Street in Charlotte. Daddy owned a men's clothing store and had done very well in real estate. Well, the hair of the dog bit him, because real estate is what really sunk my dad. He lost everything.

When the stock market crashed in 1929, I was 12 years old. Of course, everybody knows what happened then. Successful men in New York and elsewhere were jumping out of windows and committing suicide in other ways because they had lost everything.

Some said the Depression had a lighter impact on Charlotte than other areas, because Charlotte was a distribution center rather than a manufacturing center. Most people around here blamed President Herbert Hoover, since the crash took place during his term. We didn't believe him when he said, "Prosperity is just around the corner."

A lot of people lost their jobs because so many businesses went under. Although I was young and didn't know how to observe the economy, I knew enough to notice when a filling station went broke or a grocery store closed or whether somebody had to start taking in laundry or cleaning or doing alterations because the breadwinner had become unemployed.

Back in those days, there were many people coming to the house selling things—can-openers and every damn gadget in the world.

Starting in '29, we had lots of beggars. Some black people, but mostly white people. They came by our house every day or so, and my mother would fix them a meal. I never saw anyone ever turned down.

My daddy would take us in his automobile to North Charlotte's Highland Mills neighborhood, where we would quite often see white children with distended bellies from starvation. We never saw black people that way, because they were treated as if they had no control over their economic fate: they were somehow fed. Some people blamed whites for being out of work and wouldn't really help them.

A number of our friends had problems. The president of a small local bank had a $30,000 life insurance policy with a $300 a month disability clause. He had told my daddy: "The bank is failing, and I'm going to be penniless. I have gotten an agreement from my doctor that he will certify that I am crazy and will commit me to Morganton (a North Carolina asylum) in order for me to collect this." He never did say whether the doctor was going to get any part of that $300 a month.

Dad's real estate business was his downfall. He owned more than $400,000 worth of property that suddenly plummeted to about $50,000 in value—if a buyer could be found. He owed over $100,000 on the property. Back then, it was common to have a lump sum mortgage.The entire amount was owed on the due date, no monthly payments.

Almost worse than that, my father had co-signed a loan for a doctor friend. The doctor didn't pay the note and my daddy had to pay $30,000 to a bank. That helped push him closer to destitution. The pressures were eventually so great after the real estate market dropped that Daddy was forced to commit suicide. He had no choice. The only asset the family had left was a $35,000 life insurance policy. His act was one of selflessness.

It was in February of 1930 when I was called out of class at school. A neighbor, Mr. Paul Whitlock, came to get me. He told me that Daddy had shot himself. It made headlines in *The Charlotte News* that night. And after that day, everything changed for us.

Of course, Mother received the insurance proceeds. With that, she was able to eke by and support her five children. Fortunately, the Commercial National Bank forgave a note that my daddy had left and we owned the house. But we had to sell our automobile and let the maid and chauffeur go. All of a sudden, we went from

36

riches to what seemed like poverty. We had very limited funds.

We didn't have to grow vegetables to get by. We were still considered pretty high up. Farmers came around every day to sell chickens, rabbits and produce. The farmer would wring the chickens' necks right there, and Mother would boil them to get the feathers off.

To supplement her income, my mother took in roomers. We were lucky to get a few FBI agents who were gone weeks at a time and later, a Navy doctor who was never there.

My three sisters, who had never been expected to work, got only one year of college each and then had to get a job. I worked in the Piggly Wiggly on weekends, not making over $2 a day. But the dollar was worth a lot more in those days. A good meal at Thackers (downtown) was only 35 cents. For 30 cents, you could go to the movies and get all the popcorn you wanted. And my clarinet lessons after school were 35 cents each. Even so, we could afford only three lessons.

Generally, the people who came out well were doctors and lawyers, although doctors often had to be paid in produce, like a country ham or a sack of potatoes. And the physician who contributed to my father's demise eventually went broke himself.

Wealthy people who had a cushion really "made a killing." J. H. Cutter, for instance, had a good cash position in the Depression. He was able to buy up real estate for a "song," and, of course, it all became very valuable later.

My older brother, Joe, graduated from Carolina in 1927. To show you what prosperity was for us in those days, he was given a Chevrolet automobile when he graduated. There probably weren't 200 cars in the city of Charlotte then! By comparison, I partially worked my way through Duke Law School, playing in a dance band, near the end of the '30s. When I graduated in 1940, I got a silver belt buckle.

By the Grace of God, "Poundings," Roomers, Etc.
by
Mary Katherine Teague

My dad was a country preacher—a Baptist—and, as his churches could pay very little in cash, the members would give him what they called "poundings" (derived from "a pound of this and a pound of that"). Generally, it was anything edible: canned vegetables, fruits, sugar, hams, etc. I always enjoyed going through their gifts; it was like Christmas. Occasionally, the ladies of the missionary groups would make us a quilt. Each person's name and date was embroidered in the square she had made.

My parents, Rev. Jackson Uriah Teague and Burla Shearin Teague, reared my brothers, Jasper and Rudolph, and me in Henderson in Vance County, but Dad's churches were in Granville County. He preached at two one weekend, two others the next weekend and at the fifth one, which was near Virgilina, Virginia, only on the fifth weekend.

By the time I was able to dress myself, I was allowed to go with him to the Granville County churches.

For instance, we would go to Tabbs Creek on the Henderson side of Oxford on a Saturday, where he would preach at 11 a.m. After lunch at a member's home, we would head for Mountain Creek Baptist Church on the other side of Oxford, where he would preach again. A family would invite us to spend the night in their home, so that he could conduct services at their church Sunday morning. After lunch, we would go back to the Tabbs Creek church for a 2 p.m. service before returning home.

His field of churches also included Grassy Creek, Amis Chapel and Averett churches on the other side of Oxford. Usually, I attended First Baptist Church in Henderson with my mother and brothers.

With Dad, I had the best times! Those country people really knew how to cook! We'd have fried chicken or fried ham with eggs for breakfast. And, oh those wonderful preserves—cherry, strawberry and blackberry—on hot buttered biscuits! Daddy said he really got tired of fried chicken, though.

I especially enjoyed the Tabbs Creek/Mountain Creek trips. We often stayed at the Eakes home. Mary Eakes was a friend of mine. Her daddy, Bud, owned a general store. In the '30s, a five-cent Coca Cola was a real treat. He would let us have one Coke a day.

In the summertime, my father would hold a week-long revival there. The house would be full of people, lots of girls, friends from other neighboring churches who came to stay during the revival. Mary's old-maid aunt, Anna, helped her mother with all the cooking. We younger ones had to eat at the second table last. I loved to clean out the corn pudding dish, with the brown left around the edges, the best part! Mr. Eakes had ice at his store. Sometimes, we would have ice cream made in a hand-turned freezer with cake for dessert.

While we were living in a rental house, someone tried to break in when my father was away. Dad worried about leaving us alone on weekends. In 1926, he had a 13-room house built with an apartment upstairs and a separate bedroom and kitchen downstairs to rent out. Mother and Dad selected the eastern end of town, East Montgomery Street, which was two blocks from Clark Street School, so I could walk (or skate) to school. Central School, where my brothers went, was several blocks in the other direction. A cow stall and chicken house were built onto the back of the three-car garage near the garden.

Teagues' 13-room home in Henderson

Dad was paying $75 a quarter for the mortgage. He rented the apartment for $15 a month and the two rooms for $10. Although his combined salary should have been $600 a year, his churches came up short. But he came home with a lot of nickels and dimes and food. At times, couples would come by the house to be married.

My father never charged for a wedding (or a funeral), but they would usually give him $5. According to custom, he would give it to his wife.

Usually, young couples, brides and grooms, were our roomers. That's how I learned about big tummies and babies.

A particularly memorable couple was the Beasleys. Barney Beasley, who worked at Rose's, the local five-and-dime, had dark, wavy hair and a good physique. He enjoyed playing tennis at a nearby tennis court built by boys in the neighborhood. His wife, Hilda, had her first baby when she lived with us. Amaryllis was born in 1934.

Among our roomers were a newspaper man, a baseball player, and electrician. One managed Woolworth's, two worked for Rose's. The electrician fell short of paying his rent, so he left his living room suite of wicker furniture and a beautiful snow scene print in a gold antique frame.

Funny, I didn't mind washing dishes for any of the roomers when they invited me to eat with them, but I *did* mind washing for

Mother.

A homemaker, Mother also owned a farm in Franklin County, which her daddy gave to her. It was farmed by sharecroppers. Throughout the Depression, it yielded very small profits, but every little bit helped make up for Dad's low income.

She was a very good seamstress. Once, she made over a black plush coat for me that had been hers. A fur trim was on the cuff and collar. When I grew, she removed the fur around the cuff and put it on the end of the sleeve to lengthen it. She had a crepe satin-back dress, which she made into a jumper for me. Buying a small piece of silk, she made a blouse to go with it. I didn't have a large wardrobe, though. In high school, I had a green skirt, a beige skirt, a few blouses, one dress and school shoes. For Sundays, I had two dresses and a pair of Sunday shoes.

During my teen years, I still traveled occasionally with my dad. Some weekends, while at Mountain Creek, we spent the night with the Hart family. The Harts had two daughters and two sons. My hormones kicked in and focused on James Hart. He was a real "ladies' man," and I really wanted to date him.

I used to sit in church holding a mirror to one side to see where James was sitting. And I was always on the lookout at the Eakes gas pumps to see if he would come to buy gas.

Before I graduated from Henderson High School (at 16 in 1937) and headed to Meredith College, I did get my chance to date him.

Actually, he had another date in Henderson and was double-dating with Lucille, his sister who was my age. I was spending the night at his home, so we all went to Henderson to pick up his date after work. It was raining, and I slipped over to the center of the front seat so she could hop in. When he saw this, he brought her around to his side and slid her in under the wheel. After taking her home, we all went to Hilltop #1, where young people used to dance to a nickelodeon and get refreshments. This was near Oxford, and we were headed back to his home.

He had not seen me in a long time, and I had grown up. That night, I had my first and last kiss from my first love. But James Hart has always been in my heart.

With my favorite Henderson beau, I liked to go roller skating at a tobacco warehouse with a wooden floor or play tennis or go swimming in a country pond.

The truth of the matter was: when it came to dating, it didn't help much to be a minister's daughter.

40

Mama's Pride
by
Eloise Cline Ross

Raised as an only child in LaGrange, Georgia, Mama had been spoiled by a doting mother, who died when she was 14, and a father who even took her on his second honeymoon to Sea Island.

When she married my dad, he co-owned a Coca Cola bottling plant, which he sold to buy a Lime Cola franchise in Durham. My sister Doris was born in Georgia. I was born in 1923 after the move to North Carolina.

My parents, Lillian and Dewey Cline, were doing well financially until he was shipped some sour syrup; then the company began to acquire some bad debts. Soon after the Depression hit, my father's debtors could not pay at all, and in 1931, he went broke, and the franchise folded.

Mama tried to shield us, pretending that everything was okay. By then, they had four children: Doris, me, Douglas and the baby, John.

Dewey Cline in his Lime Cola delivery truck. Durham. Circa 1930.

I was in the second grade when we moved from North Duke Street to Bragtown (a suburb of Durham and considered "the boondocks" to Mama).

This was only the beginning, as we moved many times in the years to follow, probably because we couldn't afford the rent. Some of the houses were less "nice" than others. We lived in one that had "sealed walls" (horizontal narrow planks), and after some suspicious red bumps that itched like crazy, Mama discovered that we had bedbugs. The degradation of this situation was almost as bad as the itching.

Saturday was house-cleaning day, so part of the routine after this was to go over everything in that room—beds, springs, walls, etc.—with a paintbrush doused in kerosene to rid ourselves of this pestilence. Mama dared us to ever use the word "bedbugs."

Daddy worked as a salesman for various companies, and, at one time, I believe he worked for the WPA. Mama shielded us from these facts and managed to "hang in there" throughout all the transitions and deprivations. I do remember that one day I didn't hear the change jingling in Daddy's pockets and realized sadly that he didn't have any to jingle.

Although we were never without a car, it was reserved for Daddy's business. Gone were the days of the yellow roadster and summer trips to Lake Junaluska. Gone were the times when Mama would stop on the side of the road and we would all pile out and pick flowers.

She was a pianist and gave music lessons at our home, but apparently people reached the point that they couldn't afford the lessons. Eventually, the piano was sold. They did manage to hang on to the tall mahogany Edison phonograph. We listened to the classics as well as some of the popular artists, such as Caruso and Gene Austin. Mama sang a lot and so did we. Doris and I learned to harmonize. She would sometimes let us use some of her art supplies from college, and we all have pursued different artistic hobbies over the years.

After we moved from town, Daddy planted a garden and we all (including Mama) learned to chop weeds. He also bought a cow, but Mama was so afraid of it that she stood as far away as she could and still reach the udder. So Daddy finally sold it.

Food had never been a problem but became one. Meals gradually got more practical. No more huge breakfasts, with fried chicken, steak and gravy, grits and ham, etc. Mama learned to prepare our meals with what could be bought cheaply. Much of it was fried or seasoned with fatback. A small-boned woman, slim, with dainty hands, Mama began to put on weight, most likely from all the fried foods.

One Sunday, my sister invited a friend to lunch. Mama was really upset, because she didn't have a fine roast to serve to our guest. It was a good dinner, but our mother was uncomfortable serving it.

I recall the total humiliation of having to take biscuits for school lunch if there was no loaf bread.

When I had to start wearing hand-me-downs, I was already taller than Doris. In junior high, when clothes really mattered, we could not afford new outfits at all. Of course, Mama sewed for us. And she and her friends learned how to take the seams out of men's trousers and fashion them into skirts for themselves. For Daddy, Mama turned the worn-out collars and cuffs wrong side out and re-sewed them on his shirts.

Shoes were a real problem as well. You had to wear them, even when they were downright embarrassing. Daddy would manage to buy soles and rubber heels and put them on old shoes with small tacks.

Mama didn't go to church regularly but sent us to Sunday school. Now I realize that she didn't think she had the proper clothing.

Acting and speaking properly were important to her.

If one of us asked, "Where's it at?" she wouldn't answer. Finally she'd say, "Behind the at."

In the afternoons, she would change from a house dress into nicer clothes, in case some ladies would come to call. If we came in while she had guests, she'd say "Can't you speak?" We would politely acknowledge each one, and she would say, "Change your clothes and go outside." They wanted to talk, but didn't want us to hear.

As soon as the company had left, we would file in to ask, "What did we do wrong today?"

She would tell us.

Christmas must have been traumatic for our parents when money was almost non-existent, but Santa always came. We didn't get things like bicycles, but Mama managed to please us, maybe not with what we wanted, but since children seldom got toys except at Christmas, we were happy with what we got. "Big Little Books," aviator caps, dolls and paper dolls were favorites.

Mama made things as festive as possible, and it became a

time of loving and sharing in the fun. She managed to accumulate all the ingredients for her cakes, and we'd sit around at night picking out "scalybarks" (a nut with a thinner shell than hickory nut) and black walnuts.

By the time I was a junior in high school, we had to move again, this time to Bethesda, a Durham suburb that was "really the boondocks" to Mama. What a difficult time that was. I was leaving all my friends and was very unhappy.

On our way to the new house, I was sitting between Mama and Daddy sniveling.

"If you'll quit that sniveling," my dad said, "I'll buy you whatever you want."

Lucky for him I didn't stop. He couldn't afford to buy anything. Mama didn't speak up at all.

Throughout our family ordeal, Mama never let down her standards. "What will the neighbors think?" she would often ask.

I was almost grown before I realized I didn't *care* what the neighbors thought.

On the other hand, we all learned to accept our situation without complaining. The saying is that "Pride goeth before a fall," but I think that Mama's pride kept us from many a fall. As I get older, I appreciate her and Daddy's sacrifices and successes more and more.

My Father's Tears
by
Panthy Shipp Anderson

My father's head was in his hands. The fire in our fireplace was warm, but his coat was still on over his overalls, for he had just come in from taking a bale of cotton to market. Seated in his favorite straight-back chair with the cane bottom, he was crying. I was 9 years old, and I had never seen any man cry before. I watched sadly as he moaned, "I've got to pay the time bill at the store, and I owe this man and that man." He sniffed, "And there will be nothing left for us."

For Papa, William Union Shipp, the money he earned was based mainly on the price and condition of cotton, although he also grew corn and, at times, taught school. He and my mother, Mary Ann Gibson Shipp, had moved from the farm he owned in the Catawba Springs community in Lincoln County near the Gaston

County line to the land he bought outside Denver before I was born. He had heard that a railroad would be running through Denver. That happened only in recent years.

At first, they had stayed in the little house that came with the land, but he built a second one on a hill, a four-room house, where we lived. When I was born, my oldest sister, Joyce, was 17; the other one, Dorothy, 11. Papa was 50 and Mama, 42. My father really wanted a boy, but he settled for me. By the time I was 9, Joyce had gone to Bennett College and was teaching school in Caldwell County. Dorothy went to high school at Bennett and had married early. Because my father had gotten his education there, they got a discount on the tuition.

Papa had hired someone to work the old farm back in Catawba Springs for a couple of years, but by 1929, our main source of income was the "two-horse" farm on a dirt county road, which is now called St. James Church Road. Papa never liked horses, so it was really a "two-mule, two-cow, and two-hog" farm. And then there was Prince, a black collie and good squirrel-hunter, and Rex, just a dog. Both were working dogs, who looked after the cows in the pasture. In addition to the cash crops, we grew enough wheat for flour and had two potato patches (sweet and white), a vegetable and a flower garden. Mama loved flowers.

In the winter, when we had no money, she would put grains of corn in the wash pot and pour a bag of ashes in. It turned white after cooking and would be delicious corn hominy.

My mother made all my clothes and taught me how to piece quilts, sew and do craft work, when we weren't helping out in the fields or I wasn't in school.

I walked about two miles to Denver-Rosenwald School, the only local school with grades one through seven for blacks. All grades were in one room—about 50 of us with one teacher. At least one of those years, the teacher was my father. The only high school for us was 15 miles away in Lincolnton.

When I was 12 or 13, my father developed a goiter. It was the second one he had had. His first one grew on his neck the year I was 6. When he was in the Good Samaritan Hospital that time, I took my first trip to Charlotte.

Mr. Frank Kelly, who owned the property next to us, loaned his Model T Ford to our neighbors, who drove us there. "Mr. Frank," as we called him, never learned how to drive. He was a bachelor, so maybe he bought it to attract a woman. He would put gas in it and let neighbors, some of his sharecroppers, borrow it. A lonely man, Mr. Frank would dress up in his Sunday clothes and sit out on his front porch. He never was a church-going man. And he never got himself a wife.

After Papa had his second operation, neighborhood boys came to help do the plowing. A very religious man, he was used to walking the two miles to St. James Church every Sunday, but he couldn't go for awhile until he got his strength back.

I was probably 14 when the Denver bank closed, and I saw my father cry again.

He was sitting in that same chair. It was dusk and the kerosene lamp showed his 200-pound body shaking. "How could two men come in and take all the money out of the bank and not rob it?" he asked Mama and me. We could only hug him and share his grief. All our savings were gone forever.

That night seemed to bring on his bad health. The Indian-tone skin from his mother's part-Indian genes seemed to take on a sallow look. His black curly hair, which never had much gray, began to turn. His six-foot frame began to bend, as he developed heart problems and lost weight. Soon, he was a very, very sick man.

About that time, I started doing housework at other people's homes in Denver. "Day work" paid about 25 cents a day. Denver had only about 200 residents. Most were farmers like we were, as there were no mills.

Some of my friends and I cut wild onions out of a lady's yard for 10 cents a half-day. She didn't want the cow, who was "cutting the grass," to produce "oniony milk."

Christmas, 1935 was an exciting time. Dorothy was bringing her four children home for the holidays. Despite the deep snow, it was warm by the fireplace. The mantel was decorated with cedar branches, red sumac berries and cotton boll "blossoms."

Papa's bed, a fine slave-crafted antique which Mama had inherited, was in that room, but he was in his usual chair. Some days he didn't get up at all, but he was longing to see his grand-children, especially Dorothy's oldest son Wilbur, the boy he had always wanted. Papa didn't call him Wilbur. He had a special pet name for him.

When they burst into the door, Papa started crying again. But this time, they were tears of joy. "Sunshine!" he cried, drawing Wilbur to his breast. "My Sunshine!"

Only in Bullock
by
Kathleen Royster Pruitt

We were like the Waltons. We were poor, but we didn't know it. Everyone around us in Bullock were about the same. My father, Charles Gregory Royster, was "Mr. Charlie." Mother, Annie Watson Royster,was "Miss Annie" to the 20 rural families that lived around us.

In Granville County, Bullock had a post office, a church and my father's general store. If anybody wanted anything else, they had to go to Stovall, where there were a couple of drygoods stores and a bank. If you really needed something like ready-made clothing, you had to drive twelve miles to Clarksville, Virginia or thirteen to Oxford, North Carolina.

Our worst year was 1932, when my father had three children in college, he lost his mother, Mother lost her father and my 22-year-old brother died from a blood clot during an appendectomy. "I'm sure there's a way to get through this," Dad said. "If there is, I'll find it."

My mother was a do-gooder. When the government began giving out commodities, she was selected to take the staple foods to families who needed them.

One day during our difficult year, when I was 12, she said, "Let's go to the Dickens.'"

I climbed into the big Dodge and went along for the ride.

Just as we drove up, one of the Dickens girls was jumping out of the window to elope. Mr. Dickens came running out the front door with a double-barrelled shotgun to shoot the boy.

I panicked and shouted, "Don't shoot until we leave!'"

Outhouse or Hothouse?
by
Lexie Little Hill
From *Gray-Haired Grins & Giggles*

It's just not true: that you can get used to anything. I *never* got used to our outhouse. Maybe I should have been grateful our family had one; some families didn't. Even in the early '30s in rural North Carolina, those people went behind the barn and shared space with the cows.

47

Our outhouse was a three-holer with a Sears Roebuck catalog (for looking and wiping), and I hated it. I could see the spider webs and the spiders under the cut-out hole, just where I sat. I often thought, *What if a spider bit my bottom?* and *What if I fell in?*

As soon as the new catalog came in the mail, Mama banished it to the outhouse because, she said, "You spend entirely too much time looking and begging when you should be doing your homework."

What Mama didn't know was that the Sears Roebuck catalog allowed me to push my fear and hatred of the outhouse out of my mind as I browsed its pages of stuff I had never seen before.

As the big day approached, the day my cousin Mabel, a city girl, was coming to visit, I was giddy with anticipation. I helped Mama clean the house so it was spic and span and swept the yard. Then I headed for the outhouse. I scrubbed the seats, made sure the spiders were out of the holes and put a box of baking soda in the corner behind one of the seats. I knew Mabel had a bathroom in her house, and I wondered how in the world she was going to be able to use this thing.

Finally the day came. Her father was driving a sleek new Model A. Maybe they wouldn't see Daddy's old Model T under the shed of the barn where it rested because, during the worst of the Depression, Daddy didn't have money to buy gas.

Mama had cooked all the day before, and she laid out quite a spread for dinner: chicken, country ham, vegetables from the garden, sweet potato pie and chocolate cake. I bet Mabel's parents never had a dinner like this!

After dinner, all the grown folks were sitting in the yard under the shade of the big oak tree talking. Mabel and I were jumping rope, when we heard someone yell to my father, "Mr. Silas, Mr. Silas!" Everyone looked toward the sound, and we saw Henry Gaye, our neighbor who lived across the street on a hill, looking down at us. He cupped his hands around his mouth and shouted, "Mr. Silas, your sh..t house is on fire!"

I was so embarrassed I could die! *What will Mabel and her parents think of us now?*

Daddy jumped up, the rest of us following, and ran to the blazing outhouse. My brother, playing with matches, had set the Sears Roebuck on fire! Everyone stood around, hushed, and watched it burn.

Right then, I didn't care what Mabel or anyone was thinking. I was glad the outhouse was burning down. My glee suddenly turned to grief—*No! Oh no! My Sears Roebuck is burning with it!*

To Lose a Child and Then...
by
Lexie Little Hill

My little sister Clara, 2, loved everyone, especially men. She ran to them, stranger or friend, arms outstretched, and when safe in their arms, she held their faces in her hands, looked into their eyes and said, "I wuv you."

Clara Catherine Little died of diphtheria, three weeks after receiving the diphtheria vaccine. Daddy had stayed with her night and day, cradled his little girl in his arms and suffered as she gasped and struggled for the last few gulps of breath, crying, "Mama, Mama!"

The hospital forbade Mama to enter the contaminated room because she was nursing Norris. So she stood in the hall and looked through the small pane of glass in the door, her grief almost more

than she could bear.

That year, 1931, Daddy had been forced to close his small grocery store when no one paid their bills, and we had to move to a small farm three miles from town in the Union Grove community. That left Daddy no income to pay the $150 hospital bill.

They refused to release Clara's body until the bill was paid. Hoping he might recover enough to cover it, he asked each person to whom the store had given credit to pay him a portion of what they owed. No one had any money to give him.

When it seemed there was no way he could pay the hospital, an acquaintance gave him an envelope and said, "I heard you needed money, I want you to have this." There was just enough to get her body released.

Daddy assured the doctor that he would be paid if he had to sell his farm. The doctor's reply was, "I've never had anyone to offer to sell his farm to pay me. Just pay when you can."

God must have looked down upon Daddy and said, "Enough!" because he soon found a most coveted job. Every Saturday until the bill was paid, Daddy drove his Model T Ford 25 miles to pay the doctor what he could.

For the Lack of Penicillin
by
Margaret Homesley Marrash

As Papa talked with us and hugged each one from his bed, we didn't know we were saying "goodbye." A nurse and an old man who used to help Papa on the farm stood nearby. My oldest brother, Jim, Papa's "right-hand man," ushered the other eight of us to him one by one. Mama, who was pregnant, tried to be cheerful. We took our turns for Papa's attention in the bedroom we called the "front room," where we girls and Mama used to sleep. He had been moved in there, because it was the only room in the house with a fireplace. We younger ones had been farmed out to relatives while Papa was being treated for pneumonia.

At 9 (the sixth down), I had been staying with my Grandma, Elmina Homesley, a two-minute walk down the road. My sister Nellie, 2, had gone with me so that I could care for her. Mary Ruth was staying at Aunt Beulah's; Byrum, at Uncle John's.

I wandered back to the center hall and peered into the "back room," where Papa normally slept with his sons. It seemed more disheveled than usual, reflecting the confusion in our lives. I missed our family being together. Papa, who was strict but loving, used to play games with us. At suppertime and after Sunday dinner, he would read the Bible, while we were gathered around the table. We younger ones sat on our bench and sang hymns, blending with Papa's base and Mama's alto.

Our simple unpainted home in Cherryville had only one closet, for we had few extra pieces of clothing or belongings to store. In addition to the front and back room (actually left and right of the hall), there was a kitchen and pantry. No rugs were on the floors. And there was no electricity or plumbing. On a shelf on the back porch was a bucket with a dipper for drinking water and a wash pan for bathing. We had only one hearth, but our warmth came from the love from our God-fearing parents.

Mama and Papa, Margaret Elizabeth Farris and Amos Pinckney Homesley, were both educated. After secondary school, Mama studied at the forerunner of Kings Business College in Charlotte. She was an organist for the Lutheran Church before she married Papa, a Baptist. Papa finished at Cherryville's one-room schoolhouse. He was a learned man, because his father, a teacher, passed on his love of seeking knowledge. He sang in the choir at Shady Grove Baptist Church.

Besides farming, Papa owned a grocery store and a slaughterhouse. In the early fall, he would take his truck to the mountains to get apples to sell.

Moving out to the porch that stretched across the front of our house, I took my little sister's hand, waved to the others and headed up the hill back to Grandma's house.

A short time later, on February 28, 1930, Papa died. Before penicillin, many died from pneumonia. Those who survived were lucky. In our cold house, someone was always sick in the winter. My brother Robert Benjamin, the third oldest, had suffered from typhoid fever, pneumonia twice, and symptoms of tuberculosis. A doctor was not called unless there was an emergency.

Papa's death made life more difficult for all of us. My oldest sister Ann finished high school, but my older brothers had to drop out to find jobs. They worked from sunup to sundown to make $5 or $6 a week, which they gave to our mother.

We were fortunate, for we had about 60 acres planted in cotton, corn, potatoes, and sugar cane for molasses. The boys did most of the farm work, but we girls helped hoe and pick the cotton, a job I hated. We also had a cow, chickens and pigs, and our brothers had rabbit boxes and hunted doves, partridges, squirrels and possums.

Our father's store and slaughterhouse were closed. A lot of people owed Papa at the store, for he couldn't say "no" to anyone.

Mama said he was "too good for his own good." Once, when an old car broke down in front of our house, Papa made pallets for the parents and children on our porch, and Mama shared our food with them until they could get the car fixed.

Our community's Depression started before 1929, when the cotton prices dropped so low. In fact, we had to wait until the first bale of cotton sold, so we could buy shoes before starting school.

Mama made all our clothes, except the boys' overalls. Later, Ann helped her. Saturday afternoons, after scouring the kitchen, she would settle down to do more sedentary chores. Still in her house dress and apron and with her red hair pulled back in a bun, she often would be leaning over to hand-sew patches on whatever needed them. Despite all she had to do to take care of us and keep food on the table, I never heard her complain. She was always singing hymns, making us do our homework, pulling us close to her ample body and loving us.

Like other women of that day, she canned and preserved fruits, berries and vegetables. We had cornbread and sweet milk every night for supper with whatever was left over from the mid-day dinner. If the cow ate bitter weeds that day, we didn't get milk because it tasted so bad. But we all liked the "Hoover gravy" our mother made from grease left after frying fatback and some water, flour, salt and pepper. We liked to sop it with biscuits. Our favorites were her tea cakes, thick round cakes to which she added orange peel, cinnamon or preserves. Mama baked pies and biscuits every day, too. At the time, I did not always appreciate them.

While those of us who didn't go home for lunch were eating in the school auditorium, I was ashamed for my more fortunate classmates to see Mama's biscuits (the best on this earth). The children from uptown had light bread, which cost 10 cents a loaf.

We never had a nickel to spend. In my childhood, I never had a doll, and went to only two movies. But I would go with my brothers to the "junk hole," where local stores would haul their trash, and we could find things to play with. I'd go through the stuff looking for movie magazines. With what they dug out, my brothers made a contraption to ride on. One day, we discovered a big pile of candy out there that the Candy Kitchen had thrown out. We gathered it all and took it home, but Mama wouldn't let us eat it.

From the time I was 13 until 16, I stayed with Aunt Beulah as her cook and housekeeper while going to school. I got $3 and board and could go home on weekends. The hardest job was the weekly washing and ironing. Clothes were washed outside in a wrought iron wash pot, scrubbed on a washboard, rinsed and then boiled in the pot. After hanging on a line to dry, they had to be ironed with a heated flat iron.

My liberation after graduation from Cherryville High School was a commercial correspondence course, paid for by my brother, A. P. He bought me a second-hand typewriter for $4, and I studied bookkeeping and shorthand, practiced typing and sent the lessons in.

After Papa died, we had some other health scares in our family. It seemed that there was always someone in the household with one of the childhood diseases like chicken pox, measles or whooping cough—or one of us stepped on a nail or a piece of glass while bare-footed.

Mama used a lot of home remedies. For a cut foot, she would anoint the sore place with turpentine. Then she'd strike a match to an old wool rag and drop it into a bucket. The child would hold his hurt foot over the bucket, so the smoke could soothe the cut. On a burn, she would put a leaf of Jimson weed to put the "fire" out. Of course, we always had Black Draught and castor oil. Because it was so expensive, Mama would add just a little Fletcher's Castoria to the castor oil to make it palatable.

When Nellie got lice, our mother used a foul-smelling medicine that made the whole house stink. And when she had pleurisy, a serious disease, Mama packed a mustard plaster on her chest. For Marvin, who had horrible sore throats, Mama rubbed Vick's on his neck. To stop my chronic cough, she mixed white lightning with sugar.

But none of her remedies could help A. P., when he had leakage of the heart or Don, when he came home from school with "the itch."

Our mother had her share of illnesses, too: cancer of the uterus (for which she took radium and was cured), varicose veins, and a painful carbuncle on her thumb. A sliver of bone was protruding, and A. P. removed it in our kitchen.

The biggest scare was the time Robert Benjamin got pneumonia again. There was still no penicillin, but he survived. In fact, he's now 86.

OVER THE EDGE - NORTH CAROLINA

Momma, Take Me Home!
by
Eloise B. Shavitz

The screams and crying were frightening me. People were driving in and saying, "You poor child. What's going to happen to you?" I stood in the yard and watched someone pull my sister Annie Lee away from the well, as she said she wanted to die.

I looked around me at the utter chaos and asked, "What's wrong?" No one answered, but more questions rolled in my mind. Where is my mother and daddy? Why aren't they here to help me?

Just that morning, I had kissed my mother goodbye and had given her 50 cents, money I had earned picking cotton, and told her to buy a pair of hose for herself. Where is she now? I needed her. No one would tell me what was wrong and why everyone was crying. They were dead? No. No! Not my mother! She said she would be back that afternoon! Daddy? Not my big strong father, who could at one time frighten me, but sometimes be gentle. A car accident? My uncle driving drunk and hit a bridge? He lived. My parents were dead.

I heard people speaking in whispers, "The younger ones will have to go to an orphanage. Maybe the older ones can stay with relatives."

What was an orphanage? There were seven of us children from ages 17 to 1. I was about six years old that December day in 1940. Would I be one of the ones to be sent away?

The room in our farm shack was lit with kerosene lamps. People were crying and talking in that small room we called a parlor in our house in the Gallberry community in Nash County. There were two boxes in the room. What were they? Someone picked me up and took me over to those boxes and said, "Kiss your mother and daddy goodbye."

Cold. Cold. That was not Momma or Daddy. She didn't smile and kiss me back. Who was that? Not my mother. She was smiling and warm when I kissed her before she left for her trip to Raleigh.

That night after the funeral, Daddy was back and he was cursing Momma, saying he was going to kill her. Momma would soon wake me, my brothers and sisters, and we would hide in the cornfield until Daddy went to sleep. Wait! Momma was dead; who was that man cursing? I heard my older sister's voice. Christabell was talking to Skinner, the boy she had just married to get away: "Eloise is sleeping at the foot of the bed—we can't do it! She will hear us!"

More cursing. Skinner is going to kill me and my sister, just like Daddy threatened to do. I ran, like Momma had taught me. Momma would help me!

I ran to her grave and hid behind a tree praying, "Momma, please help me!" I heard my siblings yelling for me to come in. They said they weren't going to hurt me. It was cold and I was so scared. The voices got nearer, and they found me lying on Momma's grave, crying for her to come back.

After I had been shuffled in and out of other relatives' homes, the representatives from the orphanage came for me in May. I had been hiding under the house for a long time. I was tired, and the yellow dress a sister had dressed me in that morning was itching me. The cardboard and paper an aunt had stuffed in my shoes to cover the holes in the soles were hurting my feet.

By looking up through the cracks in the floor, I could hear my aunts and people saying, "It's the best thing. We can't afford to keep the three of them, and the others are older and can take care of themselves and help us, too."

Who were those people in the two big black cars? Where were they taking me? I was kicking, screaming and crying when they dragged me out from under the porch.

One lady gave me a superior smile. "Little girl, now you're going to have to behave. They won't allow that at the orphanage."

The orphanage! No! No! I wanted to stay here.

The smiling lady gave me a plaster Kewpie doll (probably from the county fair) and told me I could have it. It was so ugly. Her holier-than-thou smile and the doll's evil-looking face reminded me of the devils that I had dreamed a lot about since Momma died.

"Goodbye, Eloise. Be a good girl. We'll come see you," said family members.

The smiling lady and another woman told me to get into the car. My baby brother, Alton, was in her arms asleep. The other people took my brother, Raybion, who was 3 1/2 years old, in the second black car.

Later, we stopped in front of a big old red two-story building. The Free Will Baptist Orphanage in Middlesex was ugly, gloomy and intimidating. A portly short man with a friendly smile came up and said he was Mr. James Evans and that I would be living here with a lot of girls. They had rules and I was to be a good girl and listen to the matrons and the big sisters and do what they asked me to do.

A matron took Alton and Raybion down the road to the babies' house. I entered the gloomy building and looked around the parlor. Very dark and depressing. The floors were wood, and the lights hung by long cords from the ceiling. I was taken upstairs. Each of the bedrooms, where the girls slept, had two iron single beds and a dresser. We would all share one bathroom.

Each young girl was assigned an "older sister," who told us what to do and played the role of baby-sitter. Mine was named Hope. About 14, Hope was very soft spoken. With her beautiful smiling brown eyes, she greeted me. In future days, she would become my protector.

I soon got into the routine. We would get up very early on weekdays, clean our rooms, take out the trash and then go to breakfast, which was in a separately maintained facility. The younger children ate there, too, but on a different schedule.

Breakfast consisted of biscuits or bread and always oatmeal, which was always scorched. Sometimes, we had eggs and always fresh milk from the orphanage farm. When we were finished, we went to a chapel service.

Later, when I was in school, a bus would pick us up and take us to Middlesex Elementary. When we returned, there were always chores. We younger children would do yard and garden work; the older ones were responsible for washing, ironing and helping in the kitchen. We would eat our dinner, do our homework and go to bed.

On my first day at school, I was bewildered. Why were my schoolmates laughing and pointing at me? The other children were calling me a "dirty orphan." I wasn't dirty. The matron who helped me was up that morning before I got on the bus. I had on the yellow dress that I had worn the day my life changed forever. I still wore the same shoes, but they couldn't see the soles or the holes. Why were they saying that I was nasty and had lice? I didn't have lice! The matron had cut all my curls off and had put something that burned a lot into what was left of my hair. I didn't have lice. I yelled at them and told them I didn't have lice!

On weekends, the girls who had a living parent or relatives were allowed to go home. Sometimes, I was the only one left in our dorm. One matron, Mrs. Mitchell, would spend time with me and read me stories. I was so lonesome for my family. They had promised to come but never did. No one. Never. Why can't I even see my brothers? Everyone told me they were too young. Although we were on the same campus, I wasn't allowed to see them. As a ward of the state, I had to do what was expected of me.

One day, some of us were playing in the big parlor. "Eloise, climb up on this desk and hide," said one of the girls. "We will come and find you."

I climbed up into a roll-top desk. BAM! The top slammed. My heart was pounding. I couldn't get out! It was so dark, and I kept screaming and kicking and trying to slide open the door. The giggling and laughing had stopped. No sound, except my screams. "Help me! Help me!" I couldn't breathe.

All of a sudden, the desk cover slid open. I gasped for breath and the matron said, "Bless your heart. Whoever did this will be punished."

I never knew if they were, but I can blame those moments of horror for my claustrophobia.

Silence. Quiet. Everyone was gone. They were with their

parents and relatives for Christmas. Dark and so quiet. I was on my bed in my room by myself.

"Eloise," said a voice I loved to hear. Mrs. Mitchell sat down beside me. "Are you OK?"

"Yes," I said. I always knew her as Mrs. Mitchell, but I found out later that her first name was Mary. The only matron who was kind to me, she was a big-boned bosomy woman whose compassion and love shone in her twinkling eyes.

"Tell Santa what you want most of all," she said soothingly. "Santa Claus will come tonight and bring you a present. What do you want?"

Christmas. Santa Claus. Most of all I wanted to leave the orphanage. I wanted Momma back. I wanted someone to hug me. I wanted my brothers and sisters. I wanted my home and family. "I want my Momma back." I said. "I want to see my brothers and sisters."

She kissed me, and left the room. I had never heard about Santa Claus, so I didn't know who he was. Sleep. A package when I woke up! Santa Claus, whoever he was, had really come! A doll! A beautiful new doll! One that looked like the ones my classmates brought to school, but I couldn't touch because I was an orphan and might steal it. My own doll!

Homecoming day! Everyone was dressed up, waiting for family and the people who supported the Free Will Baptist Orphanage. I was wearing the same yellow dress, but I had new shoes! The matron had tied a yellow ribbon in my hair. I wondered what homecoming was. They told me that the families of the orphanage children came to visit on this day. No one came to see me. I had been there less than a year, but it seemed like forever. I looked and looked for siblings, aunts, uncles, another relative, any familiar face, but there were none.

All of us girls were standing together on the steps. Everyone was saying, "Smile," while they took our pictures. I was so scared and unhappy, because I had no one to visit me.

"What is your name, Sweetheart? You're such a beautiful child," said a woman from the crowd. A blonde, she was dressed handsomely. Although he didn't speak, her husband was standing nearby and seemed friendly.

"Eloise," I said.

"Do you like it here?"

I was afraid to answer.

The lady talking to me had the prettiest blue eyes. She

59

hugged me and said she would love to have a little girl just like me. She told me that she and her husband had been out riding around and saw the sign to the orphanage and decided to visit it. Both of them seemed curious and nervous. Then she asked, "Would you like to come visit us sometime?"

"Yes," I said. Did she really like me enough to let me come into her home?

Indeed she did! Nettie and Sam Bogen from Zebulon, just across the Wake County line, soon applied to adopt me. After many weekend visits and an extended trial period, their home became my home. Mother told me that God had shone a light on my face and had chosen me for her.

The poor little orphan, through the grace of God, at last had someone to love her! The final adoption papers were signed on November 17, 1943.

"Sherlock Holmes" Conley
by
Connie Conley Flynt

The economy was very tight in the little town of Wilson, North Carolina—populon 13,000. During the Great Depression of the early 1930s, families seemed to draw closer together in to survive with dignity.

J.A. and Helen Conley and their three little girls (I being the youngest) lived in this friendly community where neighbor trusted neighbor.

We didn't even have a front door key. We never locked a window in fear. Cars were parked with the keys in their switches and never stolen.

Our home had a fireplace in each room. Coal was used as fuel for warmth. Our coal supply was kept in an unlocked room behind our garage.

One day, my father noticed that our coal pile seemed to be going down drastically fast. He could not believe there was a thief in our nice middle-class neighborhood. What to do?

He took the biggest piece of coal left in the coal room, made a small hole in it and tamped in a tiny amount of gunpowder. He then returned it to its original place in the coal room.

POW!

We were all seated at breakfast a few mornings later, when

we heard that loud noise. Evidently, the next door neighbors' coal-fired laundry heater in their kitchen had thrown its two small plates in the air. J. A. had found the culprit. We lost no more coal.

In later years, we occasionally liked to tease Daddy by calling him "Dr. Holmes." He would just smile, but we knew he was pleased to have solved the case without harsh words being exchanged between good neighbors.

Chickory Trickery
by
Connie Conley Flynt

Her husband had a PhD, when nobody else had one. But he had no job. She often came to our house to borrow a cup of coffee. As they were our next door neighbors, Mother always gave her the precious ground coffee from her supply. No matter how bad things were, my daddy was going to have a good cup of coffee.

"Helen, where did you get this?" Daddy asked, when he was drinking what our neighbor had repaid.

It was chickory. Remember chickory? Chickory was cheap, but it was bitter. New Orleans people love it. Daddy didn't.

Mother told him and added, "I can't refuse it."

"No, I'll tell you what you do," he said. "You get a Mason fruit jar, and what she brings, you can put in the jar. Then when she comes back to borrow, you give her the chickory."

It took three times. She never borrowed again.

Why We Ate So Well
by
Connie Conley Flynt

I had a pleasant Depression when it came to food. It was real ironic, because I know there were people who didn't have any food.

But my daddy owned a service station on the direct route from Florida to New York. Across the street he had a repair shop for delivery trucks. Back then, many people didn't have cars, so they had to order from the bakery, the fish market and the grocery store. The shopkeepers would take their orders and deliver them.

The banks closed in Wilson before Roosevelt closed them. My daddy had $5 in his pocket. Nobody had any money. Daddy had those store owners on his account, so he went to them.

He went to the fish market and said, "You owe me this money,"

The man who owned the fish market said to my daddy, "Well Joe, I don't have any money. But I tell you what—you can take it out in trade." He had to have that delivery truck to make any money himself. That was back when fish was $5 a ton!

So, here I am during the Depression—the banks are closed—and I'm eating lobster, I'm eating shrimp, I'm eating all those good things and thinking nothing of it because it was there.

And the same thing with the bakery. We could go into the bakery and get anything we wanted! It was just one of those lucky circumstances. Daddy had a trade that was needed.

Well, I think the man from the fish market owed Daddy $89, so after a couple of years, the bill was paid off. And my father told my mother, "I never want another piece of fish in this house as long as I live."

A Very Expensive Baby
by
Rev. William Stamey Teachey
from *90 Octobers*, a memoir video*

A lot of people don't realize the situation we are living under today. In a season of prosperity, we do what we like and spend a lot of money. But I can recall back when times were not like this.

Times were tight when my youngest son was in the hospital, born there May 15, 1930. I went to check him out and lacked $15 to get him out of the hospital. I was very distressed and didn't know what to do. I didn't have the money.

I had to go to somebody, so I went to my pastor at the church and explained the situation to him. He said, "I'm sorry, Stamey, but I can't help you."

That really turned me off. I'm going to tell you the truth: it shocked my whole religious foundation. I turned around in the car and drove on up the highway for a while to figure out what I was going to do. And mind you, the baby was in the hospital and I only owed $15 more. But as I started back to town, I was angry with myself for asking the preacher, because he probably didn't have any money either.

But anyway, I went to a loan shark in Wilson. I paid that

money back $2 at a time. Usually, you have to pay extra and weekly. By the time it was all over, I had paid him $25 or better for that $15.

This story from the past can help the present generation. You are faced with situations in life—whether you are married or single—and you don't know what to do. But then you have to turn around and rely on yourself and figure out what you can do. Life is like that. You learn from these experiences.

* *90 Octobers* was produced for Rev. Teachey's 90th birthday by William G. (Tony) Teachey of Winston-Salem, the very expensive baby.

The Teachey brothers: William G. (Tony) Teachey in the Lindbergh hat and James Joseph with the Roman candle. Wilson County. Circa 1936.

Our Family Rides Again
by
Selby A. Daniels

At the onset of the Depression, my father, Ossie Richard Daniels, had to park both his Model T Ford car and truck for lack of money to buy gasoline. We either stayed at home or walked where we had to go—all except my father, who got out the old bicycle he had used as a teenager.

Early in the year of 1930, "Hoover carts" made their appearance in our farm neighborhood in northern Wayne County, near Fremont. Named for Herbert Hoover, the President of our country at that time, a "Hoover cart" was made from the front axle of a Model T Ford car using leaf springs under a single seat, with wood shafts like a cart. It was pulled by a farm horse or mule.

For a long time, my father resisted removing the front axles of his car and truck, as he kept hoping for better times. Finally, he broke over and made our first Hoover cart, allowing us to renew our visits to relatives and friends.

This action alerted me that we were truly living in "hard times."

A Soap Story
by
Selby A. Daniels

By the fall of 1930, the Great Depression had really settled in with tobacco farmers of Eastern North Carolina. Adult farm labor earned 25 cents per day, from sunrise to sunset, with lunch (dinner) thrown in.

Some farmers who owned their own land worked out a special arrangement with local Wayne County merchants whereby the merchant issued a small coupon book which was used to purchase seed, fertilizer, food and other supplies. The coupons had the normal profit for merchandise already figured in, plus an additional profit earned by the merchant for having to "carry" (or hold) the coupons until the fall of the year. That was when the farmer sold his crops and then redeemed his coupons by buying them back from the merchant.

Needless to say, the farmer had to have good weather (rain), a crop free of insects and plant diseases, and good market prices in order to redeem the coupons. Failure to do this placed the farmer at risk of losing his farm to the merchant or bank. Tenants received their dole from the participating farmer/landlord, who was then placed at the same risk of loss or profit as the merchant.

In school that fall, my teacher asked each student to name the soap used in their respective households. When my turn came, I felt embarrassed to name "box lye" but somehow felt better for being honest.

Selby Daniels, 6
and Spot

Across the aisle from me sat pretty blonde Dorothy Wheeler, a prissy girl, whose father had suffered the indignity of going bankrupt in a rural grocery store, the property rented from my father.

Out of business and out of work, Dorothy's father now labored daily for my father for 25 cents per day.

Daddy told Mother he didn't really need Mr. Wheeler but felt obligated to help him.

Dorothy, shaking her blonde curls, said, "We use Camay."

I could not believe my ears! How could her family use Camay, yet her father worked for mine, while we had to use "box lye," a homemade soap?

Arriving home from school, I asked my father about this.

He laughed and told me "Johnny Wheeler is using Camay soap and other merchandise left over after his bankruptcy."

Not really understanding the answer my father gave me, I was comforted when Mother proudly said, "We don't have to buy soap. We make our own."

The next day, I decided to feel pride in what my mother told me by volunteering to tell our teacher how we made our own soap. She promptly invited me to come to the front of the class and describe this process.

My family used a large clothes washing pot in which was poured a mixture of measured amounts of oak ashes, fatty pork grease (oil) and box lye. A fire was built under the pot, and the soap ingredients had to be stirred with a strong oak paddle. My job was to keep the fire going and the liquid stirred. "Box lye" soap was always made when the moon was "growing," as it was known that soap shrank too much after the full moon. My father would cut the soap into bars two days later. It was used to wash clothes, dishes, people and for practically every washing use—even to remove sticky gum.

Bet your ole Camay can't do that, Dorothy!

Our Family Fortunes
by
Paul Jernigan

Tubs of free barbecue and drinks brought out the crowds for the public auction but didn't sell the land. For me, at 10 years old, and my younger brothers, this was a great event. There was a country music band playing, and we had never seen so many people at one time before. We gorged ourselves on Eastern North Carolina barbecue and drank our first bottled soda, Coca Cola and Nehi. But underneath this gaiety, I knew Mother and Daddy were really worried. I had heard them talking. They were unhappy because they feared we would have to be sharecroppers again. I began to wonder what would happen to us.

Tom Norwood, a banker, and Samuel F. Teague, a lawyer who lived in Goldsboro, had owned and developed the Peach-a-Rena Farm that my father managed. This 1,000-acre farm producing peaches, dewberries, cotton, corn and poultry was in Wayne County, seven miles south of Goldsboro and two miles north of Dudley on old Highway 117. That was my home, for I was the oldest of seven boys of John Louis, Sr. and Mary Helm Jernigan born between 1919 and 1928. (Helm was pronounced hellum, like Eastern North Carolina people pronounce el-um trees.) In 1926, Brogden School was built on land owned by the farm. Then in 1929, Norwood and Teague went bankrupt. The property was taken over by the Federal Land Bank, who sponsored the auction. But they failed to sell the farm as a whole or any of the parcels into which it had been divided.

Compared with other farm families in that area during the 1920s, we had done very well financially. My father's salary had been $75 a month plus free residence in a large frame house and all the garden space we wanted. As there was no electricity, we got free wood for fuel and cooking. We also had our own hogs, chickens and cow.

We had been better off than most tenant farmers and small landowners. Their income was subject to bad weather and sometimes low prices for cotton, corn and tobacco. Our money was certain and steady; we were paid each month. Farm laborers or "hands" were paid 75 cents per day to $1 per day when needed, which was not every day. This was fairly common throughout that decade.

But now what?

The bank made a seemingly attractive offer to my father, as they had to do something with the property. For $100 per year, we could continue to live on a 40-acre tract, which contained a six-room frame house, the poultry farm, some of the peach orchards and a barn for a mule and cow. To make the deal more attractive, they made arrangements for the $100 a year rent to be used as payments on the farm, if Daddy decided to buy it. He accepted the offer. We lived there seven more years, until 1937.

Even with this arrangement, it was hard living for a family of ten. (My mother's younger brother, Starling, who was single, couldn't find work and had come to live with us. He helped out on the farm for free room and board.) After two or three years, the laying hens became too old to be profitable. The bank repossessed them and hauled them to a meat processing plant.

Daddy and I built a small roadside stand by Highway 117 across the road from Brogden School. There we sold peaches, watermelons, cantaloupes and a variety of vegetables we grew. This produce was also taken to Goldsboro to sell to grocery stores. We also made some sales on the street and by peddling from house to house.

Many hot summer nights, we older boys (ages 6 and above) helped our parents shell peas and butterbeans into the late hours. When I fell asleep, my mother would rap me on the arm with a peach tree switch to awaken me. Then we were up early the next morning to be the first at the grocery stores with them. Later, we would rush back home and load the back seat and passenger seat of our 1929 A Model Ford with watermelons, cantaloupes or corn so Mother or Daddy could take them into town.

Our family did not plant cotton or tobacco on our place at that time. Instead, we made money picking cotton and working in barning tobacco for neighbors. Those of us over the age of 12 earned 50 cents to 75 cents per day for helping in tobacco and 35 cents to 50 cents per hundred pounds for picking cotton. Adults were paid the same amount, but at 12, we were considered "of age."

Each fall until Thanksgiving, school was dismissed at noon so students could pick cotton and grade tobacco. My parents and I earned some money grading tobacco, which farmers brought to our house. Meanwhile, my father got the job as janitor of Brogden School, which paid $30 a month for eight months. With all this, we were still unable to pay the $100 per year to the bank.

In 1937, we moved to a small farm with 30 acres of cleared land in the Hornes Church community in Nash County. We took our livestock with us—one mule, one cow, one pregnant sow and about 35 chickens plus our farm tools and plows.

For two years, we farmed there on thirds. We furnished a mule, equipment, seeds and labor and got 2/3 of the crop that fall, when it was sold or divided. Our crop allotment was eight acres of tobacco and eight acres of cotton. The rest of the farm was planted in corn, hay, sweet potatoes, sorghum and a vegetable garden. Being a Quaker, my father was against the use and cultivation of tobacco but compromised his principles to make a living. As for me, I was happy about the change. I liked the friendly neighbors and the local Methodist Church. There was no Friends Meeting nearby.

We were surprised that we were the only ones in the area with a cow. While we were drinking milk, they were drinking tea and coffee. We all liked "pot licker" (what was left in the bottom of the pan when we ate the greens). Cooked with fatback, it made a tasty broth.

In 1939, we wanted a larger farm with more cotton and tobacco acreage or allotment. Unable to buy more mules or equipment, my father sold what he had. That year, we sharecropped a large three-horse farm near Middlesex with 12 acres of cotton and 12 acres of tobacco. We furnished the labor, half the cost of seed and fertilizer and received half the crops when sold or divided.

None of us were happy at Middlesex. Our landlord liked the idea of renting his large 60-acre farm to a clean and neat church-going, non-smoking, non-drinking family with seven boys ages 10 to 19. He had just evicted a family with drinking and behavior problems. To get us to farm his place, he promised to build us a new house. He never did. The shack we lived in was considered uninhabitable even then, and some of our neighbors were also sharecroppers with Tobacco Road lifestyles.

In January, 1940, we moved back to the Hornes Church community and sharecropped a three-horse farm with Mrs. Annie Biggs. That was the year I left home to work my way through college.

Our family stayed there three more years and decided to seek salaried jobs that were more remunerative. In 1940, farm laborers earned 75 cents to $1 a day. Pay for picking cotton went up to $1 per hundred pounds. The average picker would pick 150 pounds a day. That was a hard way to earn a living. Like other sharecroppers, my parents and brothers found salaried jobs during the war and left the Biggs farm in 1943.

We were part of the trend, for the demise of sharecropping as it had been known since the Civil War, occurred during and after World War II. In 1935, there were 13 million sharecroppers in the South; in 1950, less than 5,000.

My Profane and Law-Breaking Father
by
Paul Jernigan

Our automobile, such as it was, a two-door 1929 Model A Ford, was converted into a "truck" during the weekdays to transport produce from our Wayne County farm in to Goldsboro to sell. We removed the passenger-side front seat and the back seat and filled it with peaches, watermelons, cantaloupe, butter beans, green beans, field peas, okra and tomatoes. On Sundays, my parents, John and Mary Jernigan replaced the seats and loaded my brothers and me into the car to attend church and Sunday school at Woodland Friends Meeting, a distance of three miles.

A Model A would be tiny beside a compact car of today.

Sardine packers could have taken lessons from the Jernigan family on Sunday mornings. Daddy, who weighed 175 pounds, drove. Mother, also large, held the youngest in her lap. One of the twins squeezed between them. The rest of us six active boys, ages 5 to 14, crammed into the back seat, with the largest three holding the smallest three on their laps.

In the winter, our body heat kept us warm, for the car had no heater. In hot weather, a couple of us would ride on the running boards. Sometimes, two boys would ride on the front fenders, holding tightly to the radiator cap, while our father drove slowly down Highway 117.

Dad was a hard worker, made his children work, never wasted time and never took a vacation. He was very religious. A puritanical Quaker, he did not smoke tobacco or drink alcohol.

Dad loved to sing, and he sang all day. His loud and gifted voice carried across the fields and woods as he worked, joyously singing or whistling familiar hymns and World War I songs. Sometimes, midway a melody, he would shift mocking bird-like into another. It was, perhaps, his way of overcoming frustration.

Once, when things were very bad and he didn't know anyone was watching, I saw him behind the barn sobbing uncontrollably.

I only heard him use profanity once. In the summer of '33, when I was 13, we were in the field pulling watermelons to be sold. Leaning over to get another one, he suddenly jumped away, yelled words I'd never heard, ran across the field, breaking the world's record for the 100-yard dash, grabbed a long stake from a pile, rushed back to the melon and began madly beating the ground beside it. I thought he had gone berserk, but he was killing a coiled copperhead snake, which had struck at his hand but missed.

In January 1934, my father did not have money to buy new North Carolina license tags. We still went to church each Sunday but used dirt back roads and paths through sandy fields and piney woods. He knew it was illegal to travel state-maintained roads without current license plates.

By March, the gasoline tank was almost empty. One night, Daddy drove the several miles to John Waters' filling station to buy 25 cents worth of gas. The last quarter mile was on a state-maintained asphalt road. When he drove up to the gasoline pump, a state highway patrolman was parked nearby.

Dad had to come home and admit to us that he had gotten a citation and a $5 fine. The patrolman told him not to drive without current license tags unless he wanted to spend some time in jail.

This was the first and last time my father was caught breaking the law.

SOUTH CAROLINA

How a Day Trip Became a Nightmare
by
Mary Mooneyham Dixon

In February, 1931, just after I had turned 6 years old, my mother announced to me that we were going somewhere together. She didn't say where. I noticed that she was packing a suitcase with my things only, so I asked, "Why aren't you putting your things in, too?"

She picked up a pair of her stockings and tossed them in.

Soon, my parents, Elsie and Arthur Mooneyham, my baby brother Howard and I were leaving our home on Huger Street in Columbia in a borrowed car headed toward Spartanburg County. Eventually, we drove onto a campus with big brick buildings. I had never been there, but I was trustful, because Mama was taking me. Then she left me in that strange place with a woman I had never seen before. I was screaming and crying and trying to run after my mother, but that strange woman held onto me and pulled me into a room and locked the door.

After I stopped crying, I found myself among blind girls. I had never seen a blind person before. I didn't know it then, but my parents had put me in the South Carolina School for the Deaf and Blind at Cedar Spring. I had just gone from being a hearing kindergarten student to a deaf institutionalized child.

When I was 5 years and 9 months old, I was making mud pies on the front steps of our home. I stopped to run into the house to tell Mama that my neck was hurting and I felt sick.

Medical knowledge was not as advanced as today, and at first, the doctor did not know that I had spinal meningitis. Later, I was put on what I thought was an ironing board, an operating table, and given an awful smelling stuff (ether) so they could put a serum up my spine. While I was in Baptist Hospital, my parents were not allowed in my room, but I could see them through a glass door.

I recovered from the illness with my hearing gone. I could read lips from the start and was still a talkative little girl, so Mama

71

thought I wasn't paying attention when she called to me. In the '30s and '40s, the deaf were not allowed in the public schools, so the doctor advised my parents to place me in the school for the deaf and blind before I forgot how to talk. That's why they housed me with the blind children. I was considered "oral deaf." Those who could not talk or lip-read were deemed "manual deaf." Each group had separate classes. I attended classes with deaf children but lived with the blind ones.

The blind loved to hear me sing the Jesus songs I had learned in kindergarten. They would ask me to sit on their laps and sing for them. But I was very unhappy and missed my parents, my older brother, Ray, and Howard, a toddler. I did not see them for four months, when school let out for the summer.

To add to my misery, I was punished one day for stealing. A partially blind girl, whose green metal locker was next to mine, had mistakenly put her candy in mine. I saw it and was returning it to hers, when she observed me out of the corner of her eye. She told the woman looking after us that I was stealing her candy. The caretaker did not believe my version and she spanked me with a wooden paddle and made me stand facing the wall in the hall for a whole hour. Oh, how I longed for my mother! She would have believed me, for she had taught me that Jesus didn't want us to lie or steal.

I cannot remember any Christian instruction at the school during my primary years (age 6 to 9). However, I had learned about God, Jesus and His love at Mama's knee. I already knew how to pray, and I prayed often as a child.

After a couple of years with the blind, I was moved upstairs with the deaf children. I felt so much better with the ones more like me. They taught me sign language, but I still had speech language and instruction in the classrooms.

While in the primary group, we were not allowed to go outside without a chaperone. When the caretaker decided to go out, we all went out. We came back in on her command. Lights out was at 7:30 p.m. In April and May especially, it was hard to fall asleep in such light, but the rules were enforced.

The primary department for white children was in a three-story building with classrooms, dormitories and a dining area. Other children were not allowed there. The black students were housed and taught in a building down the hill from our campus. We were strictly forbidden to have any relationship with them, although a few of the boys worked as waiters or in the kitchen of our dining hall.

Mary Mooneyham, 13, seated in front of the covered walkway linking the dorms to the main building at Cedar Spring. 1938.

They also worked in the dairy. The deaf black girls did our laundry.

It was a nice change when I was moved up to the mid-age group. We had the nicest, sweetest caretaker, Miss Lucille Stone, from Filbert, South Carolina. She mended our clothes and gave us comfort when we were sad or had family burdens. We loved her, but still it was not home, and I cried often for my family. I only went home for two weeks at Christmas and three months for summer vacation. With no car, my parents could not visit. Some students who lived in towns surrounding the school got to go home on weekends.

Once a girl in my dorm was excited about going home to Clinton. When she got there, she found that her father had killed her mother and then himself. It was so hard for all of us. We felt her pain, but there were no counselors to help us.

Beginning in the fifth grade, we had fifteen minutes of chapel every morning, where we would sing a hymn, tell our favorite Bible verses and have prayer. On Sunday mornings, we went to our classroom for an hour of hymn singing, Bible study and storytelling. We were taught to sing with our hands on the piano to feel the vibrations. The manual deaf really loved the marching vibrations to "Onward Christian Soldiers," their favorite. I loved singing all the hymns until one of my relatives at home said, "Be quiet. You sound awful." After that, I would sing in silence around others and out loud when alone.

Once a month, a deaf preacher came. And occasionally, Mr. Laurens Walker, the superintendent, would decide that we would all go to a small Baptist church down the hill. What a sight we must have been: all dressed up in our Sunday best, marching two-by-two, the Baptists, the Presbyterians, the Catholics and even the Jews! Our principal, Miss Louise Walker, sister of the superintendent, interpreted the sermon in sign language with no spontaneity. She made it really boring, but I shudder to think now what it would have been like then if we had had separation of church and state. The Christian part helped to make life at the school a little brighter. I prayed often, for I knew God was with me when my family wasn't.

Maybe the Depression had something to do with our food. It was awful and mostly came out of a can, except the cooked dried beans. The miserable menus added to my homesickness. I never once ate fried chicken, roast, steak, pork chops or any kind of fried food there. On the other hand, the faculty ate like royalty. We watched hungrily as the carts went past our tables to their dining rooms. We saw fried chicken, cake, the works. They had real

74

butter. Ours was white uncolored margarine. Our milk was unpasteurized.

The worst meal in our primary years was breakfast. We would come to our chairs to find cold grits on our plates, so hard we could pick them up with our hands. We were ordered to eat them, but at our table was a retarded girl who got grits shoved on her plate. The poor girl was trying to eat all of them for us. I hope God has forgiven me for my part in it. To this day, I refuse to eat grits.

On Sundays, we had lunch at 2 p.m. Generally, it was three wieners, a slice of bologna or one sausage patty. Desserts were usually chocolate pudding, Jello gelatin or canned peaches. We always had mashed potatoes on Sunday, but that was fine, because they made good sandwich fillings. On Sundays, we had no supper. They gave the primary children one roll and a glass of milk. When we were older, we got two small apples to take to our rooms for supper. I would often sneak out a mashed potato sandwich inside my coat. When the dining room matron, who was the superintendent's mother, caught someone taking food, she would throw it in the pail for the pigs. I never got caught, I was so slick. But, like the others, I drank lots of water on Sundays to ward off hunger pangs.

I was sad when I had to leave our dear caretaker, Miss Stone, for the older girls' dorm and more restrictions. We were locked in our dorms and had to have special permission to go out. Like the primary boys and girls, we had to go outside when commanded, whether we wanted to or not or whether sick or not.

Never did I get over my homesickness. Several days before I had to head back, I started crying, even when I was 18 years old, for I hated that place so. Looking out my train window, I saw other mothers crying at having to part with their children. I never saw mine show any emotion. My dad, who was a diesel engine mechanic for the Jeff Hunt Road Machinery Company, always found time to take me to the station.

In the early years, there were ten or eleven in my class. When I graduated, there were only two of us. Many just couldn't take it any more and dropped out. One blind boy ran away after climbing out his ground-floor window. He was totally blind, but he made it to the highway, a long walk, and hitchhiked his way back home to Gaffney. His parents brought him back, but he did it again and again until the school expelled him.

I wanted to run away, too, but I was scared that Mama would spank me, and I knew she would bring me back. During graduation exercises, I was named Outstanding Student of the Year. What a shock! The students knew I was a mischievous one, but I loved the teachers and they loved me, so they voted for me. My parents were in the audience. I hope they were proud of me.

For many years after leaving, though, I had nightmares of being back at the school. In my dreams, I would feel trapped, unable to get away from the place that seemed a prison. My husband would wake me up, as I was screaming in my sleep.

And, even though I felt like a prisoner set free when I got out, my deafness made entering the outside world very hard. Although I did exceptionally well on tests for jobs or business school, I was not accepted because of my handicap. Thank God things are different now.

I wonder if God has something He wants me to do for Him as a deaf person. I ask myself, "Have I touched anyone for Him in any way?" I hope I have, but I don't see it yet. God has blessed me in so many ways. I look at the bright side. I don't have the nightmares as often anymore. I have some hearing back, thanks to the new miracle, a cochlear implant, when I was 61 years old after 55 years of total silence. My husband of 55 years, James, and I have five beautiful daughters, five granddaughters, three grandsons and two precious dogs. No great-grandchildren yet! I am truly blessed.

Let Them Eat Plums
by
Thelma Percival Kube

My parents, Milton and Maude Percival never seemed to give up hope that we would survive on our farm in Edgefield County, South Carolina. Diligently and optimistically, they plowed, planted and weeded. But without fertilizer, there was poor yield, and each year there was less.

One spring day in 1933, my mother, my sister Mary Alice, my sister Elsie, and my three very young brothers Gene, Harvey and Tessier waited for my dad to come home with something to eat. Daddy had left early that morning to sell our horse, the last remaining thing of value.

The day before, we had picked wild blueberries, and Mother had used the last of the flour to make blueberry dumplings. There was nothing left. During the winter, we had eaten all the canned fruits and vegetables and the cornmeal. We had eaten or sold all the chickens. Our only milk cow had died giving birth.

That morning, a soft sun warmed the seeds in the ground, renewing hope for a better year, as we waited on the front porch for Daddy's return. Mary Alice was combing Mother's lustrous red hair. I was dangling my feet over the edge of the porch, when Tessier, almost 2 years old, climbed on Mother's lap, and asked to be breast fed. He had been weaned from the breast at least six months. Thinking he was being playful, I laughed.

When Mother said, "He is hungry," I really felt bad.

Elise and I immediately remembered we had seen ripe field plums while playing in the woods. We asked Mother's permission to go and pick them. Dinner that day was plum stew.

Coping with "The Way Things Are"
by
Nancy Artemus Gough

"You can look at it, but don't touch it," my father, Clarence Artemus, said.

Neighbors and friends had come from all around to see our Model T. It was not new, but not many families, white or black, in Richland County owned a car in 1929. And Daddy didn't want to see a single scratch on the fine black Ford that he had bought with commissions he had earned selling insurance.

Like my mother's father, William Watson, who lived next door, Daddy owned his own home. My mother, Annabelle, never had to work. She was busy raising what would soon be seven children.

Grandfather Watson worked for a rich white man but never did a day's manual labor. Dressed in a suit, tie and hat every day, my handsome granddad, with light skin and curly hair, collected rent from tenants in Mr. Alworden's many rental houses. Mr. Alworden had a house built from the ground up for my grandparents. Their beautiful hardwood floors had to be polished with oil, but they were far better than our pine floor boards, which Mama cleaned with detergent and water.

Before and during the Depression, we never knew poverty. Even in the worst of times, most people paid their insurance. That's all they had for security, and they knew it. My oldest sister had married and moved out before my baby sister was born, so Daddy always had six children to feed during those years and never had enough left over for a savings account. But we were well fed and clothed in outfits that my mother, who didn't sew, paid a friend to make.

Grandmother, however, had managed to build a considerable savings account before the Depression hit. She cried and cried when the Victory Savings Bank closed sometime before the nationwide bank holiday in 1933. Founded in 1921, Victory was, I believe, the only bank owned and operated by black people in South Carolina. Fortunately for her, it didn't *stay* closed, and she got back part of her savings.

Later, in 1938, when my dad became ill and had no money for me to finish Benedict College, Grandmother said to me, "If you will continue to make A's and B's, I'll pay your tuition."

I was lucky to have a grandmother who was willing and able to pay tuition. There were many other students during that time who were not so lucky, but our people didn't consider higher education a luxury. It was something we were desperate to have, even though the Depression lingered on. Many students at Benedict, and other colleges and universities, paid their tuition in monthly installments. Some worked almost full-time jobs to make those monthly tuition payments and still attended classes. Often entire families would work and pool their money to send one sibling to school, and another, until all the children in a large family of modest means could finish college.

In our community, we had prestige, like many of the other families whose children attended Waverly School—the doctors, lawyers, funeral home operators and ministers. But in the community as a whole, we had to accept "the way things are."

For instance, Daddy would take us downtown to buy shoes for school. Some stores would not sell to us. One shoe clerk said we could come in, but there were not seats enough for us all in the back, so some would have to stand until the others had been fitted. Never mind that there were plenty of empty chairs in the front (white) section.

While in college, I worked every summer and part-time during the school year at Providence Hospital run by Catholic nuns. I could not have been medically treated there, but I could work there—in the kitchen. Had I become ill, they would have taken me to Waverly-Good Samaritan Hospital. Luckily for our family, that hospital allowed white doctors to come in, even though black doctors could not set foot in a white hospital.

Although our family was cared for by two black doctors in our community, we also had a third doctor, who was white. He cared for us because he liked us. By law, he could not call us in from his waiting room, but if he chose to come to our home, he could. Occasionally, a white doctor allowed black patients to sit on the porch behind his office and would call them in when no white patients were left.

The police didn't protect us much then. Whites, from any walk of life, could do whatever they wanted in our community with no fear.

One day, a white insurance agent who had lent the previous week's premiums to a black fellow got angry when the debtor couldn't pay the loan or the next premium. The agent took off chasing him—right through the house of one of our neighbors—and out the back door. When he caught him, he beat him up in plain sight. The bewildered homeowner was ill, but neither he nor his family would have called the police. The insurance agent knew it.

Though diligent about arresting our people, local policemen were not very diligent about protecting what few rights we had.

Police officers came to our house one night to arrest our father. "Clarence Arthur, you're under arrest," one barked.

"My name is J. Clarence Artemus," Daddy said politely, as they were roughly handcuffing him. His words did not stop them.

But Daddy persisted. "Clarence Arthur lives around the corner on Oak Street."

No apologies were made to the clean-living deacon. They uncuffed him and left.

When I was a teenager, Hazel Scott, a talented night club pianist, was enormously popular with blacks and whites. A movie was made about her life, but it was not shown at a Columbia theater with a balcony designated for "colored people." It really upset me that white people, shabbily clothed and unclean, could go in, but no matter how well-dressed my friends and I were, we knew not to even ask to see that movie. We had the same problem with other movies that were the best Hollywood had to offer or represented a significant event in American culture.

In Depression years, we could not control or change the *real* deprivation in our lives, but I vowed then that, if I ever reached the point when I could do something, I would.

Then, in 1954, I had the opportunity to attend the first of three five-day workshops at Highlander Folk School, located a little north of Chattanooga, Tennessee, the same school where Martin

79

Luther King got some of his early training. We called it "The Promised Land," because it allowed us to experience life as it should be, with peaceful, productive coexistence and cooperation between people of different races. Blacks and whites lived together on campus in harmony and with a purpose greater than ourselves or even our own communities.

I had to go in secrecy, for fear of losing my job as a teacher at Waverly School. Septima P. Clark, the only other South Carolina person who attended that first 1954 workshop, was subsequently fired from her teaching position in Charleston. The "power structure" made a concerted effort to fire anyone who was associated in any way with any group or activity that sought to change the way things were. I worried every time I returned to Highlander, but those experiences changed my life and, I hope, the lives of those I was able to help during the civil rights movement.

A few years later, I had to smile when I heard Dr. Martin Luther King, Jr. say, "I have seen... 'The Promised Land.'" Only a few of us who had had the 1954 Highlander experience knew what he really meant.

My Two "Little Worlds"
by
Jerri Gibson McCloud

My "little world." I actually believed that the end of the road below Winnsboro, South Carolina was where the road stopped. This is where Norma, my sister, and I lived with our aunt and uncle after our parents were killed in an automobile accident. I knew the road went north because of the places we had lived. But as for farther south—well, this was it.

Those were the days when we were given a nickel and sent to the store. Imagine! Carrying a huge sack of candy home was the highlight of our day.

Every Saturday morning, Norma and I would walk one mile to the theater in town to watch the serials and a movie. Together, we rushed out of the house so as not to be late to see Roy Rogers or Gene Autry. Norma was 5 and I was 4 years old. This went on for two years. Fortunately, there was no crime to speak of and no traffic problems.

Our house was right in the middle of a mill development that was several blocks long and several more blocks front and back. In that close community, everyone knew everybody.

At Christmas, they decorated a huge cedar tree in the middle of a circle at the end of our block. When they turned the lights on, it was the most beautiful sight I had ever seen. It seemed to make baby Jesus along with Santa really come alive.

We played mostly cowboys and Indians with the neighborhood mill families' kids, mimicking the movies we enjoyed.

More often than I care to remember, there were nights (beginning when Norma was 6, and I was 5) when we were left home with no one to care for us. We often sat out on the front steps crying. Mr. Renfrew, the school principal who lived across the street, would come sit with us until we grew tired. Tucking us into bed, this wonderful compassionate man would wait until we fell asleep before leaving the house. It must have been Mr. Renfrew who reported our problems to relatives, as we were removed from that home and left Fairfield County in 1940 to head north.

Our grandmother, Elizabeth Roe Gibson, who lived in the community of Blackstock in Chester County on a dairy farm, reluctantly took us in. After all, she had raised 24 children. Our grandfather Abe had 13 children by his first wife before she married him and bore 11 more. Imagine her, as old as she was and with so little money, starting again with two young children. At least, we were surrounded by many aunts and uncles, who lived within 100 yards of her house.

By then, Norma was in the last half of the third grade and I was one grade behind. They enrolled us in the elementary school in Great Falls. I loved to jump rope with the other kids before school would start, and lots of times, we played hopscotch, too.

Life was extremely simple and pleasant on the farm. Nobody had money back then, but there was plenty of food. Unlike today, the children always ate last, and because Grandmother was a great cook, she always had more people for dinner than the ones that slept there.

But there were some things about our "new world," that I never got used to.

Aunt Fannie fixed lunch for us every day—terribly thick sandwiches with some sort of preserves and "ukkkie" butter which was not pasteurized. Even though I helped to churn butter, I never cultivated a taste for that nor clabber, nor warm milk. After all, I had lived "up north" and then in Winnsboro, where we bought our food and pasteurized milk. On the farm, with no electricity, there was no refrigeration. The cows were milked twice a day, and dairy products stayed out on the table with a cloth over them between meals.

"Running" water from the spring was very sweet and never quenched my thirst. The bathroom was an outhouse.

There were only three bedrooms in Grandmother's house, with many beds in each one. The two front bedrooms were always neat, but the back bedroom, better known as "the boys' room," was always a mess with clothes heaped up in piles everywhere. Nobody ever went into that room except "the boys" (her unmarried sons or male visitors).

The yard had no grass, just dirt. That dirt was swept with a brush broom (tall brush from the field cut near the root and wrapped with twine) every day, front and back. Chickens roamed the yard, sometimes even on the porch from which they wandered into the house.

Our family's only transportation was a horse or horse and buggy. If the school bus came in a heavy rain, we would miss a day of school because we could not cross the creek, for the water always rose above the rickety bridge.

Speaking of the creek, the most fun of all was going there to play in the water. We always found a hole deep enough to swim in. But many times, we got stuck in quicksand, which was frightening.

A favorite playmate was Buddy, one of my first cousins. He was like a big brother, although he was only six months older. He would sit with me at night with a kerosene lamp, trying to teach me to read. Remember we were both just in the second grade. I have never forgotten the kindness Buddy showed me during this very sensitive and emotional time of my life in the second of my two "worlds."

Education, A Family Affair
by
Daisy Butler Gibbs

Mama said she always wanted her children to be educated. She had 14. Three died in infancy. I was the thirteenth, born in 1919.

Our parents, Henry Bluford and Henrietta Reeder Butler had done remarkably well. My father had sharecropped on the Hillory Long place. He did the paper work and saw how sharecroppers could never get out of debt and could never leave. He was the exception.

Years before, his mother, who worked as a mid-wife, took out a Metropolitan Life insurance policy for him. When it matured the same year he had a good harvest, he took the $1000 and bought property on Newberry's Boundary Street in the section known as Cannon Town. In its day (1922), the house he built was considered large, with four bedrooms, a dining room, kitchen and big hall. There, we raised chickens and had a garden.

Daddy rented land outside of town from Lawyer Holloway, where he grew wheat, corn and cotton. Two of my brothers, a sister and my father could pick a bale a day. Mama washed clothes at the homes of some of the "big shots" in town for 50 cents for a washing, which took most of a day. A couple of the families were very generous and gave her pretty dresses their daughters had tired of wearing. My sisters and I always looked nice when we went to Drayton High, which had grades one through eleven.

During some of the Depression years, we had to live on the Holloway property, so Daddy could rent out our fine home. That meant we had to walk four miles to school and four miles back every day except in bad weather. He had reserved one room in our town home, so we could bunk there overnight.

A professional syrup maker, Daddy traveled around from plantation to plantation in the late fall. He got paid in barrels of molasses. In the winter, my younger brother Theodore and I took a one-horse wagon to town to sell molasses and garden vegetables on Saturdays. That's how we earned spending money.

Meanwhile, Mama's dreams of educated children was beginning to come true. My second-oldest brother, H.B., Jr., who had been cooking for the Gilders family, moved with them to Washington, D.C. While there, he attended Howard University.

My oldest brother, Willie, went to Winston-Salem to seek his fortune and found work at a tobacco factory. Josephine, Jessie Mae and Addie Lee got married and didn't finish high school, but the next one, A.T., walked and caught rides to Allen University in Columbia.

To help pay for his schooling, my father took a wagon load of barrels of molasses, bushels of sweet potatoes, and bags of cornmeal and flour. A.T. also got a job at the university. He became a teacher and principal and helped pay for Elizabeth to go to Allen.

Gertrude, 13, and Daisy, 10, on the Butler front porch. 1929

To pay the rest, Elizabeth stayed in the home of a "big shot" Negro family in Columbia and worked for them. Grady soon followed her at Allen on a football scholarship. Her two-year teacher training allowed Elizabeth to teach at Drayton High until she could get her degree in summer school. But first, she helped pay for Gertrude to go to Allen. Gertrude lived and worked in another "big shot" Negro's home. Like Elizabeth, she came back to Newberry County to teach with the intent of getting her degree later. While at the Rosenwald school known as Lietzey near the town of Pomaria, she helped pay for my education at Allen.

I was lucky. I was the first to go four years straight through. In my junior year, my brother H.B., Jr., who had earned a B.D. degree at Howard came to Allen to teach Bible. He gave me the option of living on campus, which I thoroughly enjoyed. I finished in three-and-a-half years plus summer school.

I immediately got a job teaching grades three through five at Helena School before I received my degree. That small three-teacher school in Helena let out in April. I earned only $36 a month, and I had to walk two-and-a-half miles each day to get there.

The children had it worse. Even then, in 1940, we had almost no supplies. Most children could not buy or rent books, so they did their "homework" at school and had to memorize a lot. I brought lots of loose leaf paper and pencils. At the end of each day, I took up the pencils and kept them in coffee cans.

We had a cook, but the mothers had to give us potatoes and other vegetables and fruits to supplement the government foods like flour, oatmeal, prunes and tomatoes. I would usually put whatever we had in a big pot on the pot-bellied stove and cook our lunch.

The children liked to sing this little ditty while it was cooking:

"They talk about President Roosevelt
And say he ought to be dead.
But if it hadn't been for him,
We wouldn't have no government bread."

I probably learned more about teaching those few months than all the other years that I have been a teacher, principal or member of the Newberry County School Board.

Meanwhile, Theodore was at Allen University and working. He left to go into the Army, but when he got out, he used the G.I. Bill to finish at South Carolina State in Orangeburg.

Out of Mama's eleven living children, he was the seventh to complete college and realize her dream.

And They Say Northerners are Cold
by
Bob Edmonds

I might have been a Yankee had it not been for the wind.

Before my parents Ralph (whom everyone called Bill) and Onie Edmonds were married, Daddy and his father farmed in McCormick County and raised hunting hound dogs. My father mentioned in a letter to a Chicago dog customer that he would soon be wed. The man suggested that they come to the North to "make some money."

Right after their wedding in 1924, my folks struck out for Chicago in a Model T Ford. After four days on the road and not a single flat tire, they arrived in the "Windy City" where my father was employed as a carpenter in a steel mill. My mother longed for home and abhorred windy-every-day living on Lake Michigan.

After they had saved enough money for a "nest egg" ($420 to be exact), they returned in late 1925 to McCormick County, where they bought a 53-acre farm for $410. South Carolina, of course, was agrarian, and nearly everyone in that county farmed.

People said the area was just beginning to recover from the War Between the States when the boll weevil declared war on the cash crop, cotton. Even so, farming was a happy life. Then the Great Depression hit. By then, our family had grown. William, Thelma and Betty were ahead of me, and I came along in 1932.

Like most farm families, we survived on our own garden vegetables, dairy products, eggs, chickens and hogs. We grew corn to feed the animals and for cornmeal, ground at the nearby grist mill. Everyone had a cane patch. We hauled the cane to the nearest cane mill. The owner made syrup for us and took a toll of that in payment. Cotton was still the cash crop.

The folks in town controlled the money—the merchants, cotton buyers and lumber mill owners.

Daddy borrowed $60 from a merchant in March and bought garden seeds, paid for sugar, salt and other necessities until he could sell some frying-size chickens for more cash. Until we ginned the cotton and sold it, we bought nothing else to speak of.

School did not start until late September so everyone could get the crops in. When I was in the third grade at McCormick Grammar School, we were late selling our cotton bales and I had no shoes.

"Town" boys would kid me, "Aren't your feet cold?"

"No. They're not cold," I'd say, even though my toes felt like ice cubes.

I was a skinny kid, but so was everyone else. There were not many fat people in South Carolina then.

During that same year, 1940, I made friends with a "town" boy. Robert, whose father was into cotton and lumber, wore nice clothes, not denim overalls like I did. Actually, I had one pair. My mother washed them after I went to bed and let them dry overnight, so I could wear them the next day.

Finally my friend invited me to go home with him after school and play. His home was on a paved street. It was really something! It was painted white with green shutters on the windows. I could see that the house was painted inside, too. And they had electric lights.

Robert and I were headed to the rear entrance of the house,

when his mother met us. She looked me up and down and asked, "WHO is this?"

I looked her straight in the eye and proudly replied, "My daddy is Bill Edmonds!"

After staring at me for several moments, she suggested that we play in the backyard.

We had fun making horses out of chinaberry branches and riding them around, dragging the leaves along the grass. Chinaberries made great ammunition for our sling shots, and we practiced shooting. After a while, I told Robert goodbye and walked the winding dirt road to our farm home, where I had chores to do before dark.

The next day, Robert told me we could not be friends any more.

More Than a "Senior Slump"
by
Ann Spratt Wilson

During my senior year in high school (1934-35), life as we had known it changed forever.

From a friend, my father Frank Killian Spratt had rented a house on top of Paris Mountain outside of Greenville. It was adjacent to a farm he owned which stretched from the bottom of the mountain to the top. Our parents had often talked of building a home there, and I assumed that construction would begin on a beautiful house for us soon.

But Mama, Edna Garlington Spratt, was very unhappy. For the first time in her life, she had to cook, and getting groceries up there was a real problem. My two older brothers, Frank and Edward, had come home from college. They and my younger brother, Roy McRee, complained because all three of them had to sleep on a sleeping porch accessible only through my parents' room. That winter, the chateau-style stone house was freezing cold. The furnace wouldn't work. Only the living room fireplace was warm.

At the time, I didn't realize that Papa had lost our spacious, attractive home on West Prentiss Avenue in town. All I could think about was going to Agnes Scott College the next year.

Before the Depression, my father had three wholesale grocery warehouses (in Greenville, Spartanburg, Clinton and Laurens). He had owned part interest in two auto dealerships, a tire store, chicken hatchery and two farms.

Our family always had fancy new automobiles to drive, from a Buick and huge Studebaker touring car to a Hupmobile, Essex, a Whippet and Willys Knight or two and even a Lincoln Zephyr. Unlike most women of her day, Mama always had her own car. And my older brothers built T-Model "strip downs" in the back yard.

When I was 12, Papa came in to dinner one day and told us that the state had passed a law requiring people to have a driver's license. He had bought licenses for everyone in our family, including me, my 11-year-old brother, and Nannie, our grandmother Garlington, who lived with us.

That afternoon, my little brother and I took our Whippet roadster out for a spin. Around and around the block we drove, taking turns for our first experience ever behind a steering wheel.

Unfortunately, Papa was also on the board of directors and a stockholder of several banks around South Carolina.

At first, he had to consolidate the warehouses, keeping the one in Greenville. Small businesses all over upstate South Carolina owed him, but few could pay. Then most of those little banks closed. As the directors were held personally liable, Papa had to ante up to them although his debtors were unable to pay him. He sold his interest in the dealerships at a great loss. He lost his other businesses and the house. Eventually, he had to "go on the road" in his Willys Knight as a salesman for Durable Sign Company.

Meanwhile, Frank, who had to drop out of Furman, finally got a job at Piedmont Print Works. He would come home from the night shift colored with whatever dyes had been used on the sporadic jobs the company had.

Although Edward had been studying to be a preacher at Columbia Bible College, he also had to drop out. He got into a training program for S.H. Kress earning $14 a week for six 10-hour days plus many hours of unpaid overtime.

Then a recruiter for Flora MacDonald College convinced my mother that, as a 16-year-old away from home for the first time, I would "do well" at the college she represented. My mother informed her that "Ann would do well *anywhere!*" But the decision was made, and I had no part in making it. I was dropped off by Papa at "Flora Mac" in Red Springs, North Carolina, that September without ever having seen the place and knowing only one other student.

Every cent they could scrape together paid for the tuition

(about $300 in all, including room and board, paid over a period of time). A friend gave me a steamer trunk, and I filled it with hand-me-downs from a cousin. Judging by my wardrobe, the girls at college must have thought I was rich. My benefactress was. She had given me quite an array of fine evening gowns to wear on the nights we had to "dress for dinner." And her suits and coats were trimmed with furs. Every outfit had hats and shoes to match, which fortunately fit me perfectly.

The $5-a-month spending money, which was not very regular, had to cover school supplies, stockings (no runs were allowed), cosmetics, stationery, postage, movies and even blue books for exams. The $5 I had to pay for my required gym suit took a whole month's spending money. It was a big deal to have a spare nickel for a Coke.

Thanks to the National Youth Administration (NYA) program, I had a job answering the phone in the dean's office. I made $15 a month, which I never saw, for it went directly to the school.

Some students paid their fees in sweet potatoes and other produce grown by their farmer families. We got very tired of eating sweet potatoes several times every week. Other girls had to work in the laundry, so my first job looked pretty "cushy."

For the seven years after I left for college, I had no place to call home. Papa was still traveling. Mama had gone to take care of her mother-in-law in Chester during her last illness. Nannie rented an apartment in Greenville to keep house for Edward and Roy Mac, who was still in high school. Frank had joined the Army. Nannie continued as society editor for the *Greenville News.*, where she was best known for writing a column called "Facts and Foibles."

The next summer, our family's situation changed again. My younger brother said he was "abandoned at age15." Edward had been transferred to the S.H. Kress headquarters in New York. And while Roy Mac was working at a music camp, Nannie, who, at 75, became too deaf to continue her job, moved to Laurens and took an apartment with her sister. The plan was that Roy would go to Charlotte, live with Papa, and finish at Central High School.

He had won the state's highest award for playing reed instruments, and Greenville High School's band director, Guy Hutchins, was as dismayed about the move as he was. He would be missed in the choir as well as the band. That's why Roy Mac spent his senior year living with his band director in Greenville.

My mother's life changed again, too. While visiting her brother in Knoxville, Tennessee, Mama was offered a job as manager of the Faculty Club at the University of Tennessee. The Shields mansion had been donated to the University, and they wanted her to decorate and manage it as a faculty club. She could have an apartment there. After I spent two years at Flora MacDonald, she urged me to finish school at the University, which I did.

Most of the people we knew were in similar situations. Everyone coped in their own way, but one of my father's friends, who was in a business somewhat like his, did what we considered to be dishonest. Mr. P. put all his assets in his wife's name and declared bankruptcy. He came through the Depression unscathed, because he never paid his debts.

My father, on the other hand, had liquidated everything he owned and paid off everyone he owed. Papa had no more use for his former friend.

Everything Except Corn Whiskey
by
Katherine Kennedy McIntyre

My father bought an old mill on a creek in Kershaw County. I played behind the waterfall, watched it spin rainbows, stuck my toes and fingers in the splash, protected by a wall of rushing water.

My father could always find a way. The cotton business, which he loved, failed. So he sold insurance and bought a mill. To farmers without money he said, "Pay me with corn."

My father ground it into meal, and we ate corn meal pancakes, corn meal muffins, corn-on-the-cob, corn meal grits, corn meal mush, corn fritters, corn pudding, cornbread, corn pie, corn sticks and corn dogs.

While many men were jumping out of windows, my father got a mill and made us bread.

From Plain Navy to Elegant Wine
by
Irene LaGrone Thomas

Navy blue uniforms. That's what we had to wear at Winthrop College in Rock Hill. That year, 1934, we had a three-quarter-length coat added to the navy dress, suit and extra skirt that we could choose from each day. Of course, we had white blouses, too. And Mother had fashioned a variety of white collars, some with embroidery, some tatting, to go on my plain navy dress.

Winthrop did not allow national sororities, so we had clubs with Greek names. It was important, then, to be included in one of the "upper ten." I was. Mine was Tau Omega Kappa, and it was of great concern to me to have the proper clothing for parties. We would be going to one of the fine hotels in Charlotte for a banquet, and I was not sure Mother could afford to buy me an outfit. Paying tuition had been hard enough.

Mother, in fact, had become the breadwinner in our family in Edgefield County after my father, Elzie LaGrone, who had been an agricultural inspector for the government, lost his job. A Coleman from Aiken, Ethel LaGrone, my mom, had been a fourth grade teacher but now was the head of the Central grammar school between Johnston and Aiken. She had once said that, if she had to take in boarders, she would rather go to her grave. Well, she did take in boarders and was still above ground.

Mother came through for my banquet. She sent me her brand new wine-colored suit of fine wool. We were the same height but not the same weight, so I had to take a nip and a tuck or two. But I did feel elegant at the banquet.

Mother had one stipulation: that I box and ship it back immediately, so she could wear it to a teacher's meeting.

Cheap Gas
by
Irene LaGrone Thomas

On Sunday afternoons in the little town of Johnston in Edgefield County, there wasn't much to do but ride around.

From high school days, even before we were dating, four of us would pool money to buy gas so we could ride around looking at boys, hoping to find someone interesting.

We were college age when we spied one from Batesburg at a football game. Of course, we took off for Batesburg that Sunday afternoon.

On our way home, the Ford touring car with no windows started sputtering at the edge of Ridge Springs. Fortunately, there was a filling station nearby. Unfortunately, we only had a few cents collectively.

Since I was the driver, I walked up to the attendant, a kind, unpretentious fellow. "I don't know what's wrong," I told him in a damsel-in-distress tone. "This thing has died on us."

"Probably needs gas," he said knowingly.

"Oh, no, it couldn't be that," I said.

He examined under the hood and stuck a yardstick in the gas tank. It came out dry. "How far do you have to go?"

"Johnston," I answered contritely. I admitted that we didn't even have enough money to buy one gallon.

He disappeared into the station to speak to the owner. "I think we can afford to give you a gallon," he said when he returned.

When I got back to Winthrop, my conscience bothered me, so I repaid him—in postage stamps.

OVER THE EDGE - SOUTH CAROLINA

At Midnight I Cried
by
Frances Herring Shipman
Author of *At Midnight I Cried*

In the summer of 1936 on a hot, quiet and cloudless day, my mama began coughing more than usual.

She had been called "the prettiest woman in Dillon County," for Annie Herring was tall with dark hair, greenish eyes, an olive complexion and a smile that would touch your heart. But at 31, she was very fragile.

About all she could do was to read and talk to us. Of course, I could read for myself, for I was 10. My brother, Walter, Junior, was 5 then. The baby of the family, Betty Ann, was 3.

When she asked me what I wanted to be when I grew up, I shared my dream of writing music like the beautiful orchestral sounds that came from our old Philco radio.

Our home in the quaint country town of Dillon, South Carolina was a one-story frame house that sat on concrete pilings, "gray-white and old as Moses" I used to say. Like most houses then, it had a side, back and front porch, and like everything else in Dillon, it was uptown—300 Calhoun Street, to be exact, one block off Main Street near the courthouse.

Our daddy worked as a mechanic at Thompson Chevrolet Company also on Main Street. My kindly father's hours were long

92

and hard. But, unlike so many other men in our community, he had a job.

Poverty was everywhere. People couldn't find work, and even the employed were struggling to make ends meet. Some of the local farmers had already lost their land. Few had the cash to feed their livestock. With no money for food, many people had to depend on others for help. Some, I'm sure, went hungry. We at least had a garden, but we couldn't afford some other things like milk or juices.

Often I wondered if we could survive the Great Depression. It left Daddy with no money and medical bills he couldn't pay. And Mama was still sick.

My friend from across the street and I were playing in the fig tree. I heard Mama coughing. I jumped down from the tree. "Lucille," I said, brushing myself off. "My mama's sick and needs me."

I ran up the steps to the porch, opened the screen door, and saw Mama bent over an old chair in the sitting room, coughing up blood. I screamed, " Oh my God! I'm going to get Daddy! You just hold on, Mama. I'll be right back with Daddy."

We didn't have a telephone, so I ran all the way up Main Street to the body shop and told Daddy that Mama was coughing up blood again. We jumped into his old Chevrolet and drove to our doctor's office. Dr. Vick Branford was one of only two physicians in Dillon.

Daddy hopped out of the car and ran inside. "Vick, please hurry! It's Annie! I'm so worried!"

His office was only a few blocks from our house, and we were there within minutes. Mama was so weak that Daddy had to put her back to bed, where Dr. Branford examined her.

When he finished, he sighed, "Walter, I've tried everything. Let's take her to Duke Hospital. They've got a new fluoroscope there and can look at her lungs. I'm afraid it looks bad."

Daddy packed Mama's things and arranged for Aunt Lelia Bethea, who lived close by on Calhoun Street, to stay with us. Short and plump, Aunt Lelia was black as midnight with curls as dark as her skin. She had a smile that could melt the world, but Aunt Lelia wasn't smiling that day. She was shaking her head. "Sho do hate dis," she said, hustling us around her.

Day turned into night, and we three children were in our room. Daddy couldn't call, so all we could do was worry. I walked the floor. It creaked under my bare feet. I could feel the wind seeping through the wall. Finally, Daddy appeared at our bedroom door.

I always thought Daddy looked like the slender movie actor William Powell with his mustache and dimples when he laughed. But that night he seemed shorter than his 5'10" frame.

He motioned for Aunt Lelia to leave and sat down on the side of our old iron double bed. The coil springs squeaked. "I'm glad to be home with you children," he said. "I know it's late, and I'm sorry."

Betty Anne was asleep in her little bed. He put his arms around Junior and me and spoke to us in a strained but gentle voice. "Your mama has a deadly disease and won't be home for a long time, if ever."

He explained that, after they saw the doctor in Durham, North Carolina, they had no choice but to take Mama to the State Sanatorium in Columbia, where she could get the free medical care and the rest she needed. Tuberculosis, sometimes called consumption, is very contagious, so she could no longer be around him or us. He didn't tell us then that the fluoroscope had showed that Mama's lungs were almost gone.

Could it be that she had caught the disease when she had generously taken vegetables from her garden to a poor neighbor sick with consumption? That woman got no medical care at all and had died.

Daddy looked exhausted. He ran his fingers through his hair and sighed deeply. Shaking his head, he said, "I'm tired. You young'uns go back to sleep. I'm going to bed, too. I've got to work in the morning. We need every penny now. I don't know what to do, but I'm sure it's going to be okay."

As Daddy was leaving our bedroom, Granddaddy's old clock on the mantel began to chime twelve o'clock. At midnight, I cried.

HOW OTHERS COPED

Everyone could think of someone they knew "worse off" than themselves. Some pointed out relatives and neighbors who found unique ways to cope with the Depression.

NORTH CAROLINA

Grandpa's "Un-Owed" Debt
by
Lexie Little Hill

Grandpa was a man of faith, and I never doubted his Heavenly call, because there was no way he could feed his ten children on offerings from his churches.

A Baptist minister, Thomas Patrick Little of Union County divided his time among four churches in Union, Anson and Stanly. At the churches in the adjoining counties, he preached one Sunday a month, and the offering taken at the end of the year might be $25. The other churches, many times, substituted canned goods, potatoes, hay for the horses, etc.

His harvested crops primarily fed Grandpa's family. Every spring, he borrowed $1,000 from the Marshville Bank to buy seed and fertilizer for planting season. Then, in the fall, he paid the debt with profits from the harvest.

One early spring day, the bank owner stopped Grandpa as he passed the bank. "Mr. Little, I know it is your custom to borrow $1,000 every spring," he said. "Since I'm not busy, would you like to come in and sign the papers for your loan? Then when you are ready for your money, these details will have been taken care of."

Grandpa signed. The following week, the Marshville Bank closed.

Grandpa's youngest son, G.T., although married, lived at home and planned to apply his savings toward the purchase of a home. Immediately, G.T. approached the bank's owner and said, "Mr. Parker, I have $1,000 in savings in your bank. Would you take my thousand and apply it to the thousand my father never received?"

Parker became extremely huffy, grabbed G.T.'s shirt collar and through clenched teeth, replied, "Young man, who do you think you are? I want you to know I don't do business that way!"

L. L. Parker was known in the community as "Double Barrel Parker" because he was always shooting someone down.

G.T. lost his $1,000, and Grandpa raked and scraped to pay Marshville Bank the money he never received.

Anna Belle
by
Lexie Little Hill

Sixteen-year-old Anna Belle rode my school bus in Union County. She was painfully shy, always sitting quietly in her seat, head down—in sharp contrast to the seven brothers, who, every day, never left the bus without some sort of confused struggle or chaos.

I felt really sorry for Anna Belle, because she didn't have a mother. Her father lived in a drunken stupor, leaving her with responsibilities she was unable to handle.

Suddenly, there was no Anna Belle on our bus. Nobody seemed to know anything at the time, but several weeks later, I learned that Anna Belle had married a 60-year-old man from Polkton who could give her a better life.

John Camp
by
William S. McClelland

I was cutting the grass with my trusty Clemson push lawn mower when a black shadow drifted down our driveway. John Camp's dark skin glistened with sweat. He was so thin that, if he had turned sideways, I wouldn't have seen him at all.

I ran over to him, full of questions, but before I could ask anything, John said, "Mr. Bill, could you give me sump'in to eat? I ain't et in three days."

There was nothing in the kitchen but two biscuits, which I gave him. He snapped them up like a hungry hunting dog.

How long had he been gone? Several weeks, I guessed.

John Camp had been the fix-it genius, who kept everything running on the jobs for my father's construction company. Since I had turned 14, I had worked with him as the "crane monkey" (or "go-fer") previous summers. Dad paid me out of his pocket and did not list me on the company payroll, but John, who was somewhere between 30 and 40, was a valued employee.

My father had become a successful contractor after years of being a vice-president of the Tucker-Laxton Company in Charlotte. He had bought a home on East Morehead, spent a great deal of money renovating it and was happy with a large (for the times) mortgage.

When Roosevelt closed all the banks in the country (Sunday, March 5, 1933), the bank Dad dealt with, Independence Trust, did not reopen. Construction companies, in those days, paid the workers in cash on Saturdays. Dad's money was tied up, his notes for payroll were called due, and there was no recourse but to put the company into bankruptcy. This was catastrophic for the laborers, some of whom had been with Dad for years, while he was with Tucker-Laxton and then with the McClelland Company.

The men scattered all over looking for work, and we saw little of them. But one day, John Camp came to say goodbye. He was going to New York, as he had heard there were jobs for black men up there.

Dad finally found temporary work finishing up small construction jobs that were sitting abandoned, and he was gone long hours six days a week. I attended Central High School and walked home each day. The various fathers of five of us kids had worked out a schedule for taking us to school, but getting home was up to us. Mother gave me a quarter each week with which I was to buy four tickets for the streetcar. But I invariably spent it on something else, so walking was the only answer.

On the day when John Camp walked back into our lives, Mother came in soon after he had eaten the biscuits. She flew into cooking something more for John to eat. We had chickens, eggs and hog meat from the farm, also vegetables, so had fared fairly well in the food department.

While John was sitting on the back steps eating, Mother openly appraised his clothing, which, to put it bluntly, was a collection of rags. His shoes did a miracle just staying on his feet. An old suit of Dad's would clothe him. Shoes would have to come later.

John was quite vague about how long his trip from New

York to Charlotte had taken. I don't think he really knew. His only comment was, "I hadda walk mos' the whole way. Mos' people wouldn't pick up somebody like me."

He diplomatically waited until Dad got home before his next request. "Mr. Mac, could I stay here—sleep in the garage — 'til I find sump'in? I got nowhere to go, and I'll work for my keep."

Dad hesitated just a moment, then nodded assent.

We had two cars, both Series 60 Chryslers and both bought second hand. One could stay outside; one could not, because it would not run. Hoppe Motors had worked on it twice, then hauled it out to us, saying it could not be repaired.

I brought my Boy Scout cot out of the attic. Mother produced quilts from her seemingly bottomless cedar chest for John. Like all large homes built in the '20s, there was a servants' commode on the back porch, so that was no problem. We were in business.

John started the next morning and worked steadily, all day every day. With those over-sized laborer's hands, he waxed and polished the floors, beat the rugs, washed all the windows, sharpened my lawn mower and cut the grass each week. He fired the furnace, cleaned up the cellar and repaired everything that did not cost money to fix. This latter duty was important, because many things had just been let go, due to lack of time, money and energy.

We had a big yard, and the back third had been closed off by a trellis. Behind that had been a beautiful flower garden, which, for lack of attention, had declined steadily. My aunt Lala, who taught school and lived with us, had slowly replaced flowers with vegetables, but they had languished, too. John cleared the weeds from flowers and vegetables alike and even convinced the grape arbor to produce again.

In his spare time, John practiced his enormous patience on our Chrysler which would not run. His total tool kit was a screwdriver, a pair of pliers, a nail and a piece of string. Honor bright, that was all he had. I came home from school one day, and there sat John on the fender with the hood up, and the engine running. And it ran from then on—for errands, for trips, for whatever.

Dad had found a better job, so John's food was not the problem Mother had feared. And John's 5' 10" frame was filled out once more.

Meanwhile, Mother was developing fierce and incapacitating headaches. So she decided to teach John to cook. And that's when he found his talent! Mother planned the meals, and John cooked them. The simplest items were delectable.

Mother and Daddy scraped together enough money for me to go to the University of North Carolina. When I came home for Christmas 1933, John was gone. My horizons were expanding, so I thought little of it. But when I returned for spring break, Dad told me that John's fame as a cook had spread through Charlotte, and he was now a chef at a country club.

I never saw my friend again.

Beggars, Blackberries and Black-Eyed Peas
by
Herman Poole

I never went to my parents' table when there wasn't food on it, although they had to feed ten children. Many people in Randolph County did go hungry and actually searched for food.

About every train that passed on the main Southern line had hobos standing on top, holding onto the side rails or inside the open door of a box car with feet hanging down. On the spur line in front of our house that ran a daily round-trip between High Point and Asheboro, there were more men seeking work, food and maybe a little adventure, too.

A few jumped off and came to our house, which was on a nameless dirt country road (now Edgar Road). The beggars were both Negro and white. Although some offered to work, we never employed any, but Mother never turned anyone away. She shared whatever she had cooked.

A fellow from our neighborhood took off to ride the rails, and his folks wouldn't know where he was for months, even a year. A good electrician, who was separated from his wife, he seemed to enjoy being a drifter. Once, his parents found out that someone had found him hanging under a car on a brake rod, where he had nearly frozen.

Another man from our community reported much later that, during the Depression, he "broke his arm eating breakfast."

When I questioned him, he explained, "I fell out of a persimmon tree." He added, "My clothes got so raggedy that I had to put them in a sack to hang them."

Daddy raised tobacco. One year in the heart of the Depression, he lacked $2.50 out of his proceeds to pay for the fertilizer bill.

But my father, Troy Poole, was generous, even when he had very little. I was amazed, though, the day he bought a horse for some new neighbors across the road, who had moved on the land to farm but had no horse to pull the plow.

One year, he had left one field vacant, and blackberry vines had grown up all over it. I looked out our window, one day, and saw 100 people, Negroes and whites, picking blackberries. Most were strangers, although Daddy recognized some from High Point where he regularly went to sell produce. We children wanted to make them leave, but Daddy said, "No, leave them alone. Those people need something to eat."

After that, he planted that field with black-eyed peas and invited people who were out of work to help themselves. Soon, we had a field full of pea-pickers.

Mr. Crump
by
Joy Smith Burton

During the early '30s, the bottom had fallen out of the economy, and Charlotte had bread lines like many of the larger cities in the country. Needy, hungry locals come downtown to stand in line for hours to pick up foodstuffs.

Families living farther out in Mecklenburg County's small communities were unable to get to town. They either had no cars or could not afford gas. Most of the small towns surrounding Charlotte had economies built around textiles. That industry had practically shut down. The formerly working folk were extremely poor and hungry.

Mecklenburg County public health nurses would gather bags of bread and other foods and efficiently personally deliver groceries to poor families.

Twenty plus years later, I was a public health nurse, and the staff was still talking about a client known only as Mr. Crump.

Nurse Walker drove her black county car, a Ford, up to Northern Meck to Mr. Crump's clapboard off-the-ground mill house. There was a very rested, relaxed able-bodied man rocking back and forth in his straight-backed chair, his enormous feet propped up on the porch railing. He had not worked for weeks.

The nurse gently honked her horn and politely let the man know his groceries had arrived promptly.

101

Crump hollered from his perch on the unpainted wooden railing. "You got legs, ain'ten you? Bring 'em on up and set 'em on the kitchen table."

She did.

Depression Shoes
by
Joy Smith Burton

Grandmother Kitty had always been a "stretch everything" person. The daughter of poor tenant tobacco farmers from Virginia, she was my first mother-in-law, and as the wife of her second son, Robert Rhett Hall (Bobby), I really liked her.

After marrying William Samuel Hall, Katherine Smith Lester raised two boys, Snooky (a "junior" born in 1929) and Bobby (1931) in Salisbury, Rowan County, North Carolina.

Kitty told me about buying a white pair of shoes too large for Snooky in the spring. The shoes would see him through the summer. Then in the fall, she polished them with very dark thick brown polish and dyed the shoestrings. Those would see him through the winter.

The next spring Kitty would wash them good and apply a thick white polish over and over again, until she had covered the white over the brown. Then Bobby could start the spring with "new shoes."

The Old Boy Himself
by
Dr. Donald Harris

"Back during the Depression, when I was a youngster, me and my folks and my little sister lived out in the country near High Point, and we had nothing to eat in our house. We were about to go hungry when word came down to us that Mr. Harris had brought food for everybody. He left it at the little Baptist Church where we went, which was a few miles from our house. We walked over there and picked up food and then went back for more, and we didn't have to go hungry. Mr. Harris had done it for everybody in the community. You know something, Mister? In all these years, I never forgot that act of kindness on the part of Mr. Harris."

I never met the fellow who told that story with tears in his eyes. The "mister" he was talking with was my friend Don Holt. Mr. Harris was my dad, Jake Harris, better known around High Point as "The Old Boy Himself."

Jake always did everything he could to help poor people as well as his own family.

He had a store on High Point's Washington Street in Guilford County, where he was trying to sell clothes. Upstairs, he stored furniture. A friend of his, Cliff Ollis, was sick and so was his wife. They had a bunch of children and no place to go. Jake built a couple of rooms up there and furnished them for the Ollis family. Mrs. Ollis, who had cancer, died there. Mr. Ollis later died at the TB sanatorium and the children were placed in an orphanage. But, for a while, they were all able to stay together.

At his Washington Street store, he kept all sorts of interesting objects—books, family Bibles, family albums, old pictures and such, which people came in just to peruse. One day, a nicely dressed middle-aged lady came in and asked him if she could spend some time looking at the stuff he had displayed.

Of course, he welcomed her and she spent a number of hours doing just that. In the meantime, people would come in and talk to Jake. He would cut up with them and make them laugh, and they would hug him.

The lady watched it all and eventually came over to Jake and complimented him as "a really good person," one whom people loved and who loved them in return. "I'm going to give you a gift that you can always share with other people," she said. "I've been a Baptist missionary to Tibet for many years. I became very good friends with a Buddhist monk, and he conferred on me the power to bring good luck to others by giving them a small token. I'm going to confer that gift on you."

And she did, and since that time, Jake has given away countless "lucky pennies."

Being an outgoing person with an abundance of humor, he was always welcomed wherever he went. He was the only Jewish man I know who was an honorary member and on the administrative board of a white Baptist church and the only white person I know who assisted for many years in administering a black Baptist church. He anticipated removal of color barriers years before the Civil Rights Act when Ruth Moon went to work in his store as a young woman.

The Old Boy Himself gave unselfishly to his community. He

went out of his way to help feed, clothe, house, furnish, find employment, bail out of jail, try to repair relationships, pat somebody on the back and offer a host of wonderful other gestures to others.

I've seen him walk into more than one place where a man was drunk and had driven his wife and children into the street. And I've seen Jake get the fellow settled down and allow the family to come back in.

I saw him clean up a room where an old black lady was sick in bed. He emptied out the slop jars, freshened the bed and made sure the lady had something to eat and drink on her nightstand.

In fact, my twin and I helped him, and we learned that there's no honest work that is beneath you.

Living "On the Cheap" With a WHAT?
by
Margaret G. Bigger
Co-Author with J. Carter Goldsborough of
Only Forty Miles of Pavement

"You will have a check ten days from the date of this letter," stated the insurance company's reply to my father's threatening note. The letter was undated.

Just two weeks after they had returned from their brief honeymoon visiting relatives, my mother Mary Griffin (now Mrs. John Carter Goldsborough) had an appendectomy.

She had moved from her tiny quarters into Daddy's larger room at the Mansion Park Hotel in Raleigh and almost immediately became ill. After the operation, she rallied quickly, but her insurance company had been sluggish in paying. My father, who was called "Goldy" by his friends and customers on his United States Gypsum Company sales route, took action against the local company. It had been organized by some State College professors.

When he received that sly response from them, he called on his Mansion Park neighbor, Thad Eure, who was then the Principal Clerk of the House of Representatives.

"To settle our insurance problem, Thad arranged a hearing," Daddy recalled. "I helped notify others with claims. None of us got a cent, because some of the professors had used up all the money taking weekend rests in the infirmary." He cleared his throat and frowned to make sure I understood his displeasure. "At least the company was put out of business."

And so, with new bills to pay, my parents started housekeeping. Well, sorta.

Later that year, 1935, my father's monthly paycheck went up to $240. Pooled with Mother's salary from the State Prison Department, they could afford an apartment. Well, sorta. It was a quarter of the N. E. Edgerton home on Raleigh's Hillsboro Street, half of the first floor. Daddy turned the square enclosed porch into an office. Their bedroom and living room together had been the Edgerton's ornate parlor. Heavy molding crowned the walls, which had panels of pink damask.

Traveling salesman,
Goldy Goldsborough
Circa 1929

"Mary and I used to lie in bed and chuckle at the cherubs in the ceiling clouds," Daddy told me. I was chuckling then, because he always pronounced cherubs "cha-RUBS."

With their combined salaries, Mother and Daddy decided they could afford what others would have considered a sign of wealth. They hired Melissa, whom Daddy called "a godsend!" Not only was this pleasant African American woman a marvelous cook, she was thrifty, too.

Even years later, he was amazed how she handled money. "We gave her $12 a week for household needs: groceries, meat, cleansing products and our laundry and cleaning. At the end of the week, she often had a surplus in the cigar box, even when we had guests for dinner!"

He said he could still taste the delicious greens she used to cook. Unlike anything he had ever eaten, he finally teased her into admitting what they were and where they came from. Those unusual greens were dandelion leaves from the bank of a yard on her route home from the grocery store.

But a maid? During the Depression?

After they had left the Mansion Park, Daddy considered Melissa necessary. My mama, the brilliant businesswoman, who could type and sing simultaneously, could not cook.

105

SOUTH CAROLINA

Cree
by
Katherine Kennedy McIntyre
From Gray-Haired Grins & Giggles

From my playhouse window, I could see her—Cree, with all her cats, cats of all kinds, running wild and free. She lived across the fence in an unpainted shack behind a pale green colonial. The shack may have been a large woodshed at one time.

If you asked Cree her age, she would say, "Steppin' outa sebenty nine; steppin' into eighty."

And if you asked, "How many cats?" she would say, "Thuty-nine."

My father said it seemed to him she looked exactly the same when he was a little boy. He thought her name may have come from "Creole."

Nancy Zemp, owner of the colonial, wanted Cree to leave. She said the cats were too much. "But I can't make her go," she explained. "If I did, she would travel up and down the street, singing and telling everybody I threw her out. I wouldn't have a friend left in this town."

Cree earned money singing spirituals in a cracked, quavering voice. Her small body ambled everywhere. She would stand, arms akimbo, wizened head leaning to one side, hand on hip, dark face a cobweb of wrinkles, foot tapping the earth.

"Swang low, sweet cha-yu-ut,
 Coming for to ca' me hum-m-m."

People dropped money into the hat she passed around. She always announced that it was for her church, but privately admitted she kept it in her mattress.

She often climbed the fence and serenaded my friends and me. We adored her and contributed all the nickels and dimes we could get together.

One day, when she saw a young man riding horseback with me, she beckoned for me to come to the fence. "Marry him, Sugar Pie," she whispered in my ear. "His family own half the land in the county."

Moultrie Burns was a community leader, president of the local Rotary Club, a successful businessman. He was concerned about Cree.

"Cree," he told her, "your friends worry about you. If you keep your money in your mattress, someone may come in the night, knock you over the head and rob you. If you put your money in our bank, where I keep mine, it will be safe. You too."

"Thank you, Mr. Moultrie. I'll surely do that, first thing in the morning. Thank you, sir."

The Great Depression struck. Our bank failed. The money I had saved, dollar by dollar, was gone. Everybody was broke.

My father had heard about Cree's money. He went to see her. "How can we help, Cree? There was no way anybody could know this would happen. I'm so sorry about your money."

Cree bowed her head, then raised it and looked straight into his eyes. Her wrinkled face shaped into a crooked smile. "Don't you worry, Captain. I knew my money was safer in my mattress. I got it all."

She was probably the only person in Camden, South Carolina, with cash intact. At the wedding of a young white woman whom she had cared for as a child, Cree handed her a hundred dollars for a wedding present.

Looking back, I think Cree learned from her cats how to land on her feet. Or maybe they learned it from her. She was a survivor.

She finally began to trust in banks. She deposited all her earnings into a savings account and collected interest. This impressed her so much that she wrote a will and left all her money to Mr. Henry Carrison, president of the Bank of Camden, "because he took such good care of it."

HOW WE WORKED

Men, women and children worked wherever and whenever they could. Although both states were predominantly rural, the Piedmont boasted many mills, but they were not running full-time. Merchants had it tough. If they sold on credit, they might never get paid. In many circumstances, educated males found themselves doing menial jobs. If educated, females taught school or worked as a nurse. Others did domestic work or sewing. Just about everyone else found more creative ways to make money.

NORTH CAROLINA

Cotton, Our Cash Crop
by
Lexie Little Hill

In the '30s, cotton fields surrounded every farmhouse in Union County and beyond. The majority of every rural family's income came from King Cotton, the lofty title given this lowly plant. It was not uncommon to see cotton piled on front porches up to the ceiling, stored until farmers could take it to the gin.

We were poor, but we were not alone. All were struggling to make ends meet, so when the price of cotton remained low year after year, our livelihood was threatened.

Planting, chopping, hoeing, poisoning and picking cotton was a family business, and Bessie, Si and I had a part in it all. Si was our water boy until he could see above the plow handles, then he was promoted to Daddy's plow hand.

When the cotton was out of the ground two or three inches, Bessie and I walked row after row, hoe in hand, thinning it to two stalks every six inches (give or take a few inches) and digging up every blade of grass within the row. If we had had several inches of rain, we had to hoe the dreaded carpet of grass, making sure we didn't pull up the cotton with the blades. We hoed as often as necessary until the cotton was strong enough for cultivating. Daddy and Si then took over until the leaves shaded the ground, preventing grass from outgrowing the plant.

Then came the nasty, loathsome job of poisoning the cotton before it bloomed to keep boll weevils from devouring our crop.

I could smell the distinctive stench of arsenic and black molasses before I got out of bed, and I hated to get up. Immediately after breakfast, Daddy said, "Hurry now. Get on some old clothes and your worst shoes. Cover your hands with your old socks, and be sure your hair's under your cap. Don't dilly dally now. You know what to do."

I knew what to do all right, and I *hated* it. Daddy picked up the bucket filled with the poison and the short-handle mop he made from torn strips of cloth wired to a stick. I followed him to the field. Before handing me the bucket and mop, he said, "Listen to me! Keep your hands away from your face until you finish the job and get cleaned up."

I knew from his concerned look that this stuff was very dangerous, and I took his next words very seriously.

"This is poison," he said, "and you will become very sick if you don't do this." He stayed alongside me for about half the row and warned me once more before he walked away.

I was scared. I walked row after row, periodically dipping the mop into the bucket of sticky poison and dragging it across the leaves. My fingers seemed to be blistering from the weight of the bucket, and I fought discouragement, because always on my mind was, *there's ten acres of this!*

At the end of the day, my overalls were so stiff that they stood up by themselves. My shoes, covered with the gooey mess mixed with dirt from the fields, were heavy, and the mop handle stuck to the socks on my hands. Shoes, overalls and everything on my body were disposed of. But I was still revolted from the stench of this putrid mixture.

If poisoning cotton was the most loathsome, picking it was the most painful. Since Bessie's back had given her trouble for years, this was even more painful for her.

To keep the burrs underneath the cotton bolls from cutting our hands, we wore socks with the toe area cut out. Even then, our fingers around the nail area became scratched and bleeding. The tow sack (burlap bag) attached to a band and tied around our waist held the picked cotton. By the time our sacks were half filled, our backs began to weaken from bending over.

The fuller the sacks, the weaker our backs. They seem to become welded in a bent position, making it impossible to straighten unless it was done very slowly, bit by bit.

As the day wore on, the sun beat hotter and hotter on our backs. Sweat ran down our faces, around our eyes and mouth until we tasted the salt. The only welcomed relief was a watermelon patch next to the field.

I was 16 when Daddy set aside a three-acre field "just for you kids," he said. "Whatever profit you make will be yours. But you can't neglect the family fields."

We were so excited! Si plowed, planted and cultivated our field. Bessie and I chopped, hoed, poisoned and picked our cotton. At the end of the season, I had a whopping $130.

For the next 11 months, I paid for everything I bought with my own money and started my "hope chest" as well. I was in "high cotton" that year of '39!

But the following year, the price of cotton dropped to six cents a pound. Our profit was 0!

That was the year I hired myself out to a neighbor. I emptied bag after bag of cotton onto the sheet beside the field to be weighed at the end of the day. Trying as hard as I could, I never picked more than 130 pounds. At a penny per pound, I wasn't getting rich fast.

Cash crop, indeed!

Moving Up:
From Tobacco Barn to Shack
by
Julia Neal Sykes
Co-Author with Oscar DePriest Hand, Sr. of
Footprints on the Rough Side of the Mountain

Things went from bad to worse for us sharecroppers in Mecklenburg County. My soft-spoken father, Clarence Neal, couldn't take another year on the Brown farm in Mecklenburg County. He heard about yet another in Gaston County just across the Catawba River, where he could get a fairer deal. Mom, Dad and my seven brothers and sisters and I loaded all of our measly belongings on the wagon and headed to our next home.

Oh, what a letdown when we saw the house on the Forrest Gaston family farm in North Belmont! Talk about "Little House on the Prairie"—that was it! An old log tobacco barn had been converted into a house by adding two rooms, a kitchen and bedroom, to it.

We all started crying.

"How could you do this to us?" my mom sighed, as she hugged and consoled my baby sister, wiping her own tears away. "We can't live in this filthy barn!"

My older brother Clarence, Jr. declared he was leaving.

With tears streaming down his face, my dad pleaded, "I'm so sorry. I never took time to look inside the house when I came to see the farm. Please, let's stick together. We can fix up the place."

It took a lot of work. Dad was the father of improvisation. This tall, stately man was endowed with innate talents and wisdom. Those same hands that guided a plow were designed to carry out many creative endeavors then and in the years that followed.

He made a real stairway to replace a ladder to the room on the second floor and covered the exposed log walls with newspapers, using a flour-and-water paste. A perfect fire hazard. We must have had a guardian angel, because we never had a fire. And our only means of heat was an open fireplace!

We scrubbed the place from top to bottom and worked on getting rid of the bedbugs by spraying and using a blow torch on the bed springs.

All of us, except Mom, who had high blood pressure, had to work in the cotton and corn fields and tend the sweet potatoes and sugar cane. I hated sharecropping, because it seemed that we were always working for the white man and earning very little profit for ourselves.

Life on the Gaston farm was the same old story as far as making a decent living was concerned. But at least we were eating better. We had a garden, and Dad raised hogs, so we had pork as well as chicken and eggs. Dad and my brothers set out rabbit boxes, and my father's baited fishing baskets caught catfish and croakers from the Catawba River. One of Dad's responsibilities was making molasses, which was a real breakfast treat with hot biscuits.

We children started taking extra jobs wherever we could in order to buy things for ourselves. In the spring, we picked strawberries on a farm nearby. In the fall, after the cotton had been picked and ginned and a settlement had been made with Mr. Gaston, we would go back through the fields and pick any bolls that were left. We called it "crack cotton," because the bolls weren't open. My dad would take it to the mill and sell it for us.

We also took in washing and ironing for the whites, and my older sisters, Annie Lee, Blandina and Carrie Bell did domestic work.

Plagued by more hard times, we moved to the Sloan Springs farm about two miles away. The house was better, but making a living farming was impossible.

Gaston County was a textile region. However, none of the mills, as far as we knew, were employing blacks inside at the time.

By then, I was old enough to do domestic work. Mrs. Springs hired me to work for her for 50 cents a day.

Finally, Dad came to his senses and decided to abandon the sharecropping business. He found a job working as a janitor at St. Leo's Catholic School for Boys and as a chauffeur for the nuns.

Hallelujah!! My heart jumped for joy. I never wanted to see another farm—didn't even care when Mr. Springs booted us off his property before our rental house in Belmont was completed.

Dad managed to find a place in Mt. Holly for us to live in for the next couple of months. Nine of us somehow squeezed into a tiny three-room filthy shack. Even that was better than the "Little House on the Prairie."

The impact of the "Big D" (Depression) was like being kicked in the rear by "Maude," the old mule of experience. Too sore to sit down on the "stool of do-nothing," we clawed our way out of it like a baby chick pecks its way out of his eggshell in search of life.

We, too, found life. A better life.

Tobacco: Brown Money
by
Thomas Winston Pruitt

Cotton may have been king in some North Carolina counties, but tobacco ruled Granville County and affected my life—even when I got a haircut.

I grew up on tobacco farms, first my father's, three miles west of Oxford on Highway 158, and after his death (when I was 11), my grandfather's, five miles from Oxford on the same road.

Clement Currin, a tenant farmer on the Eakes' farm close by my grandfather's place, cut hair after supper. I would walk to his house. He would plow until dark, so he had a lantern on his front porch to see to cut. His price: a nickel or a pack of tobacco (RJR, the roll-your-own kind). I knew where to buy six packs for 25 cents, so I always paid in tobacco.

I did my share of tobacco farming, too. Many a fall night, I sat in a shed off the barn all night to keep the temperature about 100 degrees while the tobacco was yellowing or raising it gradually to 180 degrees when the stems were drying. We never had a tractor, only horses or mules to break the ground.

Like other kids in the community, I wore flour-sack shirts and fertilizer-bag pants. It was really embarrassing if our mothers couldn't get the "Smith-Douglas" off our bottoms. But we thought it funny to see a woman weighing 200 pounds with "Smith-Douglas" on her butt.

After our father, Allie Marsh Pruitt, died, Mama (Flora Hopgood Pruitt) moved my brother, sister and me to the home of my grandparents, Ed and Mary Ellen Daniels Pruitt, whom we called Granddaddy and Grandmammy. Our old maid aunt still lived in their house as well.

Two women are too many for one kitchen. Mama made three, so she cooked in the washhouse, and we ate out there. It was a 20' x 20' chinks-and-log room. We took the kettles out, and Mama fixed our meals on a wrought-iron range.

To make money on the side, I trapped rabbits. A painter and a carpenter in town would pay 75 cents a rabbit, if it was skinned.

One year, I raised an acre of tobacco myself. It brought $49. A local man had promised to sell me a pony, a buggy and a saddle for $50, and I really wanted them for courting. He relented and let me have all three for $49.

After I graduated from Berea School in 1934, I got a job at a gas station in Oxford pumping gas, fixing punctures and washing car windows back when all stations were "full service." I worked six days and nights a week (from 7 a.m. until 10 p.m. with an hour for lunch and an hour for supper). I stayed with my aunt, who lived a mile from the station and had a son about my age. I took my meals at a boarding house.

It was at the station that I met Kathleen Royster from Bullock. She drove in with some of her girlfriends to get some gas.

I bought my first car, a Dodge coupe, for $12. My sister, who worked for a beauty salon, and I bought it together.

Not long after that, I started measuring tobacco fields for the Department of Agriculture. After the price-stabilization law was passed, farmers were allowed to plant so many acres of certain crops. In this case, if the tobacco didn't sell, the government would buy it.

Before then, if a farmer couldn't get a decent price for his graded tobacco — or got "passed" — he took it home.

Later, I went to work at an Oxford hardware store owned by two old bachelors, Amos and Jack Clements.

For more than seven years, I clerked in the store and made tobacco flues, elbows and T's of tin. Those pipes conducted the heat that ran through a barn to cure the leaves and stems.

I was making $17.50 a week.

"Boy!" said a friend of mine. "You're making more than a teller at the bank."

That surprised me, but with annual bonuses based on great profits, I was able to marry Kathleen in 1939, buy a home in town and $800 worth of furniture.

Mr. Jack was a real character. Among other things, he sold guns. One man bought a 12-gauge shotgun, and a short time later, another regular customer bought a 20-gauge. Each decided he wanted a different gauge, so Mr. Jack took back both the guns, exchanged them one for the other and charged $50 a person to make the deal.

Both men were furious. After all, in the winter, they hung around the store heater every day.

Jack shook his head, "If you fools didn't have sense enough to get together, it's not my fault."

Some of our customers were unique, too. A woman, whose husband was the registrar of deeds, bought a slop jar. "Jack, wrap that up," she said. "I'm not going to take that to my car unwrapped."

In those days, most every family used slop jars, so Jack saw no sense in wrapping it, but he offered to carry it to her automobile down the block.

"You put it in the car," she said, "but I'm not going to walk with you."

On vacation, I visited my uncle in Waycross, Georgia, who owned a tobacco warehouse. I decided to speculate: buy cheap tobacco and sell when the price went up. I made so much that I wanted to go into that business full-time. I told Amos and Jack my plan.

"Stay, Winston, and we'll give you a third interest in the store," Amos said.

That was tempting, because they had $100,000 worth of inventory and made a good profit. But, instead, we came up with a compromise. I would work for them from Christmas until July. I stayed in Waycross until that warehouse closed. Then I commuted to my uncle's other warehouse in Petersburg. That one would close in November, and I would go back to Oxford to clerk and make flues.

Tobacco was good to me. Eventually, I bought those warehouses in Waycross and Petersburg and another in Douglas, Georgia. I ended up owning three in Petersburg and two in Douglas. We rented out our house in Oxford to move to Petersburg, where we lived for ten years. But the children wanted to return to Oxford.

From then on, Oxford was our home, no matter where my tobacco business took me.

Home Work, School Walk
by
Cedric H. Jones

At our house in Wake County (five miles from Garner; six miles from Clayton), when a child turned 8 years old, he was told, "You have a hole in your hand — to chop cotton."

And chop we did! At 12 in 1929, I was picking cotton "out," that is, at someone else's farm. For the first time in my life, I picked 200 pounds of cotton. Lafayette ("Fate") Austin paid me $2, quite a bit of money then.

When our family saved enough, we went to Raleigh to buy shoes. Although we got some supplies from Garner or Auburn, we didn't think we had "been to town" unless we went to Raleigh.

Back when farmers were paying $1 to pick 100 pounds (that's right: a penny a pound), we did all right. But eventually, the pay was 35 cents for 100 pounds. Landowners who had gotten 30 cents a pound for bales were earning as little as five or six cents a pound, depending on the grade. We were both landowners and hired help, so we lost both ways.

Our land, originally bought by my great-grandfather Eli Jones soon after the Civil War, was on White Oak Road near the Johnston County line not far from the Neuse River. My parents, Truemella and Howard Jones raised seven children (nine were born, but two died). I was the oldest. Our main crops were cotton and corn.

When we had finished our work, we could do labor on other farms for 50 cents a day from sunup to sundown. During tobacco season, I sometimes did that on Alex Atkinson's place, handing the picked leaves to whoever was going to loop them, so they could be hung in the barn to be cured. When I turned 18, my family began growing tobacco, too.

My most important "job" was to go to school, not such an easy chore. My first year (1923-24), both blacks and whites from my community walked to schools in Johnston County and Wake County. The second year, Wake County sent a school bus to take the whites to Garner. I was walking six miles round-trip a day.

When H. B. Marrow became Superintendent of Johnston County schools, he decided that buses would pick up *all* kids, just not the same buses. Soon, we were walking to a pick-up point in Johnston County to catch ours. When we got a new bus driver, a relative of our mother's, he came within a half-mile of our house. Later, he moved to Wake County and could pick us up at our door en route.

Most of that time, I was attending Pleasant Hill, a Rosenwald school. After the sixth grade, I took a district test in Garner and a county test at Berry O'Kelly Training School in Method to determine whether I could move up to high school. I never saw seventh grade, just enrolled at Clayton High School in Johnston County. On May 17, 1935, I graduated.

I farmed until soon after Charlie McCullers, an uncle by marriage, asked me to help him deliver wood to Shaw University. Once on the campus, he said, "You go up to that building and talk to the President." I found President Stuart Nelson, who told me how to enroll. When I was able to save the money, I started college in

116

January, 1937. Dr. Robert P. Daniel was President by then.

I had to miss a semester and find different relatives to stay with different years. Part of that time, I worked in a boarding house. My mother worked extra days in peoples' homes to help out, too. But in 1941, I graduated as an English major.

Degree in hand, I went to North Carolina State College in Raleigh to do the only job I could get—as a common laborer. Of the $12.50 for five-and-a-half-days' work, I was expected to pay fifty cents to buy my lunch and eat in the kitchen. Instead, I usually brought my lunch in a pail. My cousin, Emma Ligon, fixed it for me. I stayed at her house and roomed with her son that year.

Later, I got my first white-collar job—as an insurance agent in Durham.

In February 1942, I joined the Army. While at Fort Benning, Georgia, I finally got to use my degree, teaching elementary education to black boys who had not been to school much. The Special Training Unit administered a test, which, if they passed, made them eligible for regular Army duties.

After the service, my first job was at Perry's High School outside of Louisburg in Franklin County. Later, I got my masters at Columbia University before heading to Second Ward High School in Charlotte.

All that working and walking was worth it!

Shattered Dreams Woven into Rainbows
by
Helen McDade Linder

One August evening in 1935 when Mama and I were preparing supper, Mama said, "Helen, we've got to talk. The mill is going to start up full-time in September, and we really need you to stay home this year." She sighed. "I'm sorry, Helen. I know how much you want to go to college, and I've always wanted you to go...but we do need you here. I've talked with Mrs. Davis, and she said you could have a job in the Draw-In Room with me."

I stared at Mama. I couldn't say a word. I knew I was going to burst into tears, and I didn't want anyone to see me crying. I had worked so hard and done without so much! My dream of going to college was shattered.

Since graduating from high school in May, I had been working in the office of a printing company in Lexington. Normal-

117

ly, at 16, I would have had a summer job at the mill, but it was not running full-time. On my job, I earned $5 a week. My parents had agreed to let me save that salary, even though they could use financial help. My earnings would go for college expenses.

I had already been accepted at Mars Hill College and granted a $250 scholarship. I would have a job at school when classes began in September. With five of us children at home, I knew it would be hard for my parents to send me money, so I had written to ask about extra work there during the school year.

We had lived in Erlanger, a mill village community in Davidson County since 1928. My parents, Rena Alexander and Eston McDade, were skilled mill workers. Daddy was a weaver, and Mama was the best "draw-in hand" in the mill. During the Depression, the mill was often on "short time," and when those periods came, no one worked regularly. Mama and Daddy had gone without full pay since spring, and I knew they really needed more money. There was no getting out of it. I was 16, and I had to go to work in the mill. I didn't cry, but my heart was running over with tears.

It was just like last year!

During 1934, when the mill was on "short time," Mama was pregnant with her fifth child. She had worked, when needed, until the last few weeks before the birth of our newest brother, Carroll, in August. In September, I started my senior year in high school.

One night, my mother came into my bedroom. "Helen, I hate to have to say this, but we need your help. The mill is running full-time now, and I've got to go back to work; we need my paycheck. I've tried, but I can't find anyone else to take care of the baby." Her sad brown eyes met mine. "We wish we didn't have to ask you to drop out of school your senior year, but things are going to get better, and you can always graduate next year."

I couldn't believe she was asking me to do this! I loved school. I had worked hard and made good grades so I could go to college. I had already earned 15 of the 16 credits I needed for graduation. There was nothing I could do but accept the fact that I must stay home to care for Carroll.

When I reported this to Thomas Stokes, our principal at Lexington High, he was surprised. "Let's see what we can do about this, Helen," he said. "You're a good student and should graduate with your class. Tell your parents I'll be out to see them tomorrow afternoon."

In talking with them, he learned that Mama's department

would be working a four-day schedule, Monday through Thursday. The next day, Mr. Stokes told me his plan: I could attend school on Fridays to take only one subject, English. Miss Dorsett, my English teacher, agreed to give me a study outline for daily lessons. On Fridays, she would test me on all the assigned homework and give me periodic exams.

I was elated!

I worked hard that senior year, and in April, I was inducted into the National Honor Society, on a Friday. I graduated in May with my class.

On the Monday after Mama told me I must work at the mill, I explained all this to my employer, Ralph Moffitt.

"You'll never go to college if you go to work in the mill," said my sympathetic boss. "Stay here with us."

"Can you pay me what I'll make at the mill?"

"How much is that?" the printer wanted to know.

"Ten dollars a week."

"I can't double your pay, now," Mr. Moffitt said. "Perhaps sometime, but not now."

I told him I would work until the end of August.

Helen McDade

In September, I went to work at Erlanger Mill. I gave my parents the $75 I had saved.

Mrs. Charles Davis, the personnel director who became my mentor, assigned me to the Draw-In Room, with Mama as my teacher.

After a few weeks, I knew I'd never be the skilled worker my mother was. I did not like the work at all. I made too many mistakes, and Mama spent too much time correcting them. I asked to be transferred to another department. In the Weave Room, I was a shuttle filler. I tried, but I hated every minute of it. I asked for another transfer. I didn't like the work as an inspector in the Cloth Room any better. My next assignment was to the Winder Room, where I stayed for more than a year. This was "piece work," and by working hard, I could earn more money.

Actually, something very good *did* happen that summer of 1934. I met a tall, good-looking young man with curly brown hair, a cleft chin, laughing blue eyes and a beautiful smile. A farm boy from Spartanburg, South Carolina, Dozier Linder had come to visit relatives at Erlanger and stayed the summer to work in the mill. Although he went to Clemson to major in textile engineering, we kept in touch for those two years. We fell in love and married in September, 1937.

My take-charge mentor ordered a three-room house fixed up for us on one of the prettiest streets in the village. We continued to work in the mill and took correspondence courses.

Two years later, I had a miscarriage. When I went back to see Mrs. Davis, she suggested a change. "Would you like to work for me?" she asked.

Those words were as melodious to me as Mama's words about needing me at the mill had been discordant.

You bet I would! That was my first step along a path to bring new life to my shattered dreams. The second step would be bus rides to a business college to hone my office skills. The third, a fun job at a radio station. The fourth, a home of our own away from the mill village! The last, section editor and feature-writer positions at our local daily newspaper. Despite the hard journey, rainbows appeared all along the way!

You Work To Live
by
James Milton Johnson

"You work to live"—that was the typical expression in my home even before the Depression. We sometimes changed the words to "You live to work."

Will T. and Ada Womble Johnson had three girls and three boys. For most of my growing-up years, we lived in a large three-story home in Pittsboro that had belonged to my grandfather, J. J. Johnson, a former sheriff of Chatham County. The house was heated by fireplaces, water came from a well in the yard, and we used an outhouse for a toilet and an out-of-date Montgomery Ward catalogue for toilet paper.

Before I was part of the family, my father owned a store in Pittsboro. He had a heat stroke while helping out during a wheat threshing, then he got typhoid fever and pneumonia. While he was bedridden for several years, an associate ran the store until it closed in 1915, the year I (child number five) was born. After that, he seldom held a steady job. He could operate a sawmill (for $1 a day), but he was not strong enough to cut timber (at 75 cents per day).

120

As soon as I became steady on my feet, it was my job to keep small pieces of wood in the wood box for Mother to use in the kitchen stove. A few years later, I was assigned to keep the larger wood supplied for fireplaces. By then, I had to tend the garden and hoe the small (possibly five acres) of cotton.

In June, 1925, the Hagedorn Construction Company completed a stretch of road from a few miles below Pittsboro to the Moncure Fork and was beginning to build one from the northern border of Pittsboro to the same fork. That summer, I got my first job outside of the home. I was the waterboy for the construction company. I do not know what I was paid, but Mother was able to order a pair of roller skates from Montgomery Ward for me. When school started that fall, it was fun to skate on the new concrete road with no traffic.

After the new road opened to traffic, Mr. Gordon Burns started a filling station near our house. This became my summer hangout. He would ask me to do things and then give me something to take home to Mother (never money). I was a small boy and can never forget people laughing when I tried to return the gasoline hose to the hook.

Four downtown buildings burned in 1929. Mr. Charlie Poe constructed a semi-portable hot dog stand and moved it to the lot where the old courthouse had stood. He asked me to help him. Hot dogs and Coca Colas were five cents each. Mr. Poe would stop by to pick up money and check supplies. I had to sleep on the floor because the Cokes were stored outside, so we could not just close up and leave. I do not recall being paid for that.

The next summer four of us boys (a brother and two friends) loaded a Model T with camping items and headed for a few weeks at White Lake, where we worked at odd jobs.

My next job was to help Mr. Jennings Phillips in the Siler City Hardware Company's Pittsboro store on the east corner of Hillsboro Street next to the present courthouse. Again, there was no pay, but he would give me something to take home.

My last job before graduating from high school in the class of '33, was with Mr. John Bell in the Progressive Store. I worked at the grocery store a full year. I would leave school at 11:30 a.m. to let Mr. Bell go to lunch. I would walk back to school at 1:30 p.m. (I never had a bicycle). I would leave school again about 3:30 and go directly to the store. We did not observe set store hours. Anyone could buy something and arrange for pick-up at any time.

Each truckload of supplies from the Sanford warehouse

contained numerous 100-pound bags of sugar. People could buy as many as they wanted, then pick it up at a prearranged hour. Many times, I would dress (arrange items in) the show window until I could not stay awake. I would then go and sit on the curb until I could hear the bootleggers' horses or Model T coming to get their sugar. We sold a half truckload a week to them.

Salmon was 10 cents a can. If the label came off, Mr. Bell would say it was worth five cents and tell me to take it home. Somehow, Mother would make enough salmon cakes for eight people from that one can. The rest of my "pay" was other food items for my lunch and supper and more for my family.

I was small for my age and not too well. My next oldest sister, Frances, said I had to go to college. She made arrangements, and, in September 1933, I enrolled in Appalachian State Teachers College at a total cost of about $75. I was to teach math and science.

Frances was a secretary in Raleigh and heard that N.C. State was looking for students. She arranged for me to transfer to their Department of Chemical Engineering the following September. I lived in the YMCA basement and waited on tables in the dining hall (called Bull Hall). Later, I moved to a house basement and tended the furnace to pay for my room and the folding Army cot I slept on.

The next summer, I worked for a professor in the Physics Department and tended the forestry professor's house while he was away. After our junior year, we were to seek summer employment with a chemical or paper company. I got a job with a laboratory equipment and chemical supply company in Richmond, Virginia. I was to use small machines to make items of laboratory apparatus and do some repairs.

During my four years at college, I attended no movies and only one football game. Life was work and study, with possibly one weekend at home each year.

Two companies were interested in me, one in Philadelphia, one in New Jersey. At a Chemical Society Meeting in Chapel Hill, I met with Mr. Tom Simpson, from the New Jersey oil company. I liked his offer of $140 a month, $15 more than the Philadelphia refinery. "You're hired!" he said. "When do you want to start work?"

I reminded him that I had been away from home essentially for four years, so I would like to start on July 1, 1937. Graduation was scheduled for June 8.

With that, Mr. Simpson jumped from his chair and pounded on the table. "I want you NOW!"

After he calmed down, I proposed June 15th. However, this was unsatisfactory, and he repeated his act.

As a result, when my name was called at graduation, I left my chair to receive my diploma, then walked off stage to a waiting taxi (suitcase in the trunk) which took me to the depot to catch a train to Philadelphia. Next, I took a taxi to a rooming house in Paulsboro, New Jersey. It was a short night, but on June 9th at 8 a.m., I was at the gate, ready for work. And I worked for Mobil Oil for 45 years.

My "Almost" Career
by
Alice Blue Lowder Honeycutt

As a student at Albemarle High School in Stanly County, I thought I wanted to be a nurse. In the eleventh grade, we could choose to be in a vocational program. We earned no money but would get experience and academic credit.

Four of us girls chose nursing and spent a couple of hours each day at Yadkin Hospital, talking with patients, emptying their bedpans and bringing them water. One of our classmates, a slim blonde boy named Paul, would drive us to the hospital and one girl's father would bring us home. A neat dresser, Paul was also in the vocational program and worked for the Chevrolet dealership.

Our family didn't own a car. We didn't need one, because we lived on Third Street within walking distance of the school and the barber shop uptown where my father, Henry D. Lowder worked.

The year that I was 8, one year before the beginning of the Depression, Wilbur Saunders offered my father a large house for the small one we lived in. He and Fred Gaddy were managers of the Wiscassett Mill and wanted to build an office on Daddy's property. The big house was ideal for a boarding house, which Mother ran with the help of Marcelle Swaringen (a young white woman), who lived with us and did all the cooking and cleaning. Young women would come into town from farms to work in the hosiery mill during the week. A father or brother would pick them up on Friday afternoon and return them on Sunday.

An only child until my sister, Idalene, was born in 1930, I never felt deprived. Mother always paid a woman to make my dresses, six at a time (five for school and one for church). Idalene always had pretty dresses, too. We ate well. Mother would order the groceries, which would be delivered. If she had ordered chicken, the delivery boy would get one out of the coop on the back of the truck. Either he or my father would kill it.

Both Daddy and I could come home for lunch. One memorable meal during my high school years was the day I walked in and Daddy had invited a former co-worker to eat with us. He was from Henderson, where Daddy used to work in a barber shop before moving to Albemarle. The shoeshine man sat down and ate with us at the dining room table. I hurried back to school and told everyone, "We had a black man at our house for lunch!" It was the talk of the school.

Because we had no car, I seldom went on trips. Occasionally, a woman who lived with us would take me with her for the weekend. That's how I got to see cows and other farm animals.

My aunt lived in Thomasville. When I was about 11 or 12, I rode the bus to see her. I had to change busses in Salisbury. On the way home, I bought some candy in the bus station. When I went to get on the bus, the driver asked, "Where's your ticket?"

I had spent my money! I forgot I had to buy another ticket. I was real scared. "My father is Henry Lowder," I said calmly, assuming he would know who Daddy was. "He will pay you when we get to Albemarle."

The bus driver, Mr. Ritchie, let me get on the bus. As soon as we got to the station, I called Daddy and asked him to come pay Mr. Ritchie before he left for Badin.

The year after I was supposed to graduate, Albemarle High School was to add the twelfth grade. We had the option to stay an extra year or get our diploma in 1938. I chose to graduate, so I could start my nurse's training at Watts Hospital in Durham.

At Watts, we mostly studied that first semester. I could not go home the weekends we were off, because we didn't have a car. Even if I had had the fare, I did not want to ride a bus and change in Salisbury, so I stayed at the hospital on those weekends, unless a friend who lived in Durham invited me to visit with her family.

In early December, I called home and asked for money. My parents thought I wanted to buy Christmas presents. I didn't tell them differently. I packed my trunk and found someone to take me to the bus station. I bravely made the trip through Salisbury.

I wanted another "chosen career:" housewife. I was in love with Paul Honeycutt, who, by then, was working for Davis Motor Company and would someday have his own dealership.

My new career lasted 58 years.

I Lost My Job!
by
Dr. Wesley Wallace

My first mistake was not asking how much I was going to get paid. My second: I never got a contract.

I was so relieved to find a job at Louisburg College and so inexperienced that I did not ask the president the right questions during the interview.

My education at North Carolina State College did not cost much, because I had signed an agreement to teach in North Carolina public schools for two years. I did my practice teaching in Cary. The high school there was also a boarding school. I taught history and, while the principal was away for a week, Latin.

After I graduated in 1932, I did a year's graduate work at State toward a master's degree and was a graduate assistant to Professor Hugh Lefler. I started looking for a job in the fall of 1933. I climbed into Mother's old air-cooled Franklin and drove around our part of the state to see who was hiring.

At last, I found an opening at Louisburg College in Franklin County. The president of the Methodist junior college and boarding school for both males and females hired me to teach history and French. He asked me to lead a class in Spanish, too.

"I had only a half year of Spanish in high school," I protested.

"That's okay," he told me. "The class is mostly football players and girls. You have the book. Just keep order."

When he found out about my music background, he asked me to serve as director of the band.

That was a joke. The school had only three instruments!

Mother had two friends who were teaching at Louisburg. She introduced me to them, so that I would feel at home when I got there. Neither woman mentioned that they had not been paid in quite some time. Both were single and stayed because they got free room and board.

The president neglected to tell me in the interview that I had duty in the boy's dorm or that the window was broken in my third floor room. Cold wind whooshed in, and the heat didn't come up that far.

At the end of six weeks, I got paid $10. Other than being housed and fed, I had only one "perk." I could charge items at the bookstore. That store never had a book in it, but I ate a lot of candy and crackers from there. At Christmas, I got another $10.

After the holidays, Mother's two friends asserted that they had a written agreement but the college owed them money, so they quit.

Meanwhile, unbeknownst to me at the time, a Duke graduate told the president that he would come for no money, but he wanted to bring his wife, who could teach history and French.

And so I was told in so many words, "You're done!" The president gave me $20.

I was delighted! I caught the first bus back to Raleigh.

"We Would Pay *Them...*"
by
Dr. Wesley Wallace

I was supposed to be a school teacher, college professor maybe—in history or possibly French.

Mother was a linguist and taught history at Meredith College. In 1932, I earned my B.S. degree at North Carolina State College and was prepared to teach. But I could not find a job in that field. I did have a fine avocation, though.

While in high school and later at State, I played cello in the school orchestra. At 15, I made my radio debut as part of a trio at a reception for a new bank. Mother was the pianist. During my college years, I played for many parties and functions, including receptions at the Governor's Mansion.

A union musician, my mother had advance knowledge of the professional cellists who were coming to town with a major silent movie. She would arrange for me to study with them while they were in Raleigh.

If I couldn't teach, I could play cello.

It just so happened that, as I was riding a bus in Raleigh, the program director of WPTF Radio Station, Mary O'Kelly, told me there was an opening in the studio orchestra. She asked if I wanted to play bass. When I had worked there in my undergraduate years, they needed a cellist for more time than I could give, so I agreed to try bass. Soon, I was working at the WPTF studios in the basement of the Cross & Linehan men's clothing store and the S & W Cafeteria, across from the Sir Walter Raleigh Hotel.

Part of our $7.50-a-week job was to do "voice work," which was really fun. We did announcing and read parts in radio

126

plays. On "Good Evening Judge," I was a character player. Whatever character I was assigned, I played. With a black accent, I was Old Man Mose. In the same play, I was also a drunk. Then I would read commercials in a normal voice.

One of the announcers was leaving for the New York "big time," and I was asked to audition for his job as a staff announcer and writer. Richard H. Mason, the general manager, hired me. The first two weeks, I earned $15 a week. From then on, it was $20 a week, big money for me. One of my assigned duties was to be in charge of the daily schedule. I also enjoyed being an announcer, writer, clerk and producer.

The job was a real challenge. I normally worked 13 consecutive days, then had a Sunday off. In my eight years there, I never had a Christmas, a New Year's, a Labor Day or any other holiday off. Generally, I worked 60 hours a week and, a few times, as many as 80 hours (before the wage-and-hour rules).

Even so, Graham Poyner, the program director who replaced Mary O'Kelly, and I agreed that, "If we had any money, we would pay *them* to let us work there."

I met the challenges at WPTF from April '34 until I enlisted in December '42.

Once in a while, the Army assigned a man to a job that fit his background. After I got my commission, I was sent to the Solomon Islands to run a radio station for the Armed Forces Radio Services. Later, I was sent to the Philippines to manage another of their stations. After the war, I stayed on as a paid civilian to close down all 14 stations in the Southwest Pacific area.

The president of the Manila Broadcasting Company, who had been liberated from the Japanese by our forces, asked me to join his company.

Wesley Wallace
Solomon Islands, 1944

For three years, I was the general manager.

I eventually became a college professor and, later, chairman of a department at the University of North Carolina at Chapel Hill. The Department of Radio, Television and Motion Pictures, that is.

Summer Pittance
by
John Gill

My salary would be five cents an hour for ten-hour days, seven days a week. And I was lucky.

The City of Charlotte had a program to give work to the unemployed, at five cents per hour, trimming trees between the sidewalks and the streets or doing other light jobs cleaning up city property.

My father worked for the P & N, a short electric railroad started by J. B. Duke in the early days of his involvement in the power business. In 1933, his friends, Herman Wolf, John Chapman and Frank Moser created a job of that type for me. I would work for Duke Power, and my expenses would be paid if I were working out of town. Most of the jobs, however, were in Charlotte.

We lived on the east side of town. The streetcar fare to the Duke Power's warehouse and repair shop on West Morehead Street was seven cents each way. There was a small cafe in the old Carolina Trucking Company on West Morehead where I could get a 35-cent lunch. My take-home pay was a penny for each day's work!

It didn't take long to figure out that my mother's sandwiches were really good. And water tasted just fine.

President Roosevelt had NRA labor laws passed just in time for my last week. I was paid $12.50 for 48 hours of work.

Laboring for pittance paid off in the end. After I worked five summers for them, Duke Power had a job waiting for me when I finished Clemson College. I never considered working anywhere else. My 40 years of service (with time out for World War II) ended June 30, 1978.

Only a Summer Job
By
Lois Moore Yandle
Author of *Spirit of a Proud People*

One of the most traumatic experiences I had as a teenager was the first time I went to the weave room of Highland Park Mill #3 for a summer job. On entering that part of the mill, I felt overwhelmed by all the machinery, and the noise was deafening.

My parents, Joe and Madeline Moore, and many of their

family members had worked there since they were young, making colorful ginghams, but at 15, this was my introduction to what really went on inside the mill on the hill.

My job as a battery filler required quick work to be able to keep up putting full bobbins of thread into a large cylinder wheel. I was assigned a certain number of looms, and it took some hustling to keep up the pace. Thank goodness, some of the weavers came to my rescue many times.

What really bothered me were the smells of oil, machinery, and the sweat from those hard-working men and women. The odors penetrated, it seemed, every pore in my body.

There was no air-conditioning, and lint filled the air as well as the hair of everyone there. Dirty rags used on the machines and lint collecting on the floor added to the messy look. Sweepers came around as often as they could, and this helped, but the weave room was a very large place with so many looms that it was impossible to keep everything "spic-and-span."

Snuff was used by many men and women, and some were not able to control it as it seeped out of the corners of their mouths. This was something I could not get used to. I knew that was one habit I never wanted to develop. Spittoons were available, but the workers were not always able to leave the machines as quickly as they would have liked. The officials had painted large white spots at the corner walls near the floors. They were there for a purpose: no one was to spit in the corners. I must admit that some men did use the floors, but this was frowned on.

Not many days had passed when I realized that this was not a place I wanted to work for long.

Saved by a Cow and Crazy Crystals
by
James R. Clark

The Depression in 1935 was dancing around us like leaves falling from a tree. President Roosevelt was telling us that "better times" were just around the corner. Our problem was we never could find the right corner.

Our family of seven was living on the edge, but two things we never had to do without was milk and butter, because Mother had a cow. Although we lived within the city limits of Charlotte, there were no restrictions on barnyard animals, so we had chickens, too. Occasionally, she sold a chicken, but eggs were a more important source of income, and she sold butter and buttermilk to neighbors. My mother worked very hard. My father was a policeman, and they didn't make very much money back then.

In the spring of '35, I graduated from Tech High. I stuck around home a while to help Mother. A few months later I was walking in the 200 block of North Tryon Street and stopped in a shop in the Mayfair Hotel building. I got to talking with the manager, James W. Fincher, and asked if he were hiring.

"I could use some temporary help," he said.

And that's how I came to work for the Crazy Crystals Company (also known as the Crazy Water Company), "where Charlotte drinks its way to health." Their headquarters was in Mineral Springs, Texas, and I had never heard of them before.

If you added these miracle crystals to your drinking water, you were supposed to have a drink that could cure almost any ailment you might have. In fact, the ads claimed that this natural mineral water product could cure "constipation, stomach trouble, colitis, neuritis, rheumatism, common colds, etc."

To introduce this magic potion to the people around Charlotte, they hit upon the idea of giving away free samples. This is where I came into the picture. Mr. Fincher was running the show. He hired four young boys including me. We loaded his old Studebaker with boxes of crystals. It was so full we hardly had room to sit down.

Our first stop was Gastonia. We parked at a large textile plant with many mill houses. We filled our bags with samples and walked up and down the streets, knocking on doors from early morning until late afternoon. If anybody answered the door, we would tell them we had free samples of Crazy Crystals. Since we offered them something free, it was easy to get them to listen to our pitch. Many of them invited us into their living rooms.

"Do you know Grady Cole personally?" more than one would ask.

"Tell me about the Briarhoppers," others would say.

Many of them had pictures of these folk heros on their walls. Grady Cole was a WBT personality with a down-home voice and an "ordinary Joe" style. Likewise, the Briarhoppers were country singers who sang on the radio and, as someone said, "everywhere a crowd gathered."

I guess a lot of people could say they knew at least one Briarhopper, because the singers in the group kept changing. I didn't know any of them.

Grady Cole and the Briarhoppers heavily advertised Crazy Crystals. Frequently, the Briarhoppers sang in school auditoriums near the mills. They gave the product—and us—real validity.

There was a large water cooler in the office that had Crazy Crystals in it. I tried it, but I didn't like it. It didn't cure me, because I was in good health. The company claimed that the "crystals" were removed in factories from natural spring water, and consumers were to mix the crystals with water and drink one-to-eight glasses a day depending on the recommended "cure."

I found out later that the July, 1935 issue of the magazine *Hygea* had quoted Dr. Arthur J. Cramp, head of the AMA Bureau of Investigation, who revealed that the main ingredient was "Glauber's salt or the 'horse salt' of the veterinarian." He cited several companies producing it.

In 1940, the Federal Trade Commission ordered the Crazy Water Crystals Company to cease and desist from misrepresentation concerning their products recommended as a treatment for certain ailments and sold under the trade designations "Crazy Mineral Water," "Crazy Water Crystals" and "Crazy Fiz."

Over a time of two months, we covered ten textile towns. We wore out our knuckles knocking on doors, since mill houses did not have doorbells.

One afternoon when we returned to Charlotte after a long day, Mr. Fincher told us that was the end of the free samples. I was out of a job.

I went looking for those better times around the corner. Lucky me! I made the right turn and the S. H. Kress Company, about a block from Crazy Crystals, pulled me into their stock room.

MINERAL WATER PRODUCT

DRINK to Your Health---
A Natural Mineral Water Product—
for Constipation—Stomach Trouble
—Colitis—Neuritis—Rheumatism—
Common Colds, Etc.
Just Add them to your Drinking Water.

Crazy Crystals

CRAZY CRYSTALS add years to Life and Life to Years
CRAZY CRYSTALS bring a noted health resort to your home

CRAZY CRYSTALS CO.

Mayfair Hotel Building, 239 N. Tryon Street   Phone 5716

Not Everyone Wore Rags
by
Jack Wood

I had to leave town to learn a trade.

When I graduated from Charlotte's Central High in 1930, I had a track and field scholarship to Duke, but I didn't accept it. My father, J.C. Wood, was a homebuilder and didn't have any homes to build. I wanted to contribute and decided to get a job until the economy got better.

Soon, I was a file clerk in the credit department of McClaren Rubber Company, a manufacturer of automobile tires, and playing on their baseball team in the Twilight League. By 1932, there were rumors that the factory would be closed, so I knew I would need another job somewhere.

I had always been interested in clothes and, while at Ed Mellon Company on West Trade one summer day, I saw in a *Menswear* magazine an article about a fine store that supplied the best-dressed men in New Haven, Connecticut. I wrote to Roy, Ltd. telling about my interest and experience and listing some references. I was waiting for a letter when I got a phone call from the owner, Herb Ratner. "So you're interested in getting in the men's clothing business, are you?" he asked.

"Yes sir."

"I'll have an opening when Yale opens this fall. But how well do you know Bob Lassiter?"

"We played football together in grammar school and junior high before he went off to prep school, but we've kept in touch," I told him. Our families knew each other, as my father had built his family home, a real showplace. I had listed Bob as a reference because he was a student at Yale.

"Well, he's the captain of the football team, and with your connections up here we ought to hire you. You could bring us some business," said Ratner.

I gave my two weeks notice and headed north. My fare to New York by all-day-all-night bus was $10; to New Haven, $2. Mr. Ratner met me and took me to get a room at the YMCA for $5 a week.

At Roy, Ltd., we had a master tailor named Frank Williams. Frank had an Italian accent, and I soon found out that he was actually Francisco Guglielmo, the cousin of Rudolph Valentino. Several years before I got there, Rudolph had come to New Haven and drawn a crowd of 60,000. Needless to say, Frank attracted business.

Some of our customers were still wealthy: notably Jack and Rust Heinz of the ketchup and canned food family, Paul Mellon, Alfred G. Vanderbilt, Svasti (the Crown Prince of Siam) and, of course, Bob Lassiter.

Svasti had a fetish about the number nine. And so he would buy nine neckties or nine shirts, nine sport coats, nine suits. He even ordered nine topcoats. One was raccoon.

After spending one season there, I returned home to open my own "made to measure" clothing business in the city's tallest skyscraper, the First National Bank. I was able to rent office space for $7.50 a month because the bank was in receivership. It had closed before the bank holiday. My new partner, Bill Trotter, who had tried working on a ranch in Colorado for awhile, and I borrowed the first month's rent from his mother.

We would measure a customer and fill out a form with all his measurements. He would give us a $5 deposit, which we kept. We sent an order to the company that would make the suit. They would ship it to the customer COD for the cost of the suit (typically $23.50) plus shipping. Our first full month in business, we took eight orders, mostly for sport coats or trousers, not full suits.

It was soon apparent that I needed a second job. I applied to become a reporter in *The Charlotte Observer's* sports department. Jake Wade, the sports editor recommended me.

At the interview, the editor Ernest Hunter said, "I've heard that you have an outstanding knowledge of all sports, and I know you're a high school graduate. But can you type? To get this job, you've got to be able to type."

That was a Thursday. I said, "Just give me until next Tuesday and let me come back."

He agreed and I rushed to Pound & Moore, rented a typewriter and spent all weekend learning the keyboard. On Tuesday, I showed him that I could type the story he gave me. I was slow as Hell, but I finally did it.

"Practice builds speed," Mr. Hunter said. "Take off your coat and go to work."

That day, I became the third man in the sports department along with Jake and his assistant editor Fritz Littlejohn, the son of the future police chief. The pay: $75 a month. From then on, I worked until 3 p.m. at my clothing office and 3-11 p.m. at the *Charlotte Observer*. Bill Trotter kept our office open the rest of the day.

133

Well-dressed men in Charlotte liked to mimic male stars' Hollywood clothing. Heavily padded shoulders and a snug waistline gave
them a "he-man" look, they thought. From these photos of Clark
Gable, Jack Wood drew a sketch of Gable's half-belted jacket with
the shirred yoke and outside bellows pockets to send to the made-to-
order tailor for a customer. The first two photos are from "It
Happened One Night" starring Clark Gable and Claudette Colbert.
On the back of the third: "Julian Flowe, 105 Central Avenue,
upstairs apartment." Photos from Jack Wood's collection.

His involvement gave us one memorable order. When Fred Waring came to town to play at the Carolina Theatre, Bill went over to meet Fred and told him that he was John Scott Trotter's brother. John Scott had been an arranger for the local Hal Kemp Band before he headed for Hollywood to be a musical director for the Bing Crosby Show. Fred Waring knew him and was impressed with Bill. He brought most of his band over to our place that night to be fitted for suits.

Frank Williams wrote to me in March of 1933 soon after I had returned to Charlotte. He was out on his own and wanted me to work for him on commission. But Charlotte was home. And someday I would open my own fine men's store, Jack Wood, Ltd.

The Industry That Sustained a Community
by
Joseph C. Grogan

Because of the growth taking place in the tobacco industry, Winston-Salem was better off than other North Carolina cities. Most residents hardly knew there was a Depression, because they continued to work right on. People were still smoking, and business was growing like "gangbusters." The tobacco companies were not laying off. They were hiring.

With eight children, my own family struggled. I was a middle child of Irvin W. and Eva Bell Grogan. We were able to keep our home at 2353 Elizabeth Avenue in the heart of Forsyth County's largest town.

My father was a building contractor, but construction "went to pot." He did minor repair work, whatever he could get. Mother had a good reputation as a cook, so grocery stores asked her to make cakes for the well-to-do. This was a good source of income. We lived near the Westover Golf Course, and my brothers and I caddied there and sold the golf balls we found for spending money.

One of our neighbors, Walter Masten, was the manager of Brown & Williamson Tobacco Company, which was best known for Golden Grain smoking tobacco. He found jobs in his company for both my older brothers, Irvin, Jr. and Harold.

Shortly after I graduated from Reynolds High School in 1935, I attended Lees-McRae in Avery County but was taking the same courses I had in high school, so I left. I was working at a local grocery store, when I met an R.J. Reynolds Tobacco Company employee, who said, "Why don't you apply at our company?"

I applied for a job and was accepted. At first, I was in the leaf house, shaking dirt off of Georgia tobacco. (The first crops of the season came in from Georgia.) After all the incoming tobacco was received, I was transferred to the plug-wrapping room. At that time, they had just started wrapping plugs in cellophane. After eight or nine months, I was sent to the George Washington smoking tobacco room.

Although similar to the better-known fine-ground smoking tobacco, Prince Albert, George Washington was flavored differently and had a coarser, rough cut. Soon, I was sent to the office of the George Washington unit, where I worked as a timekeeper for a year.

Part of my job entailed taking production records to the main office two or three times a day. I knew several people there from my neighborhood or from my caddying job at Westover Golf Club, and I often stopped to "chew the fat."

The assistant treasurer, whom I knew real well, asked if I'd be agreeable to transferring to the main office. Of course, I was, so I moved to their accounting office. I enjoyed it, but I generally didn't get involved with figures. My principal job involved getting checks certified at the bank and taking them to the post office that handled the revenue stamps and customs payments. An armored car would pick up the revenue stamps every day.

After that, I worked in the purchasing department for R. C. Haberkern. He carried the responsibility of acquiring practically all the materials used by the company with the exception of leaf tobacco. Though gruff, he was the man behind the orphanage at Germanton. Many times he made arrangements for them to go to the circus when it came to town, and he saw to it that each one had a box of popcorn or Cracker Jacks.

R. J. Reynolds was the finest company in the world to work for. All they ever asked for was that you give them an honest day's work and be there on time. The president was James A. Gray, a devout Christian. People said that the two smartest men who walked the streets in Winston-Salem were Malcolm McLean of McLean Trucking Company and James A. Gray.

As part of my job, I saw Mr. Gray in his office every day. As busy as he was, he always took the time to say hello and ask about my family. He was a most pleasant, fair-minded gentleman.

Our company had splendid executives and I had the pleasure of knowing all the local ones. It is said today that most large companies could not care less for the average hard-working employee. Not our company in the '30s.

I know of several instances in which management took someone who needed alcohol rehabilitation, placed him in treatment, paid for it and held his job open until he got straightened out. There was always someone to give an ear to an employee with hardships or a personal problem. Later, they hired a chaplain and had a chapel on the premises. This was an extremely benevolent company, more like family.

Unlike businesses today, R. J. Reynolds Tobacco Company had a big heart and was well-known for fairness, and those of us in purchasing were told never to take advantage of anyone. We were explicitly instructed, "If it comes down to a division of the dollar, you take 97 cents and give $1.03 to the other person."

My career at R.J. Reynolds was interrupted by Pearl Harbor. Feeling that I would be declared 1-A, I enlisted in January, 1942 in the Signal Corps. In September 1942, my outfit was shipped overseas to participate in the invasion of North Africa. Later, we entered the Italian campaign. I was still there when the Germans surrendered in 1945.

I was the only man in my outfit with white civilian underwear. It was my most prized possession, a constant reminder of life as it used to be. Angelia Mackie (who later became my wife) worked in the production office of Hanes Knitting Company in Winston-Salem. She kept me supplied.

While I was in the combat zone of North Africa, I complained in a letter to Mr. Haberkern that I couldn't find a cigarette. Every month or so after that, I'd get another reminder of home and the company with a heart: a box of 50 Camel cigarettes.

Cash Money
by
Paul Jernigan

In the 1930s, cash was practically non-existent for the ten-member Jernigan family of Wayne County.

At age 12, I started doing a man's work. Well, sometimes.

Occasionally, when we were caught up with our farm work, I would help a neighbor with plowing or other farm jobs. My pay was 50 cents a day. A day was from 6 a.m. until sunset, with an hour off for lunch. I never saw any money; it went to my parents to help us survive.

That year, 1932, we picked cotton for other farmers for 35 cents a hundred. One Saturday, I picked 75 pounds. For this, my family received 26 cents.

In the fall of 1935, at age 15, I got a job at a nearby dairy. I was a high school graduate, for Brogden School had only 11 grades. For a 12-hour day, seven days a week, my family received $5.25.

One day, my boss, Bernice Williamson said to my dad, "John, I don't have any money, but I can give you a ham or a shoulder."

I heard my father reply, "Well, we've got to eat, so that will be all right."

That happened more than once. If he didn't have a ham, he paid with some other cured pork. Sometimes it was side meat like bacon.

After I worked there for about six months, Mr. Williamson told me he could no longer afford to pay me at all.

In 1937, we gave up trying to run a small farm in Wayne County, moved to Nash County and started sharecropping, where we saw even less cash money.

Later, my brother, John, Jr., who had infantile paralysis (which we now call polio) received tuition payments to Guilford College through the North Carolina Vocational and Rehabilitation Department.

At a Quaker meeting near there, he had met Dr. Ada Field, who, according to him, held the first PhD in nutritional chemistry given to a woman. She had gotten her degree at Peabody College, where she taught before retiring in North Carolina. Her aim was to promote nutrition through organic foods and whole wheat flour and meal. She owned a farm on which she had built a grist mill to make whole wheat flour and cornmeal plus a hammer mill to grind feed for neighboring farmers. John knew that Dr. Field's farm was about two miles from the campus and that she needed someone to help her.

Thanks to John, I got the job. My next younger brother, Bill, had just graduated from high school and could take my place on our farm. I could work to earn tuition.

And so, on the morning of June 1, 1940, I got a neighbor to drive me to Highway 264. All my clothing and personal items were in two cardboard boxes tied up with binders twine. I hitchhiked to Greensboro, caught another ride to Guilford College and then walked the last two miles to Dr. Field's farm.

This was quite an adventure for a poor farm boy, who had never been over 20 miles from where we lived. Those first few days were frustrating, too. I was 20 years old, but I had never spent a night away from home. I was accustomed to being with a large family with seven rowdy boys. Suddenly, I was very homesick, alone in an old farmhouse with an elderly spinster and no near neighbors or social life.

Another frustration at first was having to do farming by hand, spading and hoeing. I was used to doing this with mules and plows. Heretofore, I had worked sandy loamy soil. Her soil-depleted land was hard clay when dry and slick red mud when wet. She was trying to rebuild it to its original topsoil by adding humus.

Dr. Ada M. Field was a unique lady, gifted intellectually and academically. Her complexion was that of an outdoors person, which she was. As she worked beside me in her field or garden, she always wore the same clothing: simple blouse and sweater, plain wool skirt, cotton stockings and sturdy shoes. Her gray hair was drawn straight back into a bun.

Dr. Field paid 25 cents an hour. For room and board, she would deduct 21 hours or $5.25 per week. This sounded good to me, as farmers back home were paying laborers 75 cents to $1 a day. Needless to say, the federal minimum wage did not apply to farm labor.

I worked long hours six days a week and saved enough money to enroll in Guilford College that fall.

In those three months, I wasted only $3.47. That went for razor blades, haircuts and soap. I was doing my own laundry and ironing. When school began, I walked the two miles, sometimes twice a day, a total of eight miles. Dr. Field advised me to save money by buying an old bicycle. I purchased one for $3, although I spent a lot more time and money buying parts and repairing it.

My employer was a straight and no-nonsense person, but I owe a lot to her. Without her help and goading, I would never have succeeded in college, for which I was totally unprepared.

Not the usual college student, I had to work or study on Saturdays or in the evenings when athletic and social activities were taking place. Some might think I made great sacrifices to get a college education. Neither then or now do I feel that way. I considered it a great opportunity to improve myself.

I once read a quote: "Anything that is great and noble costs much."

OVER THE EDGE - NORTH CAROLINA

Any Job Was Better Than None
by
Lucielle Gwaltney Hunter

I was chosen to teach because I was an organist, but I never saw an organ anywhere in that town. Our dean at Queens College had told us that, if we could get a job teaching English, we'd better take it, so I accepted the first offer—at Hoffman School in Richmond County, between Rockingham and Hamlet on Highway 1. Unfortunately, later offers were better, but, had I not honored my contract, I would have missed an experience of a lifetime.

Lucielle Gwaltney at Hoffman's "hotel" Richmond County, 1940

When I arrived at what locals called the "old hotel," where some of the teachers would be staying, I was stunned. In my room was a double bed, which I was expected to share with someone I had never seen before, and one dresser with a basin and pitcher on it. There was no closet, only a metal rack to hang our clothes on. A pane was out of the window that faced the railroad track, and there was a big hole in the floor. An old iron wood stove provided heat for the room (and we later found out, would boil water to pour over the outdoor pump so we could fill the basin). Our "bathroom" was an outhouse. About the only thing else in that tiny town was a general store and a post office across the street.

Some of the local residents lived in small unpainted homes, five for the whites, five for blacks. This was the fall of 1940, not 1920!

One of the first things my roommate, Sarah Frances Nichols, and I did was to find newspapers to stuff the window and floor holes. That was not easy because Hoffman had no newspaper.

The first night when the diesel train roared through town, I sat straight up in bed. But after a few jarring nights, I slept through

140

until morning.

Meals, prepared by Miss Daisy, the owner of that "hotel," were boring. Dinner was always black-eyed peas, some sort of meat (usually ham or beef cut up in small pieces) and, often, boiled potatoes. Miss Daisy and her niece Deane did not eat with us, and we wondered if they had the same menu. The people around the dining room's one large table were more interesting, especially the newlyweds named Lingerfelt, who both taught at Hoffman School, and the trapper.

At the nearby government game reserve, the trapper tagged and tracked certain animals, and also trapped minks and other furry creatures for pelts.

Not far from the reserve was the Army's Camp Mackall. As war was developing, paratroopers and helicopters were practicing their skills. A Civilian Conservation Corps camp was adjacent to the Army installation.

Teachers today complain of heavy loads, but when I arrived at Hoffman, I faced an exhausting schedule. Not only would I teach English and French, but also typing classes *simultaneously*. That is, I would give the typing class an assignment to keep them busy while I was instructing an English or French class. Only one period did a typing class have my complete attention. In addition, I was the advisor/publisher for the school newspaper and played the piano for all school programs, grades one through eleven, coached girls' basketball and tennis and directed commencement exercises. For all that, I earned $95 a month, and I lost the first month's paycheck!

Although his name was Mr. Powers, our principal did not exert much authority over his students while he taught classes, too. One day, when four boys in my class were protesting assignments by lying on the floor, I did not send them to the principal. One of the fellows was over six feet tall. A mere 5'1", I was not going to pull them up. I just ignored them until they got up and returned to their seats.

As we had no social life, I volunteered to teach two nights a week at the CCC camp. And I thought the "hotel" was rustic! I met with students one-on-one in something like a barracks, made of wooden boards. Those healthy, strapping guys worked on forestation and wherever needed.

At a simple wooden table, I taught English to fellows my age (of 20) or older, who struggled because they had little experience with good grammar. (What I taught was not what they were used to hearing.) The government provided small high interest/ low vocab-

141

ulary paperback books and a grammar textbook. Forget spelling. I brought my own books, too. Most of my students never liked English wherever they had attended school. Some were from Charlotte or Fayetteville and places in between. But a few, who were truly motivated, did seem to learn.

Springtime in Hoffman was beautiful. The moon shining on white sand through the peach orchards with blossoms in full bloom made a spectacular sight.

Nothing was more spectacular than the fire. A brush fire of unknown origin burned out of control for days. Despite all the CCC workers and paratroopers could do, it leapt from one pine woods to another, exploding here, turning a tree into fireworks there.

Near the end of the school year, our graduating class was to do a play. I had selected "A Ready-Made Family." All 15 of the seniors had parts, except four, who were put in charge of the sets or had other behind-the-scenes jobs.

The chairman of the school board confronted me. "If you put on a play that leaves out four students, you can leave!" His daughter and niece were among the four.

Dutifully, I found another play that required 15 actors. But the students refused it. They loved the laugh-a-minute first one.

Oh well, I was ready to leave anyway. My schedule made me weary. I was tired of riding a bus that stopped at every cow path going home to Charlotte every other week for a hot bath, and I suspected that someone had been stealing books and clothing from our unlocked room. My boyfriend, Charlie Hunter, whom I had met through the Presbyterian College Students Association, would be coming in his old Chevy to get me soon. And I already had a contract to teach at Charlotte's Piedmont Junior High School the following year.

We put on "A Ready Made Family."

While the boys and girls performed a great show without all the backstage help, the school board chairman took his daughter and niece to a movie. The audience liked our play so much, we had to repeat it the next weekend.

Two years later, as a newlywed, pregnant with the first of seven children, and the fifth wartime French teacher at Derita High School in Mecklenburg County, I directed seniors in the same play for its third full-house performance.

One of life's pleasures is that some of my students from Hoffman later moved to Charlotte for job opportunities and have become my friends.

Earning While Learning
by
Selby A. Daniels

When I was 12, I got sent to the woodpile by my teacher—and I was glad!

One day in the winter of 1930-1931, Miss Evans, my teacher at Fremont High School, called me aside and asked if I would like to earn some money. Would I?! Opportunities for a young tobacco-farm boy to earn money were few and far between. "Yes!" I said eagerly.

She then wanted to know if I knew how to split kindling and wood for her small heater. I was already doing this chore at home, so I assured her I could do it.

After she determined that I usually arrived at school on a bus before 7:30 a.m. every morning, she promised to "pay well." The lady who always smiled as she spoke gave me her room number and described exactly how I was to split and cut the kindling and wood.

Fremont School had a teacherage on the school grounds operated by a Mrs. McCall. This teacherage was a two-story frame structure, divided into single rooms, very much like a hotel. All the teachers were single, as it was against the law in North Carolina for a female teacher to be married in those days.

Mrs. McCall had a large wood pile or wood lot. The kindling came from fat pine trunks and stumps of long leaf pine trees.

On the morning I started this chore, I found an old rusty axe, stuck in a block of oak wood. That surprised me, for we never let our axes get exposed to rain. It was dull and had gaps in the cutting edge. In spite of those encumbrances, I managed to get the job done.

I took the kindling and wood upstairs to Miss Evans's room and called her name. She invited me in and told me to hurry and build her a good fire. She was dressed in a nightgown and bathrobe, something I had never seen in my young life on the farm. Within minutes, I had a roaring fire going in her little pot-bellied heater, and she gave me a buffalo and Indian head nickel!

Shortly afterwards, I was asked by several other teachers to do the same chore for them, as they saw me working for Miss Evans. I ended up doing this for two single men also. That was a puzzle, too. In my young mind, I couldn't understand why those grown men couldn't chop wood themselves!

What did I do with all those nickels I earned? For one thing, I sometimes splurged and had a Pepsi Cola and a large cinnamon bun covered with white icing. Together, those cost a dime for lunch. That was a welcome change of diet for me from the pint of fresh whole milk and ham biscuit I usually had.

More importantly, I discovered I could earn money from working, doing something I already knew how to do, and this gave me great satisfaction. Finally, I had a warm feeling inside that, at long last, I could get some inexpensive things in the local stores without having to ask my father for money.

After this, when I heard farmers talking of "hard times" and that money was "hard to come by," I really could not understand what they meant. Miss Evans had freed me from that kind of problem.

How Perseverance Paid Off
by
Selby A. Daniels

No one in my family had ever gone to college, but during my years at Fremont High School in northern Wayne County, my mother would talk with me about making good grades, so I could be the first.

Our tobacco farm family was no different from any small farmer at the time—no richer, no poorer. Money was not discussed. We would just wait until that time came and then worry about it.

Tobacco was our primary source of farm income, so in my senior year (1936-37), my parents decided that I should have three-fourths of an acre of tobacco, which would hopefully generate enough money to pay the $150 first-semester fee at Atlantic Christian College in Wilson, just 12 miles north of my home.

Daddy worked out a plan whereby I was to assume the status of a tenant farmer with that three-fourths of an acre: I would pay for two-thirds of the fertilizer cost and furnish all field labor. He would provide the land, mule, plows, barns, etc. Daddy was to receive one-third of my land's total net sale on the Wilson tobacco market. The remainder would be mine to apply toward college tuition. It was a fair arrangement for the times, and I was excited just thinking about it.

I worked hard to make sure my allotment was as good as my personal care could make it, and it really did turn out quite well.

The last week of July 1937, just as we were finishing the last cropping (harvesting) of tobacco for curing, my father told me he was sorry but he was going to have to take my tobacco from me. He explained that he had just received a letter from the Wayne County Tax Office notifying him of nonpayment of back taxes on our farm that went back seven years (since 1930 when the Depression first started). The tax office threatened to confiscate the farm and sell it at auction on the court house steps in Goldsboro unless it was paid by that fall.

I was crushed, devastated! I had been looking forward to matriculating the last week of August, but all my hopes and dreams about college were now dashed. What could I do?

Mother came up with a new plan. Her mom's only brother, Joshua T. Aycock, who lived in Fremont, was reputed to be quite wealthy by everyone who knew him. Stories abounded of his thrift, frugality and miserly ways, usually told with derision at the mere mention of his name. The one good thing I knew about him was that he allowed my mother to live free with him and Aunt Net, his wife, so she could finish her high school education there in Fremont. Mother's plan was simple. We would visit Uncle Josh together and ask him for a loan large enough to cover my first year of college.

When we went to see Uncle Josh, he showed no outward sign of interest. He just let us talk. Finally, he looked squarely at Mother and said, "Annie, if I had the money I would loan it to you, but I don't have it."

My hopes were dashed once again.

I should mention at this point that Uncle Josh died exactly two years after our visit, and he left an enormous amount of money and property for that time: $350,000! In his 16-page will, he named nine nieces and nephews (my mother was one) to receive yearly interest and dividends from his estate. And with the death of the last niece or nephew mentioned, the whole principal of his estate was to be divided among 21 grandnieces and grandnephews. It was years before I actually received my share. Today, in retrospect, I realize Uncle Josh really had all his money "tied up," but I still feel he could have helped me, if he really wanted to.

In the spring of 1937, my father had hired two young white boys fresh from the U.S. Army, who had been honorably discharged from their tour of duty in Panama. Daddy had them doing everything on our farm. Word had apparently spread beyond our neighborhood about these men, for on the last Sunday of July 1937, John Pool, a fellow farmer from Black Creek whose farm was eight miles from us, came to see my father. He had a late crop of tobacco, and having heard that we finished early, he asked to hire one of them for four weeks to help harvest and cure. He would pay $10 a week with "free room and board" at his home.

Daddy quickly saw this as an opportunity for me to partially solve my college money problem, so he called me to join in the discussion. After talking with me, Mr. Pool seemed satisfied I could handle the job. He shook hands with my father and said, "Selby will do fine."

Mother helped me pack my bag, and I went home with Mr. Pool.

Little did I realize what I was getting into until 2:30 Monday morning, when he called me to get up and go help his black tenants take out a barn of tobacco. Looking at my watch, I said to him in a low voice, "But it is 2:30, Mr. Pool."

He responded that we had to take out four barns of tobacco by sunrise and be ready to go to the field and crop (break off) green leaves all day. I was used to hard work, but nothing like this! The earliest my father ever started in the morning was 4:30 to do the same job. By mid-afternoon, my energy was almost spent. After finishing the cropping that day, I thought surely Mr. Pool would call it a day for me. But instead, he sent me back to the field alone to "pull suckers:" (breaking off all new young tobacco shoots) until sundown. By that time, I was dragging, so galled I could hardly walk. After a supper provided by his wife, Sarah ("Sally") Pool, I went to bed at 8:30, the earliest ever.

Promptly at 2:30 the next morning, Mr. Pool called me to get up. That second day was a repeat of the first, and so it went the whole four weeks from Monday through Friday. On Saturday, my boss had me work in his garden all day. Nothing had been said that day at my home about working in the garden! On Sunday, I rested.

At the end of the four weeks, I felt like a slave with a hard taskmaster, but I was determined to persevere. It was my only chance to matriculate that year. I knew that the $40 would only cover the entrance fee and that I'd have to work wherever I could to make up the difference. I would clean dormitory floors, wash dishes in the dining room, barber other students, even babysit—or whatever it took—to stay, but I couldn't disappoint my mother.

On Atlantic Christian College's opening day, I handed the registrar four wrinkled, sweaty $10 bills, my ticket out of the Depression.

SOUTH CAROLINA

Top Pay
by
Estelle Jordan Downs

In all our growing up years, we six Jordan children never had spare change to spend.

We were lucky. Our father, Lewis Jordan, had a job and transportation. He worked for Cooper Furniture in Greenwood as a salesman and collector. In the worst of times, he was more a collector than salesman. And I have known of times when he took money out of his own pocket to make a payment for something a family really needed.

Our transportation was his truck, an open pick-up vehicle used to haul furniture. It was not intended as a school bus, though, for we all walked from our home at the edge of town nearly five miles to Blake School. But for us older children, it had another purpose. About every two years, Daddy would tell all of us to go sit in the back of the truck. Sometimes, we'd be there for hours, playing, fussing and fighting. Something was going on in the house. We didn't quite know what, but when we could go back inside, we would find a new brother or sister.

Although going to the movies was the favorite entertainment of the day, we could see one only if we had saved enough bread wrappers. For ten wrappers, one of us could get into a movie theater free. But with five brothers and sisters, my turn didn't come around very often.

Our lack of cash became most painful when I was in Greenwood High School and it came time to buy our class rings. Every two weeks, our teacher would call out the names of those who had not paid for a ring. Only two of us could not. Madeline and I sat humiliated in our seats, burning with shame which we thought that teacher deliberately caused.

Finally after graduation in 1931, I got my first job. At Park Seed Company, I was to pack seeds. Older workers used scoops to fill packets. But my group had to hand-count the seeds. Eight of us young girls sat around a table with Mr. Parks at one end. The number of seeds to go into each packet was determined by Mr. Parks according to the species.

Every now and then, he would call one of us over. He would count the seeds in that person's packet. If it was the wrong

147

amount, she would be fired on the spot. No mercy. No room for mistakes.

For that unpleasant work, I earned eight cents an hour. After a 60-hour week (10 hours a day, 6 days a week), I earned $4.80. At the time, I was living at home and my family needed my help, so I was glad to get it. But it seemed a pittance when I found a job at Nantex for $12 a week.

Perhaps because I was a high school graduate, I had been getting "top dollar" at Park Seed. I found out that the other girls at our table were earning only six cents an hour.

Thanks, Sis!
by
Cleo Alford Yongue

As the daughter of Darlington County farmer, the ninth of twelve children, I was grateful to my married sister, Alma Denley, a beautician in Columbia, for helping me go to nursing school.

My father, Grant R. Alford, had money in the bank from a good cotton crop. Mama had wanted to use it to buy a car, but Daddy wanted to save it. The bank failed, and his savings were lost forever. Needless to say, my sister's assistance was crucial.

Actually, all we had to buy at Columbia's Good Samaritan-Waverly Nursing School were books and uniforms. She helped pay for my books.

I was soon settled in their nice home for nurses, where we had rooms with twin beds and ate as well as the private patients in either of the hospitals for blacks (Good Samaritan and Waverly). Private patients did get better food than those in the wards, such as grapefruit, a

Cleo Alford and Helen Wilson, a classmate. 1937.

poached egg, bacon and toast for breakfast. Ward patients would likely have canned salmon made into a gravy and poured over grits,

148

Cleo Alford

toast and maybe a piece of Spam.

The nursing school was near both Benedict College and Allen University, so we nurses dated when our schedules allowed. I met my husband, Addison B. Yongue, in Columbia through my sister, Alma, but I didn't like him much at the time. I went out with other boys to movies, where we sat in the balcony, and maybe to a drug store for ice cream.

We nurses saw some great shows, like Cab Calloway's, at Township Auditorium, chaperoned, of course. The doctors would buy us tickets. That seemed only fair. They were making the money, but we were doing the work.

Even as freshmen, we worked a nursing shift. I noticed that some of our worst cases came from nearby towns and adjoining counties, such as Bishopville, Newberry and Greenwood. Their medical care seemed to have been neglected. Some of those with diabetes came in needing amputation of a foot or an entire leg because of lack of care.

More than once, someone in need of a tetanus shot died because his family couldn't pay $5 for the shot. That happened one Saturday night in 1934, when a man was brought in after a fight on Assembly Street. Without the tetanus, he became toxic and got violent. We had to use a restraining jacket to keep him in the bed. While we were buckling him to the bed, he was combative, and his toenail cut me on the back of my hand. He died a short time later.

As we freshmen had to do all the dirty work, I should not have been surprised when I was told that I would have to pack every body opening before the undertaker picked him up. I went down to the morgue with him to begin the task.

He was tremendous! At least six feet tall, he must have weighed between 250 and 300 pounds with big feet and huge hands. He had died after having 50 stitches in the stab wounds all across his back and down his shoulder and arm.

I had already packed his ears, nose, and mouth with cotton before I strained to roll him over. As I pushed him, gas in his tummy made a sound.

I left.

"Something's wrong!" I told the head nurse on that shift.

"He's not dead!"

After I described what happened, she said to me, "If you can't go downstairs and carry out your orders, you can leave."

I went back to my room and packed. We could not leave campus alone after dark, so I took off for my sister's house soon after dawn.

Alma took me right back.

I had to face Dr. D.K. Jenkins, the superintendent of the hospital, and L. A. Norther, the head of the nursing staff.

When I explained the events of the night before, they said that the head nurse should have sent someone with me because I was still on the first three months' probation and had never done that procedure before. They welcomed me back.

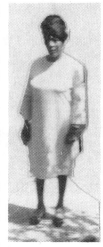

Alma Denley

All the time I was on duty, I was still scared of dead bodies and afraid I would do something wrong. I lost ten pounds those first three months.

But Alma kept encouraging and reassuring me until I graduated three years later. Thanks to Alma, I had a long career as a public health nurse.

The Man Upstairs
by
Edna T.J. Koon

Maybe he was just doing his job, but for a long time, I resented the man upstairs, the man who did the payroll upstairs from where I worked.

Soon after I was graduated from Frank Evans High School in Spartanburg, Congress created the Federal Emergency Relief Administration (in 1933), which gave states money for the needy. Because I had taken a commercial course, I could type and was given a job in the local FERA office on North Church Street—but not before someone was sent to our house to be sure no one else there was working.

My father had had an accident and could no longer hold down a job. While in high school, all three of us older girls had worked in the summertime at a sock mill (10 hours a day for $1 a day). But Powell Knitting Mill, where we also worked after

150

graduation, had closed. As the oldest child still at home, I was the most eligible for the position.

For $12 a week, my job at FERA was to type cards for applications from people needing jobs, relief money or food. If they qualified, I could give them slips of paper which they would take to the community house behind the office, where they could pick up commodities (surplus foods such as cheese, flour, butter, powdered milk and other products that farmers could not sell). Later, a Mrs. Edwards was hired to determine the needs of people who couldn't work. That was the beginning of our social services.

About three months after I was married in 1935, I was investigated again. It seems that the man upstairs in payroll was a neighbor of someone who knew how many farms my father-in-law owned along Greer Route #1.

Even though I was still taking my paycheck home and living there during the week (and only visiting my husband, Roy Johnson, on weekends), I was immediately disqualified. Instead, Mama was given a job in a sewing room.

Of course, I moved to the Johnson farm, which had eleven houses. Whenever the bank took over a neighbor's farm, my father-in-law Thomas Johnson would buy it, so he had acquired considerable property.

Meanwhile, Roy, a recent Wofford graduate, had been looking for work. Trained as a teacher, he nevertheless took a job in a grocery store in Washington, D.C. Until we could afford a place of our own, we would live there with my sister. His brother, Lee, who had driven him up to D. C., had come back so that I could pack some clothes to move.

That was when Guy Rankin, the chairman of the board of trustees and two others from Campobello District One Public School, came to Mr. Johnson to ask if Roy would be willing to teach the sixth grade.

"I don't know," my father-in-law said. "But his wife is here. Why don't you ask her?"

I told him I would call Roy that weekend. The next thing we knew we were renting a house on the Asheville Highway across from Campobello School.

For $7 a month, we rented that four-room house with plumbing and electricity. The only drawback was that it had no pump on the well, and the next-door neighbor would not furnish us water. The Campobello Building & Loan, which had gone out of business, did not have the money to clean the well. But one of the

151

men who had worked for the closed company found someone to clean it for us.

About three years later, Mr. Rankin stopped in to see my husband. "Roy, they're going to sell your house at auction tomorrow," he announced. "I'll drive you to see if your daddy will pay for it."

Roy's father had a different idea. "It's not a good business policy to loan to your children. But Uncle Leal makes money from loaning to people who are in a good position to repay. Go see him. I'll sign the note."

Uncle Leal Ross asked Roy how much he would need.

"For one acre and the house, probably $800," Mr. Rankin told him.

Uncle Leal disappeared into a back room and returned to hand Roy a roll of money. "All I ask is that you pay the interest."

Precisely at $800, the bidding stopped. And so, each year for eight years, we paid $100 plus the 6% interest until we owned our own home.

All my life, I have believed that the REAL Man Upstairs not only watches over us but cares for us in our daily lives. Maybe He had something to do with that other man upstairs in charge of the FERA payroll.

Forty Cents a Pound to Nary a Nickel
by
John B. Sligh

My daddy owned our farm as long as I could remember. At that time, there was not another black person around who owned his own land.

My parents, Wade Hampton (everyone called him Hamp) and Sally Maze Sligh, had nine boys and lived in a six-room house in Newberry County off Highway 219. I was the sixth son.

When I was only 6 years old, in 1916, I started working on our farm, chopping cotton, a hard job. Later, I helped pick cotton by hand, a job made even more unpleasant by saddlebacks, strikers and stinging worms which infested the bolls and stung or pricked our hands and bodies. The only thing worse was the boll weevils. Daddy never could buy the spray that other farmers used, but I don't think the spray did much good anyway. But in good years, we could make a decent living off cotton at 35 to 40 cents a pound.

While attending Mt. Bethel Garmany School off Highway 34, I met a real nice-looking girl, who was about my height (5'6") and two shades lighter than I. Her name was Tulie Griffin. The school year then only lasted six months, so it took more than a year to complete a grade. I got to the sixth grade. Tulie and I were both in our teens then.

I courted other girls, too. I went with Gertrude Butler a while, and when we broke up, I asked her best friend, Ruby Quarles, who lived in town, to find me another girlfriend. She never did, but I saw Tulie at St. Matthews AME Church on the Sundays we had preaching. We lived in the same community and went to parties and visited each other's homes, so eventually I asked her to marry me in 1938, when I was 28.

My daddy had died, so Tulie moved in with us and we worked his farm for a year until we moved out on our own and began sharecropping on Bluford Gilbert's land. For the house with three rooms and a kitchen, we each brought a bed from our homes, a table and two or three chairs. That was all we had. And we had to walk a half a mile to get water from a spring. We raised chickens, and one year, Mr. Gilbert gave us the use of a cow.

Tulie worked in the field with me and took in washing for other people, making $1.50 a load. Sometimes, I got to help out at other farms for 50 cents a day—for a 10-hour day, usually plowing with a mule or hoeing cotton.

Cotton prices fluctuated, so we never knew what we would make. One year, they were ginning cotton in October when it was 35 cents a pound and the word got out that it would go up to 50 cents after Christmas. Some people held theirs back. Others bought from their neighbors and warehoused it. But after the holidays, it went down to 25 cents a pound.

Another year, we made $15 for all that labor. Still another year, the cotton came up late. Then it rained a lot, and we yielded only 25 pounds! We made nary a nickel! The only cash we earned off the land we got that spring, when Mr. Gilbert paid me to plant at $15 a month for March, April, May and June. We never used cash to buy clothes. We got flour, meat, sugar and other foods not grown in our garden.

Five years of sharecropping was enough. In 1944, I went to work for Lawyer Johnstone as a butler and yard man. Keeping a yard looking nice, even with a push mower, was a better way to make a better living.

Tulie died after we had been married 17 years. In the very

same month of the very same year, Ruby Quarles lost her husband, a dentist. She was the one I had asked to find me another girlfriend. This time, I didn't look any further. After a short courtship, Ruby and I were wed.

Only the Rooster Fared Worse
by
Maggie Fletcher Wood

I told the Lord, "Don't let me go through through a depression again— I'd rather be dead." I meant it.

My husband, Carroll, and I married when we were 16 on December 24, 1930 in Cherokee County. Both of us were working 55 hours a week at "The Big Mill" in town, Gaffney Manufacturing, and made $7 each a week. We had no furniture, except what our families didn't want. For a while we didn't have a single chair with a bottom. We took part of our first pay to have the chairs bottomed.

On December 13th of the next year, we had our first child. We saved 25 cents a week to help pay the doctor's fee. Each of the two times I got pregnant, he tended to me until my baby was born and looked after both of us for six more weeks for $25.

At first, we did not have to pay rent for our mill house, but then they started cutting back on hours and charging 30 cents per room per week for our three-room home. For a while, the mill closed down all but one day, and Carroll got $1.25 for ten-and-a-half hours of work per day. Of course, 90 cents was subtracted for rent. We needed the other 35 cents to pay a nickel a day for ice to keep my baby's milk cold.

Mr. M.E. Higgins ran a dairy farm, and he said, "I'll not cut off one of 'my' babies as long as my cows are fed." He gave free milk for many babies in the mill village during the worst of times.

One day, Daddy brought a friend to Gaffney to pay taxes, and they came to our house. I didn't have as much as a quart of flour, so I told them, "I'll have to make some more bread." Fortunately, they decided not to stay for supper. I was embarrassed. The next day, Carroll went to the Salvation Army to get a sack of flour. That's the only time we ever got anything from there. It was the only time we ever asked. But I admitted to Mama what we had done.

If it had not been for Mama and Daddy, we would have starved. Some people around us were, but my parents had a farm in

154

Cowpens with a cow, hogs and chickens. Every Saturday, they'd bring us meat, milk, butter and eggs.

A farmer came knocking on my door one day wanting to sell sweet potatoes. I love sweet potatoes, but I didn't have any money. I asked him, "Would you take a guitar for your sweet potatoes?"

"Yes, ma'am," he said.

Mama and Daddy had given me that guitar, but I bartered it for those sweet potatoes. Then his potatoes were rotten, every one.

Then there was the matter of coal. Grandfather was visiting us one night and was sitting next to a window. "I see somebody in the yard," he said.

I looked out and couldn't see anyone. But the next morning, all the coal that we had piled near the window was gone.

Back then, people were not murdering like they do now, but they would steal.

Another time, we had a little house out in our back yard. Our neighbor, who participated in cock fights, asked us if he could put his rooster inside the little house that night. It was real cold and the rooster was hurt bad. We let him. But the next morning all our coal was gone from the house, and we didn't have money to buy more. Whoever took the coal got the rooster, too. It probably made him sick.

Anyone who lived like us back then still thanks President Roosevelt for what he did. He cut the hours for a day's work to eight and set a minimum wage of $11 a week for five-and-a-half days. At first we didn't think the mill owners could do it, but they did.

And we thought we were billionaires!

The Value of Education
by
Mamie Copeland Norris

I've been financially safe all my life.

When the Great Depression began depressing others, I was teaching at Lowdnes Hill, a Rosenwald school in Greenville County. I was making less a month than teachers are making per day now, but everything was cheaper then, and $57.50 was "good money" in the early 1930s.

Although I was in my 20s, I lived on "Copeland Hill" near

the railroad station with my parents. A fireman for Southern Railroad, my father had a dangerous job but got decent pay, which enabled him to own our home and allowed our mother, Mittie Young Copeland to stay home with us four children (all of which, by the way, went to college). Since 1924, we always had a car.

After I graduated from Union High, I had to go to Asheville College to summer school to complete the 12th grade in double sessions. To get my teacher certification, I took summer courses at Allen, the local Methodist college, and Benedict, the local Baptist college.

Like many schools then, Lowdnes Hill was operated by trustees, most of whom were white. About the only thing they supplied were signatures on our checks and an occasional visit. We did get plenty of coal to keep the stoves warm in winter. Our boys would find enough kindling in the afternoon for us to fire up the stoves in the morning.

By the time I was teaching there, Lowdnes Hill (which was built in 1917 as a two-room schoolhouse) had four rooms. I taught the primary grades, first through third. We went up through the seventh grade. Our books were provided by the state but were generally used ones.

That was better than when I was in school. After the white children had bought their schoolbooks at Houston's Bookstore on Main Street, we black children went in Houston's back door on Brown Street to buy the used books white children had turned in.

None of my pupils were children of sharecroppers, so their families were not desperately poor. Most worked in the Watson peach orchards. Generally, I had about 35 children each year. Although I divided them into grades, there were lots of large families with brothers and sisters who studied together.

In 1937, Howard Norris, who also worked for the railroad, and I were dating. If we weren't sitting on the front porch, we were going to the movies (comedies, mostly—no shoot-'em-ups for me), attending Tabernacle Baptist Church (the black one) or just talking with the family. Even though I was 31 years old, my mother was strict, and I had to be in by 11 p.m., even if we went to an adult affair.

Really, there was not much to do in Greenville except on special occasions. We did enjoy vaudeville entertainment back then, like the Whitman Sisters and Bojangles. Big bands like those led by Jimmy Lunsford and Fletcher Henderson sometimes came for a major event such as the Christmas charity ball at Textile Hall. I got

Duke Ellington's autograph. When he played at Clemson, he and his band had to sleep in a Pullman car, because they weren't allowed to stay in a hotel.

Howard and I decided to get married on a Friday, but then I got invited to a bridge party, and he went to work on Saturday, so we didn't marry until Sunday. It was over three weeks before my mother knew about it. My cousin told her.

I never had to live in rental housing, but for four years, we stayed with my parents until Howard could build us a house across the street.

Our son, Robert, was born in 1940, but I never missed a year or even a month of teaching. Yes, we worked under the same rules as white teachers. We could not be "showing" and still teach. Robert was born in May.

It's true that I did not show much at first. But black schools then only operated for six months. We finished in March.

McCormick Oddities
by
Irene LaGrone Thomas

The five trustees of the McCormick County school where I taught sixth grade after finishing at Winthrop "didn't trust anybody," we used to say.

At the end of the 1936 school year, they sent out a questionnaire with queries such as "Do you play cards?" "Do you dance?" and "Do you date on school days?"

Of the five of us at the McCormick teacherage, I was the only one re-elected to teach the following year. The other four (one grammar school teacher and two women and one man who taught high school) wanted to know how I had answered.

"I answered 'yes' to all of them," I told them. They had, too, but I had added, "but not to the extent that these activities would interfere with my job."

I didn't choose to stay anyway. I had an offer to go to Graniteville, South Carolina to teach biology, my major.

My roommate Dot Nicholson and I agreed that the most memorable thing about our stay in the teacherage was the wall hanging in the parlor. The widow, who ran the teacherage, had a wreath with little florets of the hair of her husband's other three wives.

157

Oh, To Be a Mill Worker!
by
Fred Whitten

Soon after Franklin D. Roosevelt came to office, a National Recovery Act code specified a 40-hour workweek and a minimum wage of 30 cents an hour. Suddenly, mill workers who were working 55 hours a week making $6 would be working 40 hours and getting $12! Preachers and the ladies of mill communities around us began organizing prayer meetings in different mill homes and all around. They were worried about what the men might do with all that extra time and money, fearing that they would gamble and drink it away. They prayed that their men would not go wild.

As a farm boy, I was jealous of the mill workers' children. When I got home from school, I had to work until dark. They didn't.

I was the ninth of eleven children of Miles Norton and Ella Harbin Whitten, who were sharecroppers. We moved from place to place but always in Anderson County. I attended Concord School, where one teacher taught first through tenth grade. Although there were two rooms, we used only one. Our teacher would call different age groups up to the front pew and teach them, while the rest of us did assignments. I probably learned more there than I would have in a separate grade, because we could listen to the other lessons. In fact, when I went to the larger Lebanon School and was a fifth grader in a class for fourth and fifth grade, I mostly sat and waited for the others to catch up. Later that year, we moved and I went to Hammond School for the fifth through seventh grade. After that, we had to go into town to get a high school education.

Fortunately, my first year at Anderson High School, we had school buses—one from the Hammond area; one from Roberts School. I graduated in 1935.

For college in 1936, I chose the Textile Industrial Institute (TII) in Spartanburg. It was the only way I could have gone to college. A Methodist junior college, they had a plan that allowed us to go to school two weeks and work in a mill two weeks. At Arcadia Mill (a branch of Mayfair) my first year and Saxon Mill the second, I made $12 a week for $24 a month. My board was $5 per week or $20 a month. Our tuition was $2 a month, which left us with $2 spending money.

In 1937, when the Social Security Act went into effect, they took one cent out of every dollar. To compensate, the mill gave us a two-cents-an-hour raise (from 30 cents to 32 cents). After Social Security took 13 cents, we had 67 extra cents to spend each week. Most of the students at TII were studying for the ministry. I took English, Bible, math, French and other general courses. I was also on the basketball team.

After graduation, I went to work in the Gossett Mill bleachery at Toxaway Park. Most mills had sports teams, but Gossett didn't have basketball, so I played for Orr Mill. Of course, we played other mills, but we also challenged the Clemson freshmen and Erskine College. Won a few times, too!

Baseball was the most popular mill sport. In 1937, the St. Louis Cardinals sent pitcher Bob Bowman to play with Orr. Two years later, he won 14 games for the Cardinals.

Maybe mill work wasn't the best job around, but I worked to support my parents until they died, with an interruption for the Navy in World War II.

My next job was more satisfying. I served as Anderson's assistant county treasurer for 30 years.

Liberated by Two Mules
by
Lilla Childs Durham

I knew about his little girl, Louise, but Larthun didn't tell me he had boys. The slim-faced widower I had gotten to know at our Baptist church in Simpsonville didn't look like he was in his 30s, but he was 33 when we were married. I was 20.

After we went to the preacher's home to marry, we went down to his house. Little Louise, his mother Frances and sister Essie were there, and that's when I met my stepsons: John Herman, Theodore and 3-year-old Willie Raymond.

Like my father, Larthun worked at the Simpsonville cotton mill. Daddy fired a boiler, but Larthun scrubbed floors for $9.05 a week. He had a little cotton patch and a T-Model Ford, but not long after that, we began sharecropping for "halvers."

In 1926, we were at the Holland Farm, when the man said he couldn't give

Lilla Childs Durham

159

Larthun the money to plow. "I can't feed five children and my mother and wife on this," my husband said.

He had tried working in Hendersonville, North Carolina, during the week and coming back on weekends, but he figured he could make more in Florida, so he went there.

We had a garden, of course, and I was picking blackberries and apples and canning them. I had a new baby but I said, "I'll plow." Louise was 10 and his oldest boy, John Herman was 8, so I let them help me keep the plow going.

Larthun Durham

By fall, we had made four bales of cotton, picked it and put it in the house. We had planted corn and had gotten two rows, but it was hard, and we couldn't make good meal.

In October, Larthun called and told me to move. On December 22, we went to Florida and stayed until April. When we got back, the man had rented our house, and I didn't get a penny for all that cotton or the corn.

By 1929, we were farming on the T. E. Jones place near Simpsonville in Greenville County. We peddled what we raised and stayed in a four-room house. His mother was living with us, and our family was growing. I had three children in the '20s, twins in '33, a girl in '36 and another girl in '37. Louise was married and had a baby in '34, but my other stepchildren were still there. Sometimes, we had four to a bed. All that time, I worked in the fields and plowed with the rest of them. We raised chickens, hogs and cows. I made the children milk the cows, so I could churn the butter and make buttermilk. We also grew potatoes, cabbage and beans. The cash crops were cotton, corn and peas.

One of those years before the twins were born, when we "settled up" for cash, there was no cash. To buy shoes and other necessities, my husband worked down at a furniture store, delivering furniture. The older ones got odd jobs and I took in washing.

Then, in 1938, we bought two mules. No more sharecropping for the Durham family! We rented a place on East Georgia Road, and all we had to give the man was five bales of cotton. If that was all we made, then we would get nothing. But if we made more, we got it all. That year, we made ten bales.

160

By 1942, with the help of a government loan, we bought 98 acres in Greenville County between Mauldin and Greer, and Larthun built us a house. They told us we could take 32 years to pay for the land, but we did it in four years.

I raised four of his children and gave birth to 13 more. I'm 96 and have 71 grandchildren, 160 great-grandchildren, 140 great-great grandchildren, and I hope to have more in the next generation. I don't really know. Until two years ago, I was still plowing my garden—with a motorized plow instead of a mule.

Was Reverend Bettis Really Right?
by
Cato Edward Coleman

Reverend Alexander Bettis once said, "If a man is trained or educated, he will do a better job at whatever he does."

My father, Nelson Coleman, a World War I veteran, only finished the third grade at a school that ran a mere three months a year. Guess you could say he got a lot of education on the job. He worked for J.W. White, who owned a bicycle shop, a tin shop, was a gunsmith, a keysmith and ran a plumbing business in Newberry. Mrs. White had a millinery shop that also sold blouses, knitting and crocheting items and notions.

Daddy, my mother Earlean, my little sister Ethel and I lived in a three-room house on Newberry's Benedict Street. Mother took in washing. I'd pick up and deliver the clothes in a wagon I pulled through the neighborhoods. Most families paid $1.50, but she did laundry for singles at 40 cents a basket. At the height of the Depression, Mother would make $3 a week. I would hoe cotton for 50 cents a day when I wasn't at Drayton High School.

When I finished in 1939, I had few choices for college. The tuition was too high at South Carolina State and Benedict College. Instead, I attended Bettis Academy in Edgefield County. The tuition included a $5 entrance fee and $8 per month, and I could work my way through cutting firewood for the fireplace and heaters in the auditorium and doing other odd jobs on campus like raking. At the end of each month, I'd be handed a check for $12 to sign and give back. I never did find out what happened to the other $4.

The school needed the money. In the building where my classes were held, I used to say that "we could study astronomy

through the roof and zoology through the floor." Not only were there holes in the roof, but we could see the chickens through slits in the floor. Wind blew through the walls.

More important, the teachers there were excellent. Our English teacher made us tear sentences apart, tell four things about a verb and state whether a noun was abstract or concrete. Teachers today don't do that, and children can't speak or write English correctly. They don't even know Latin, which we had at Drayton. At Bettis Academy, we learned about the hard books in the Bible, like Revelation and Song of Solomon, an allegory. Preachers today don't like to discuss that. They just want to sing and shout and preach about the easy passages.

Bettis Academy shows how God works. Its founder, Reverend Alexander Bettis, has been called "a Moses for his people." Born a slave, he was taught to read by the owner's wife, who was breaking the law by doing it. He loved reading the Bible and wanted to become a minister. No one in South Carolina would ordain him, so I've been told, but a Georgia preacher did it. Before his death in 1892, he had established more than 40 Baptist churches, which formed the Mt. Canaan Association. All the churches in the association contributed to found Bettis Academy in 1880.

When I was there in 1939-41, it was a high school and junior college. My diploma enabled me to teach school like my future sister-in-law. But she was getting only $50 a month in Newberry County, and I thought I could do better up North.

When I moved in with my uncle in Roselle, New Jersey, it took a while to find a job. I went to work for Hubaney Brothers, a company that made practice bombs and rockets.

Was Reverend Bettis really right? The teaching job I prepared for did not pay enough to support a family. Hubaney Brothers probably would have hired me even if I did not have a college diploma. It was wartime.

My education opened my mind to keep learning. While in New Jersey, I met an Italian, who taught me how to repair shoes. I stayed there long enough to earn enough money to buy the machinery I would need to start my own shoe repair business in Newberry, the business I still run today.

I am 80 years old, and I KNOW Reverend Bettis was right.

Lessons Learned. Lessons Taught.
by
Annie Belle Wright Chappelle

The best lesson I learned at Bettis Academy was how to save. It was not taught in a classroom. It was from life experience.

The junior college in Trenton, South Carolina, had a store with candy, canned sardines and other things to entice us. Grandma and other family members would give us a little change for spending money, but I learned to resist temptation. Well, most of the time.

My parents, Joseph and Ada Culbreth Wright, didn't have to go to college to figure that out. Sharecroppers with a crowd of children who moved from farm to farm in Saluda County, they knew how to scrimp. For instance, Daddy had a shoe lathe. He bought leather and fixed our shoes when they were worn out.

All of us 12 children (seven girls and five boys) worked— planting and gathering crops, mostly cotton, corn and wheat. At times, we would go to a neighbor's house and work for him picking cotton. We got cash for that: fifty cents for 100 pounds. Yes, that's a half-a-cent per pound!

When I was a teenager, the boll weevils ate all the cotton, and Daddy got a WPA job working on the roads. Through the National Youth Administration, I cleaned classrooms at my school

163

and got a check, which helped buy books and clothes.

After completing 11 grades, I graduated from Saluda Rosenwald in 1937. My father gave all of us the opportunity to go to college. Only three of us girls took him up on it. Our oldest sister, Laura, who is 95 now, went to Bettis. Another older sister, Christine, attended that Edgefield County college one semester. She dropped out to go to New York, where she eventually went to a beauty school and became a beautician.

When it was my turn, Daddy loaded me, my belongings, a lot of cornmeal, grits, peas and store-bought rice in bulk bags into a neighbor's car, and we headed for Bettis. He took very little money. My tuition was food.

At mealtimes, we had plenty of what we had: grits for breakfast, peas for lunch and rice for the evening meal. The most plentiful meat was fatback. Those sardines in the school store were mighty tempting to go with bland breakfast grits.

A degree from Bettis Academy allowed me to teach. Like Laura, I later went to summer school and took extension courses at Benedict College and Allen University in Columbia to get a four-year degree.

My first teaching job was at Pittsburg School. Both Greenwood and Saluda Counties supported our little one-room unpainted school that stood high on a hill near Willow Springs Baptist Church. As the only teacher, I taught first through seventh grades to about 12 children. The larger kids helped the smaller ones, while I taught the others or worked one-on-one. On cold mornings, I sent some of the children out to the woods to find trash, wood and sticks to burn in our wood stove. A mother fixed our lunches at her home and walked to the school to bring them to us—usually, soup or sandwiches.

I made about $50 per month, but I had to pay $15 to $20 to board at Mrs. Byrd's home in that community during the week. The first year, our brother Mitchell would drive Laura's new car every Monday and drop her off at her rural school and me at Pittsburg. He would pick us up on Fridays. In our part of Saluda County, everyone knew each other. Our family was well-respected, and we had some white friends. That's how Laura could get a brand new Ford from Cromley Ford in the town of Saluda.

After I married Thomas Carroll on December 6, 1941, he would deliver me and bring me home. I still boarded at Mrs. Byrd's. On weekends, I returned to the farm Thomas owned outside of Ninety Six, near Epworth in Greenwood County. We shared our home with his elderly father, niece and a sister.

On my last day at Pittsburg, we had a School Closing Celebration. The children put on a program of speeches, dialogues and a play, and the whole community turned out. Everyone brought food for the picnic.

I am convinced that, although I was teaching seven grades in one room, those children learned just as much as they do today. Probably more.

What a Great Deal!
by
Thelma Percival Kube

Roosevelt's New Deal really benefitted our family.

Franklin Roosevelt became President March 4, 1933. On March 9, Congress began a special session which became known as the "Hundred Days." The President at once began to submit reform laws, calling his programs the New Deal.

While the laws to speed recovery were being formed, food was being given to the people. I was 13 when a man from the town of Edgefield would bring a truckload of food to Red Hill School. In the first package we received, there was flour, something we hadn't had for quite a while. We all ate heartily. Harvey, my 5-year-old brother gorged himself on four biscuits, then announced, "I don't like them ole government biscuits!"

One of the first New Deal agencies was the Public Works Administration (PWA). My dad, Milton Percival, worked on PWA for $1 a day repairing roads. When he used his mule, Sam, he received $2 more per day. When he was promoted to foreman, he was on equal pay with Sam: $2 a day!

My brother, Frank, joined another New Deal agency, the Civilian Conservation Corps (CCC). Like the others in his division, he worked to check soil erosion and restore the land. Doug, another brother, joined the division that restored forests.

In 1935, the National Youth Administration trained youth for jobs in fields such as housekeeping, sewing, typing and many others. My older sister Mary Alice and I joined the NYA. Mary Alice went into nurses training. I worked as an aide with the County Health Department. We were paid $3 a week.

The New Deal still wasn't quite enough for me. Although only 18, I got another part time job waitressing and housekeeping at the Edgefield Hotel for $3 a week

HOW OTHERS WORKED

Unique jobs were not uncommon. Some people worked harder than others; some hardly worked at all. All have interesting tales to tell.

NORTH CAROLINA

A Plea For Empathy for the Textile Worker
by
Betty M. Hinson
Author of *From This Red Clay Hillside*
The Eagle 1924 - 1950

Several years after Mother's death, I was cleaning out the attic and came upon some yellowed newspaper clippings. From the '20s to the '40s, my mother, Catherine Miller, wrote the social news of Eagle Yarn Mill. She and my stepfather worked there, and we lived with my grandparents in the mill village on the hill. (We called it "on the Eagle.") She wrote for the *Gaston Gazette* and the *Belmont Banner*, but it was a letter to the *Charlotte Observer's* Open Forum that caught my eye.

Although it was signed only by "Worker, Gastonia" and is undated, it obviously appeared during the Strike of '34. As it was with all the other stories she wrote (including another for the *Observer*), I believe she is that worker. At that time, Mother, a spinner, would have been working approximately 11 years, having dropped out of school in the eighth grade to start out at Cramerton Mill.

To The *Observer*:
I've been a mill worker for the past 11 years, have been considered one of the best of "spinners." But the load has almost got the best of me, for the machinery has been speeded to the highest notch, more cleaning up has been put on us, till we can't hardly bear any more.

There has been so much criticism on the part of

the strikers, that it has aroused my temper, and I want to tell from experience what I know about a mill worker.

Now you folks who read this letter, just picture a poor, frail mother getting up at 4 or 4:30 o'clock in the morning; watch her as she slips on her best printed dress and flour sack apron; imagine this poor little mother making bread enough for breakfast and dinner, then she slices about half dozen pieces of fat meat, makes each member a cup of hot coffee and goes to the table and asks God's blessing on this humble food. Then she leaves her children in the hands of their grandma, while she goes to work to help their daddy pay for this food which has been bought on credit and also to help buy clothes for them to wear.

I've seen women so wet from perspiration that it could be wrung from their clothes. I've seen them go to a window for a breath of fresh air, only to be whistled at by a section hand and made to get away from the window. I've been in a rush to get a drink of water, only to be watched by this same boss, watching every move. I've carried a bite of lunch to eat and would sit down with dirty hands, not even taking time to wash the oil and grease from my hands. I've swallowed only a few bites when this same boss comes and orders me to get back on the job, while he goes and takes a rest at his desk. I've seen "speeder hands" running like a scolded dog, trying to do his "creeling" and doffing. The work is speeded so high since the short hours began that the mill men are getting off more production in a 6 or 8 hour day than they got off in 11 hours per day.

They claim they are not making money. Well, if they are not making money, I ask you how can they afford to build those fine mansions to live in? How can every member of the family own his or her own car? How can they spend hot summers at the sea shores? How can they afford to take trips to foreign countries? How can they afford to send their children to college and obtain the best education? When the poor mill worker can't make enough money to buy milk for his under-nourished children and can't buy books to send them to school, and the mothers much watch the flour sacks like a hawk watching a chicken, to get hold of them to make little undergarments for her children.

Now picture this mother unable to work, and with only the father to make a living. He toils and sweats his 6 or 8 hours and comes in ready to fall over in his "straw tick bed." Now on pay day, look at this man draw his $9 for a week's work after the rent has been taken out. This leaves him only $8. That is, if he occupies a four-room house. After he pays $8 for a ton of coal, where is his groceries coming from?

Now I want you to see this mill worker going to the store asking his grocery man for a week's rations on credit. Watch him order 3 lbs. fat meat at 16 cents a lb.—48 cents; 24 lbs. flour—$1.10; about 50 cents' worth of Irish potatoes, 25 cents' worth of pinto beans, 1 pk. cornmeal, 24 cents, not to speak of all the other things such as milk, butter, coffee, etc.

Now do you people want to know for what reason are the textile workers on strike? Read carefully this letter and you will find out we want decent wages, shorter working hours and a right to organize and join a union and do away with this damnable stretchout system.

WORKER, Gastonia.

Through the Ears and Eyes of a Child
by
Betty M. Hinson
Author of *From This Red Clay Hillside*
The Eagle 1924 - 1950

"The only thing we have to fear is fear itself," President Franklin D. Roosevelt told us over the radio.

Although I had been born in 1929 and was too small to realize the devastation of the Depression, I joined my parents and others in the Eagle Mill Village in Belmont, North Carolina, to hear Roosevelt's speeches.

Like other families, we gathered in the front room of our five-room mill house and hunched around our Philco radio.

Even I understood that our President's goal was to pull our nation out of the economic chaos. But I could look and see that those who had jobs were working only two or three days a week.

When I started to school at Belmont Central in 1935, a lot of parents had no lunch money to give their children. One little boy brought a baked sweet potato in one pocket of his overalls and a biscuit in the other.

I remember my embarrassment the day I took crackers and a pint jar of tomatoes that my mother had canned. I could not open the jar and had to ask a bigger boy to unscrew the lid.

Through the Work Projects Administration (WPA), some people were hired to work on our school grounds setting out rose bushes along the fence. Miss Ruth, a widow, came each day with her work gloves and little spade. Her premature white hair showed beneath a broad-brimmed straw hat that shielded her face from the sun. She always wore a clean plaid apron and would smile at the children and say "hello," as she set rose bushes in holes dug by WPA men. When Miss Ruth finished with her planting each day, she would come into the basement of our school and clean the toilets.

My dad always said that no job is too small to do with pride. He was insistent that it is always better to work at any honest job than to take a handout from others.

At least *she* had a job.

A Different Kind of Washerwoman
by
Paul Jernigan

During the Depression, people helped each other in times of need.

While I was working my way through Guilford College in Greensboro, one of my classmates was DeArmon Smith, whose mother operated the college laundry so her son could get an education.

One Sunday at a Friend's Meeting, Mrs. Smith, who was a widow, asked me, "Paul, who's doing your laundry?"

"I am," I replied.

"Why don't you let me do it?" she asked in a motherly tone.

"I can't afford it." I replied.

Laundry services were included for the boarding students, but others had to pay per piece.

I was living and working off-campus on a private farm to pay tuition and buy books and watched every penny. I did my own washing and ironing.

The plain but friendly matron in her 40s persisted. "Why don't you try it?"

I told her again that I couldn't afford it, but this conversation was repeated several times until, one day, I dropped off my work clothes, school shirt and pants, towels and underwear at the laundry.

When I picked them up, I asked how much I owed.

"Twelve cents," said the plain lady, who suddenly seemed beautiful, straight pulled-back hair and all.

For the remainder of the year, I used her services. Mrs. Smith's prices—that is, the ones for me—ranged from 10 cents to 17.

His Compulsion
by
Dr. Wesley Wallace

At Hugh Morrison High School in Raleigh, we called ourselves The Three Musketeers—Hubert Crow, Banks Young and I. We did almost everything together. Along with our expanded group of eight to ten boys and girls, we would pile into one or two cars and go bowling or out to play tennis or to swim in the country club lake near Hubert's house.

After Hubert and I entered North Carolina State College in the fall of 1929, the two of us often studied physics together at his home. His mother, who was of the prestigious Dinwiddie family of Virginia, would graciously say to me, "Stay and spend the night," and I'd gladly do so.

The Crows lived in a mansion with a broad front and a side veranda above an expansive yard. We would study in his big room with a high ceiling, sleep and return to school the next day.

Through that friendship, I got to know Hubert's father, too. Edmund Burwell Crow, a vice-president of Commercial National Bank, was known for his impeccable character. He taught the most popular Sunday school class in Raleigh, 200 men or more at the First Presbyterian Church.

Before the bank holiday in 1933, Commercial National Bank failed.

Although no one spoke of it, I could tell that the family was having a hard time. They moved to a less stately home on Blount

Street near Peace College. Mrs. Crow was what we would call a "good scout." She did not show her feelings and made the best of her situation.

I learned later that Mr. Crow had a compulsion for the rest of his life. He somehow felt that he had let his customers down, people whom he had encouraged to rely on his bank. He felt that he owed them what they had lost. At first, he had no job. Then he tried selling insurance. According to Hubert, he paid what he could when he could.

Eventually, he got a position as a bank examiner in Virginia. I visited him and Mrs. Crow there. They lived in a very small apartment, a drastic contrast with their fine home near the country club.

Did he pay everyone back before he died? I don't know. But I admire him for trying.

Our Musical Breadwinner
by
Dr. Wesley Wallace

My mother, Lillian Parker Wallace, was the bread-winner of our family.

Our parents were separated, so my sister, Marian, and I lived at 3201 Hillsborough Street in Raleigh with our mother. Her parents came to live with us soon before my grandfather, a retired Methodist minister, died. Grandmother, Saidie Feetham Parker, stayed on to help Mother keep house.

My mother calculated that Grandmother could spend $5 a week on food. Cabbage was only a nickel a head and a peck of potatoes was just 20 cents, so the $5, with Grandmother's careful planning, could be stretched.

Mother's primary occupation was history professor at Meredith College. She was strict, but her students were very loyal. Unfortunately, as the Depression progressed, her monthly check was reduced to about 20-30% of her salary.

A fine pianist, Mother reveled in the joy of music.

In the early '20s, she played dinner music in a five-piece orchestra at the Sir Walter Raleigh Hotel, after she finished her teaching duties.

Often, she hurried to the nearby Superba Theater to play with a different five-piece orchestra for the silent movies. At the theater, the violinist had already seen the movie so that he could cue the others. He used a foot pedal which blinked lights to tell the pianist, trumpeter, clarinet player and cellist to shift to the next piece.

By the time the Depression hit, the hotel no longer provided dinner music and the theater no longer needed an orchestra. Mother was, however, able to supplement her income by playing the piano.

As the capitol city, Raleigh still had many social events, and Mother often earned extra dollars playing for an afternoon tea or reception.

She still made union scale on every job. The scale wasn't high, but it was paid.

I could always tell Mother's mood by the selection she chose to play when she came home. Around midnight, if I heard a difficult piece being attacked, I would know that things had not gone well. But if her fingers lightly played a lyrical piece, I knew it had been a wonderful day!

From Architect to Map Salesman
by
H. Edward White, Jr.

In the '20s, my father, Hugh Edward White, had a thriving architectural practice in Gastonia. He was noted for having designed Gastonia High School, City Hall, the S.P. Stowe residence in Belmont and other fine houses in the region. But when the Depression hit, all that "went to pot." Building construction, and especially architectural work, became practically non-existent.

To help put food on the table for Mother, my three sisters and me, he came up with the idea of drawing a local map, which he called "The Industrial and Farm Map of Gaston County."

He did a lot of research and traveling all over the county to locate the large farms, cotton mills, county schools and churches, so he could properly map them. He believed that, particularly in the case of the farmers, if they could see their names on the map, they would want to purchase one. In 1931, Dad had 200 copies printed.

Two types were available: one on a heavy grade of linen paper; the other on plain paper.

When I was about 17, my father and I drove all over the county in his '24 model Hudson Brougham, calling on farmers, mill owners, and various business establishments to peddle the map. The

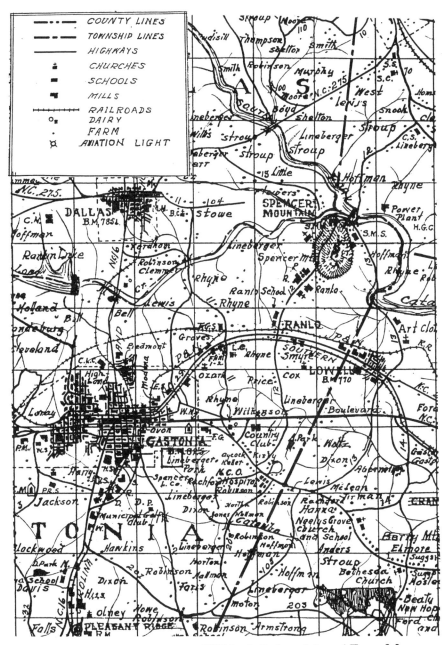

A section of Hugh Edward White's Industrial and Farm Map
of Gaston County, 1931

173

price was $1 for the linen paper version or 50 cents for the plain. If they didn't have the money, they would give us corn, tomatoes, cantaloupes or whatever produce they had. We did all right—after several weeks, we got rid of most of them.

Known for his fascination with figures, Dad included a variety of tables. In the commercial weight table, he reminded us that 12 gross make one great gross; 20 articles, a score; 24 sheets, a quire; 20 quires, a ream; a league is three miles; a hand, four inches; a span, nine inches. In the Pounds per Bushel table, he informed us that a bushel of dried apples, for instance, weighs 24 pounds, but a bushel of green apples weighs 56 pounds.

At random, he sketched native wild life and farm animals common to the area. Along the border on all four sides, he named the county's important features and attributes (from mineral waters, fine climate and four railroads to barite, galena and sphalerite) as well as industries and products (horticulture, iron work, castings, textile machinery, tire fabric, ginghams, flanneling, sheeting, rayons, silks, hosiery). He stated that Gaston County was the "combed cotton yarn manufacturing center of America" with 1,243,277 spindles.

Our county was settled by Scotch-Irish, Germans and Highland Scots, and, on the map, Dad took delight in pointing out that it took less than 30 years for cotton mills to supplant distilleries as the principal industry. By his count, Gaston had 103 textile plants,105 churches and more than 50 schools.

The population of the county in 1930 was 78,049. He listed how many lived in the towns: Gastonia-17,094; Belmont-4,121; Cherryville-2,756; Bessemer City-3,749; Dallas-1,486; Stanley-1,085; Mount Holly-2,225; Cramerton-3,000; Lowell-1,665 and McAdenville-914.

My father left spaces to write in those towns' population in 1940, but he died in 1939 before filling in those numbers.

After only one year at Davidson College in 1932, I helped my ill father struggle to keep a one-architect office open. I soon became his "right hand man." I learned to letter, cross-hatch wall sections and copy details and eventually enrolled in the International Correspondence School of Architecture. What allowed us to survive besides a few houses, were some small school buildings under PWA and a couple of patient ward additions at the North Carolina Orthopaedic Hospital.

After eight years of learning at Dad's side, I entered the Georgia Tech School of Architecture. Unfortunately, I couldn't put

174

my new-found knowledge to work immediately because I served in the Navy three years during World War II. But I did finally follow in my father's footsteps.

Breaking the Gender Barrier? My Mother?
by
Margaret G. Bigger
Co-Author (with J. Carter Goldsborough) of
Only Forty Miles of Pavement

Daddy was telling me about how North Carolina's future Secretary of State had helped him try to collect from an insurance company during the Depression. He knew Thad Eure and his wife as neighbors in Raleigh's Mansion Park Hotel, where he had met my mother in the early 1930s. He added an "aside" about Eure that I had never heard: "Thad had been the Principal Clerk in the House of Representatives when I first met him." Daddy chuckled. "He read out a bill before the House to raise the Secretary of State's salary one month and filed for that office the next."

"Did you say Principal Clerk?" I asked.

"That's right."

"But wasn't Mother a Principal Clerk?"

His "yes" made my heart stop. When I was growing up in the '40s and '50s, the term "clerk" was a rather lowly one. An office clerk or a sales clerk was generally the lowest person on the salary totem pole. Knowing that she had taken a one-year business course at Greensboro College and having heard about her being able to type at an incredible rate and sing at the same time, I assumed my mama had been a mere secretary with an even lesser title.

After all, my aunt—her sister Margaret Griffin—had been the one in the family to break the mold of a woman allowed to hold only the most menial of corporate jobs. Aunt Margaret had been the Chief Purchasing Agent for the Norfolk Shipbuilding and Drydock Corporation during World War II. Men were unaccustomed to dealing with a woman in a business relationship then, and she held her company's fourth top position, having to negotiate with top Navy personnel and suppliers important to the war effort! Our family was quite proud of her accomplishments. But no one ever mentioned Mother's former job.

"Principal Clerk" in legislature language was the top position of a department run by the state. My mother had been the Principal

175

Clerk of the—of all things—Prison Department!

Daddy explained how that happened. When she was still Mary Griffin, Mother, who was originally from Roanoke Island in Dare County, was looking for a job. Her cousin, State Legislator Willis Smith, found her one with another legislator, Edwin B. Jeffress of Guilford County. Yes, she was a secretary then.

My father delighted in relating a parallel tale to the one about Thad Eure: "Soon after typing a bill to put the Prison Department under the State Highway Department, she was named Principal Clerk of the Prison Department. Jeffress became Chairman of the State Highway Commission."

The Highway Department used prison labor to build roads, so Mother and Jeffress were still working together, but she did much more than type and sing.

I had never heard that! But Mother did tell me about how she had to keep up with where every prisoner was working. Not only could she name all 100 counties, but she knew which highways in each one were under construction. She also was in charge of all the local "trusties," prisoners who had earned the privilege of working in and around state buildings, including the Governor's Mansion. She had her own trusty, who served as a "runner" to deliver messages. How could I have been so naive to think that she had all that responsibility as the secretary (principal clerk) for Jeffress?

Maybe I did not realize her importance because I was aware that, before she became Mrs. John Carter Goldsborough, she and Daddy could hardly make ends meet.

The original Meredith College building, the Mansion Park Hotel was grand, though old. Located halfway between the Governor's Mansion and the Capitol, its architecture was similar to that of the home of the governor.

A traveling salesman for the United States Gypsum Company, my father chose Raleigh as his territory headquarters and the Mansion Park because he could get meals as well as a room there. He arrived soon after the bank holiday in March, 1933.

Recuperating from a nearly-two year bout of tuberculosis, Daddy found himself with only $9 in his wallet and an empty bank account, two good reasons to return to work. He notified the company that he no longer needed a leave of absence and would go anywhere on the East Coast. The general sales manager informed him of a second 10% salary reduction across the board and sent him to North Carolina. "I would be starting at $186," he recalled. " But I had a job. So many others did not."

Almost immediately, Daddy, known as "Goldy" then, was attracted to 31-year-old Mary, who was nearly as tall as his six-foot frame. She had a trim figure and short brown hair with the stylish finger waves of that era.

Generally, he saw her only on weekends because he was out trying to make a commission selling building materials. Even the sensational Sheetrock, which could be quickly nailed to studs for instant walls, was hard to sell. Dealers seldom bought, because builders had no customers.

"Very few dealers could afford a carload of stock, " he said. "Stopover cars seemed the best selling method, but I never let a customer know he was the first. In other words, I let him think I had at least one order in my pocket. Sometimes it would take a whole week to make up one car."

He explained Mother's dilemma. "Mary's financial situation was graver than most, for she was helping to support a motherless nephew and paying off a major hospital bill. Her state salary had been cut over 30%."

Although he never mentioned a figure, he did show admiration for the legislators who, by drastically cutting salaries, saved many a job. Was Mother's take-home pay any more than a secretary's? Possibly. But that may have been why they selected a woman. She would not expect an executive's pay. Whatever her monthly salary had been, when cut to less than two-thirds, it did not last 30 days.

Mother and her roommate, Bobbie Cobb (sister of Beatrice Cobb, the distinguished editor of the *News-Herald* in Morganton), who worked for the Department of Revenue, would be down to their last few cents at every month's end. When that happened, they always walked to the S&W Cafeteria, where they could eat breakfast for a dime. Toast and coffee were a nickel each. Once seated at a table, they could get free coffee refills and complimentary sweet buns not much larger than a cookie.

By August 1933, Goldy's salary had been raised back to $207 a month, sufficient to live on, with some left over for entertainment.

For fun in the fall, the Mansion Park gang carloaded to football games. Within a 25-mile radius were North Carolina State, Duke, Wake Forest and the University of North Carolina, so they cheered for at least one a weekend.

By 1934, practically all construction of any consequence was on what Daddy called "made" jobs: that is, government

177

buildings and WPA jobs. He explained why his commissions rose, "James A. Farley, a former USG salesman, saw to it that new post offices were built in Durham, Rocky Mount, Goldsboro and Chapel Hill. In 1933, he had become the new Postmaster General."

One Saturday night in the spring of 1935, Daddy and his district manager, Frank Miller, met Mary and one of her Raleigh friends at the seaside resort in Atlantic Beach, North Carolina. As neither Mother nor "Sugar Pie" Jones had a car, they rode down with others from the Mansion Park.

In receivership, the two-story frame hotel's entire complex, and even the bridge to Morehead City, was operated by Chase Manhattan Bank. Nevertheless, the elegant ambiance still dictated that everyone wear evening clothes for dinner.

Daddy recalled how stately his Mary looked in her long black gown. "The fabric fluttered as she walked with dignity into the dining room. After a sumptuous meal, the four of us followed the boardwalk to the hotel's pavilion, where an orchestra played. Mary's Methodist upbringing nixed the dancing idea. I had a better one anyway. We ditched Frank and Sugar Pie."

He mused that maybe the moon over Atlantic Beach was what prompted him to propose. On second thought, maybe she was the one who asked him. Whatever the case, they were married that May 11th.

Too much in debt to buy a traditional wedding dress, Mother wore a brown silk gown which she had used as a bridesmaid's dress a month earlier. They were married in her brother's home in Norfolk.

Daddy says that, when the Methodist minister asked whether they took each other for "richer or poorer," he accepted her debts. When he spoke of "in sickness and in health," she accepted his arrested case of TB.

Unlike a traditional wife, however, Mother continued to work as the Principal Clerk of the Prison Department until Daddy was transferred in 1938 to Baltimore, Maryland. That's where I entered the scene.

Now, I grieve. Of course, I have missed her ever since her death in 1977.

But I ache to be able to look into her gray-hazel eyes and say, "Mother, I'm so proud of you! You were ahead of your time; you made history. You set a precedent for women all over the state! Principal Clerk! Wow!"

The Pursuit of Cleanliness
by
Lois Moore Yandle
Author of *Spirit of a Proud People*

It was exciting to go to Granny Smith's and feel the wonderful flow of warm water coming from a spigot over your head and covering your body.

The owners of Highland Park Mill #3 paid Clara Jane Smith to run a bath house, and she did a super job. In her 60s, this short, chunky woman, in her long work dress of Highland Park gingham and white apron, was pleasant most of the time.

Margie and Lance Martin in front of Granny Smith's bath house

But her voice could be loud when she was aggravated with those who did not leave the stalls as clean as they should have or when the boys in the neighborhood turned on the hot water spigots and drained all the warm water from the tanks.

I knew better than to misbehave. Not only would I reap the wrath of Granny Smith but my parents also. She was no kin to me. "Granny" was just the name all the villagers called her.

The nice thing about this bath house, it was free.

There was another bath place—Sid Rouse's Barber Shop. The outgoing, likeable guy had a good thing going.

You could get your hair cut, shoes shined, have a bath and leave your cleaning to be done. The bath cost a quarter there.

When I had my hair cut, Mr. Rouse would put a board across the arms of a barber chair, drape me with a big striped cloth and cut away. Back then, we girls had haircuts similar to a boy's cut (bangs, sort of long on the sides, with a shingled look on the back).

During the Depression, not many people in our neighborhood could afford to spend much time with Mr. Rouse. The

the children's hair and gave us baths in an old tin tub.

So, you're wondering, did the mill village houses not have bathrooms?

Yes, and no.

When the houses were built, they had outhouses and hand pumps. In 1923, water and sewer lines were run to the kitchens and back-porch toilets. This was an improvement over pumps and outhouses—but just a little.

We still had no built-in wash basins nor bathtubs. The toilets were freezing cold in the winter, so chamber pots were necessary items for the nights. And just imagine how tough life was with no way to take a bath except in a #2 washtub or a sponge bath at the kitchen sink.

In 1904, when the mill was built, there was some type of facility for washing up available for the mechanics, loom fixers, card room workers and others who worked on machinery. It was not until the 1950s that showers were installed for those men.

In the '40s or '50s, the women finally got stalls in their bathroom at the mill. When I worked there as a teenager, the restroom was a large room with commodes with no separations between them. The women did enjoy gathering there for short periods, sharing things about their families and always a joke or two. They needed that time to keep their sanity while working in such a noisy place—and surviving the Depression.

Meanwhile, thank goodness for Granny Smith and Sid Rouse!

Eight is Enough
by
Lexie Little Hill
From *Gray-Haired Grins & Giggles*

In 1935, our government instituted a program to provide work for the needy. Unemployed men in our rural area of North Carolina signed up for this program called Work Projects Administration, better known as WPA. Local farmers dubbed WPA as "We Piddle Around."

I remember watching trucks filled with men, equipment and always a portable toilet go by our farm. These men built bridges, public buildings and parks and repaired roads. They even did landscaping.

180

A prominent lawyer in our area arranged for these workers to maintain his spacious lawn for the summer. Every Thursday, neighbors watched as eight men unloaded two lawn mowers and two outhouses from the truck.

One neighbor, amazed at all the commotion, asked the head man of the crew, "Sir, why does it take *eight* men with only two lawn mowers to mow the lawn?"

"Why that's simple," he said. "There's two a-comin,' two a-goin,' two a-sittin' and two a -mowin.' That's *eight*, ain't it?"

Yep, the more things change, the more they remain the same.

SOUTH CAROLINA

The Ledger
by
Edna T.J. Koon

Our family came to Spartanburg in 1918 from Atlanta, where Daddy had been learning auto mechanics. (Imagine that! Fire engines were still drawn by horses back then!)

Two weeks after we got here, Mother died of the 1918 flu she had brought from Atlanta. That left my father Thomas Jiles Taylor with four children. At age 4, I was the third daughter. My baby brother Donald was the youngest.

In due time, Daddy married Lolita Maria Cobb, whom I call Mama, and they had three little girls.

During the early years of the Depression, I was in high school. We lived at 497 Front Street one mile from the Daniel Morgan monument in the center of town. Frank Evans High School was beyond that. There were street cars, but we had no money to ride them, so we walked.

Each of us wore out our shoes and had to put cardboard inside until our father could afford to get a sheet of leather about the size of a newspaper. He would gather us around the heater, put our shoes on the leather, draw around them, cut the shapes and then tack them on our shoes. He did a good job.

When Carolina National Bank in our town closed, Daddy had little money in there, but his customers did.

My father worked every day and many nights for doctors and lawyers in town. Many a night, I held a light for him so he could finish fixing the car of someone who needed it the next day. Most of the work he did was "on credit." He logged what people owed in a black legal-size ledger.

That was before The Accident. Daddy was working under a transfer truck one day in 1934. Usually, he had a cushion on wheels beneath him, but he was in a hurry and, as he labored, his hand slipped and the transmission dropped. It smashed his head against the concrete floor. The serious brain injury that resulted left him like a stroke victim without the ability to express himself. He was no longer able to work.

But what about all those debts owed to Daddy? Those car owners *surely* could pay *some*thing. Some did. Most did not.

But one day, after I had married, I was visiting there and watched as my father took down the ledger and held it. With tears streaming down his face, he struck a match to it.

Crook vs. Crook
by
Tunk Ancrum

My father, Andrew Ancrum, was very nearly wiped out by the Depression, and he and Mama managed to scrape by on very little. Daddy lost his concrete business in Spartanburg, and Mama subsequently went into the antique business, gradually selling or bartering off many of the fine pieces of furniture that had belonged to her own parents.

When my sister, Harriet, and I were little, nothing was ever wasted. They would even stop along the road to pick up coal that had fallen from the delivery wagon.

Interestingly enough, it never occurred to most Southerners to lay off their kitchen help, as those people were desperate to eat, too. However, even in the worst of times, we children were cautioned never to take the last of the food in the serving bowls but always to "leave some for the help."

One night, Daddy had to go bail one of his friends out of jail, and Mama teased him and claimed that he and his cock-fighting cronies were all crooks.

"Who's a crook?" he countered. "Everyone knows antique dealers are crooks. You're a fine one to talk!"

From then on, their pet name for one another was "Crook."

182

Rags to Riches?
No, Just Suits to Overalls
by
Tunk Ancrum

My sister Harriet clearly recalls seeing Daddy out hoeing in our aunt's garden, while wearing a wool suit!

Our father, Andrew Ancrum, had a surplus of them, since our uncle in the Marines had turned over his civilian clothes to him, and there was no money for work or leisure clothes after his concrete block business went down the Depression drain.

He eventually got a job with the WPA, helping build Spartanburg's Duncan Park and the football stadium at Pine Street School. At that point, Mama got him some overalls and a lunch basket.

Harriet says that when she first started dating Clarence, he snagged her by telling her how he had once met Daddy out on that football field. Clarence said, "I know it must have been your father, because I could tell he wasn't like those other people out there."

That *did* it, naturally, and it wasn't hard for Clarence to win her hand after that.

Three-Way Comparison
by
Mary Mooneyham Dixon

While I was in the intermediate age group at the South Carolina School for the Deaf and Blind in Cedar Spring, I adored our caretaker. Perhaps my affection for her was greater because I compared her with two others who held similar jobs at the same institution.

When I lived in the primary dorm for white deaf girls, our caretaker was Miss Cutter.* In her fifties, she used to just sit in her chair in a room, watching to make sure we were okay and behaving.

She often asked one of us children to rub her forehead or her feet. Later, I took that to mean she may have had headaches. From what I can recall, Miss Cutter did not play with us at all. Mainly, she got us in line for bed, for meals, for playtime outside and to go to class. She reminded us to take our baths, brush our teeth, get in or out of bed, etc.

Once we became intermediates, the deaf and blind children

of the same gender and race were integrated. My favorite caretaker, Miss Lucille Stone, was in her thirties. She sometimes played with us, listened to us, and comforted us. She would mend our clothes and do special little deeds of kindness.

Miss Stone was a little on the fat side, about 20 pounds overweight and about 5'2" tall. She had a wonderful sense of humor and was quick to laugh.

The campus was, in those days, mostly surrounded by trees, kind of country-like. One Saturday, we walked for six miles. We were tired but had a great time. What a wonderful way to banish our constant homesickness for a while!

Miss Stone helped us through our adolescent problems, as we were ages 10 to 14. Once in a while, we would get mail from home mentioning domestic problems. We would go to Miss Stone for comfort and encouragement. She was great at comforting us, even quieting other girls who were gossiping about our situations.

Unlike the others, she never locked our dormitory door except at night. Never too strict with the school rules, she trusted us. So, you can see that we loved her.

The caretaker for the older white girls was Miss Alice Young.* We called her "Miss Alice." We never felt comfortable discussing any problems with her. Tall with a stiff walk, Miss Alice wore her hair pulled back in a tight bun behind her head. She had a bad case of incontinence in the days when there were no sanitary products. She kept her room closed at all times and did not allow us inside. Of course, she could not take us for any long walks or treat us to games when we went outside.

The older girls' dorm had one very long hall with bedrooms on both sides and a study hall. The one and only bathroom was in the middle. Some rooms held two students; others housed up to five of us. Miss Alice would always be sitting at the end of the hall with the doors to the outside locked. We had to have permission and a good excuse to go out and always in twos.

There was no rapport with Miss Alice. We just tolerated her.

Did the other two hate their occupations? I don't know. They didn't complain to us.

Did Miss Stone love hers? She loved *us*—and that's what mattered.

* Names changed

Cooperation, Caring and Sharing
by
Ida Goff Fields

As one of the four grandchildren of Tom and Julia Goff, who lived on a farm in Saluda County (two miles from Sardis Baptist Church), I learned how rural families worked cooperatively for the good of all.

My parents, Clarence and Iree Goff, moved our family of five to the town of Batesburg in 1928, so that we children could get a better education. But my sister Julia, my brother Jack and I joined our cousin, Everlee Goff, at our grandparents' farm in the summers.

Everyone helped out at their outdoor cannery. When the garden vegetables were ripe, it was time to build the fire under the canner. Twenty-four oversize cans were lowered in a metal basket into the boiling water. They boiled until done, the hot vegetables pop, pop, popping until the time was up. Meanwhile, some of us would be sitting around snapping beans or chopping tomatoes while others filled more cans with whatever vegetable was ready. When the cans were removed, an adult would solder the tops securely.

In the same way our family worked together, the community had an informal co-op. When a farmer killed a cow, for instance, he would quarter the meat and give some to certain neighbors. Although almost everyone had a smokehouse for pork, there was no way to preserve beef, so they would share. When the farmers who received beef from Granddaddy slaughtered a cow, they would give him an equal share. No money changed hands.

If one family's garden didn't turn out well, the others would give what vegetables they had in abundance. If another family had an illness and couldn't gather the ripe peas (corn or pole beans), neighbors would come in and help pick before they rotted in the field.

Occasionally, there would be a barn-raising during "lay-by time." That was around the first of August when most of the crops had been harvested and there was less work to be done. Churches had revivals then. Families had reunions and people visited more relatives and friends.

In 1933, we attended the Furman Matthews reunion, for the descendents of my grandmother's daddy. From 50 to 100 relatives spread food on boards under the shade trees at Sardis Church. They had singers in the morning and speakers in the afternoon. All the Matthews, Goffs, Lakes, and Corleys gathered for the all-day event.

185

I really miss those times and family members. We didn't know we were poor. Those were the good days, when people weren't so selfish.

A Profitable Trip to Washington
by
Nancy Artemus Gough

Although an insurance salesman, my father, J. Clarence Artemus took correspondence courses in carpentry to learn that trade.

In 1938, our national leaders could see what Adolph Hitler was doing in Europe and, knowing that war was inevitable, began to prepare. The decision was made to rebuild the idle Camp Jackson outside of Columbia, which had been little more than a fine place for a picnic after World War I.

Daddy gathered seven or eight friends and acquaintances, who had been building homes in the area, to apply for construction jobs at what would become Fort Jackson.

"You can haul sand and carry bricks," they were told, "but you have to be in the union to get any other job."

Of course, no matter how skilled those men might have been, they were not allowed to join the all-white union. So my father went to Washington to meet with our senator, Ed Smith.

Senator Smith was frank. According to Daddy, here's what he said: "As far as I'm concerned, you did not see me, because you could not vote for me. And the people who did will vote me out. But I will help you by sending you to the Fair Employment Practices Commission (FEPC)." He saw to it that someone took Daddy to the right office.

The FEPC was powerful, but they could not change the laws of South Carolina. Instead, they helped my father set up a black union which would entitle them to be hired by the people who turned them down.

In 1939, they formed Local 2260 of the United Brotherhood of Carpenters and Joiners, a small group of ten but a part of the American Federation of Labor. My father never hammered a nail after he became a union officer. Our beautifully dark-skinned dad, with a great speaking voice, became their business agent, who traveled from New Jersey to Florida to recruit more skilled workers and locate other jobs for them.

Yes, they were accepted on the Fort Jackson project. And by

186

1940-41, their union had well over 200 men and had worked on the new DuPont plant in Camden and at Shaw Air Base in Sumter. Instead of the pittance they would have gotten for hauling sand and moving brick, they were making BIG MONEY.

That was the end of my father's insurance days. He was getting a good salary, too.

Founding members of Local 2260, United Brotherhood of Carpenters and Joiners (AFL). Back row (LtoR): J.C. Artemus, Business Agent and Financial Secretary, Charles S. McIntosh, Treasurer, ___ Corbin, D.D. Mozie, Henry Belton. Front row (LtoR): Fred Sammons, President, Herbert Center, Vice-President, Boston Brice, Recording Secretary. Not pictured: Willie Mack, George Singleton

NORTH CAROLINA/SOUTH CAROLINA

One Man's Story from Three Bibles
Courtesy of
Harvey Michael and Lucille Michaels Nash

"I wouldn't be sitting here telling you this story if I had a job to work at," declared 70-year-old Joseph Asbury Michaels of

187

Burlington, North Carolina.

He had been asked by John H. Abner, also of Burlington, who was working for the WPA's Federal Writing Project, to "tell about his life as a cotton mill worker and a tenant farmer."

Michaels had labored in cotton mills for 50 years, off and on, falling back on farming between jobs and to supplement his meager income.

"I would still be working in the textile trade," said Michaels, "except that I got laid off when the Social Security law went into effect. They found out I was 68 years old, so they laid me off. I have not been able to find a job since. I am only 70 now, and hale and hearty, as you can see. There is plenty of work going on that I can do, but no mill will give me a job on account of my age; so I am forced to live off my sons. I get the old age pension, but it is only $9 per month, and that is not enough to live on."

To tell his story, Joseph Michaels went into another room to fetch three Bibles overflowing with family records of his life, of his wife, 12 children (10 living) and 16 grandchildren. "This old book," he said, holding up the smallest, "is the beginning. I bought this Bible in 1879 and I have kept it ever since. I was only 11 years old at that time, but I paid for it with my own money."

His life of low-wage toil made the Great Depression seem only another difficulty to be overcome. Born in Burke County, North Carolina in 1868, he began crushing rock by hand in the gold mines there at age 9. In 1887, he and his father went to Glendale, South Carolina to help build a cotton mill. "They only paid 70 cents a day, and a day was sun up to sun down, but it beat gold mining," he recalled.

He and his dad helped construct another cotton mill in Clifton, South Carolina, where he got a job. "I worked two weeks for nothing, then I was paid at the rate of 25 cents a day. Finally I got a set of looms, but wages were so low I could never earn more than 45 cents a day. The work was so hard and wages so cheap that I quit and went back to Burke County. For some time, I mined gold in Burke and Catawba counties."

By 1896, he was married with one child and working in a cotton mill in Converse, South Carolina where he could make 70 cents for a 12-hour day. But, as was common in mill villages, the hands had to buy groceries and supplies from the company store, which charged high prices.

He told of mill owners who would seek out tenant families who had had bad luck, pay off their debt but put them into deeper debt by charging for moving them, not paying during the "learning period," and overcharging for supplies. At 75 cents a day for a man and 25 cents a day per child, they found it impossible to pay off a $100 debt. "On payday, the father would be given a blank ticket, showing the family earnings for that month and the amount of the debt."

Speaking in generalities, not about any particular mill, Michaels compared mill workers' plight to that of slaves, except slaves had it better because they were "usually treated as well as the mules or other stock." He noted that "mill operators did not own the hands and, consequently, felt no responsibility for their well-being. Sometimes, a hand would get sick and die from lack of medical attention."

There could be severe consequences for buying from another store (discipline or dismissal), verbally protesting (supplies cut off), physically fighting back (the chain gang), trying to leave the village (they would be stopped or brought back until the debt was paid off).

Michaels knew of a man whose whole family got typhoid fever from their well. Those who didn't die returned to work but couldn't stand the hard work and long hours. "All winter, they dragged around in the mill, and the debt grew and grew."

That spring, the father wrote to a friend in another state, asking him to find a farm where his family might sharecrop and, hopefully, return to good health. With assurance from his friend, he explained his case to the superintendent and promised to pay the debt, offering to give the mill papers against his planned crop. The superintendent refused to let them leave, so they plotted a getaway. As their new landlord was to pay the freight bill, they loaded their household goods on a railroad car by night. Before the boxcar was picked up by the train, the mill deputy sheriff served papers attaching the contents of the car for the debt. In the end, the unfortunate man was liable for the demurrage on the car and the costs of drawing up and serving the attachment papers. To get the superintendent to release the goods and let them move back into the house, they had to cut their supply bill "to the bone" and accept the addition of another $50 to their debt.

Although resolved that he would never let a mill company get him in debt, Joseph Michaels saw the advantage of tenant-farming: fresh air. "The mills of that time had no ventilation, and people breathed the same foggy lint-laden air over and over again. Naturally, consumption, or T.B. as they call it now, took a heavy toll from the cotton mill worker."

He moved his little family to a farm in Spartanburg County

in 1898. But in that "red land" and "bad year," he raised only three bales of cotton which brought 5 cents a pound for the first bale and 7 cents a pound for the other two. That's when he began working in a mill in the winter and farming the rest of the time, never longer than five years in any one place.

Between 1900 and World War I, the steadily-increasing Michaels family lived in Burke County, North Carolina (to mine monzonite), Spartanburg County (to farm), Fairforest, South Carolina (to farm), then Belmont, North Carolina (to work in a mill) back to Spartanburg County (to farm and do mill work) and over to Boiling Springs, North Carolina (to farm), where one child died in infancy. Soon, they had returned to Spartanburg County (to farm) and on to Chesnee (to build and work in a mill). After brief stays in Pacelet, South Carolina and Saxon Mills in Spartanburg, they went back to Converse, where their 15-year-old daughter died of diphtheria. Discontented there after her death, they decided to try farming again.

Soon after the Army began drafting men, mill wages went up, so they moved to Apalache, South Carolina. "That was the first time in my life that either me or one of my children has earned anything like a decent wage," said Michaels. "Cotton mills were making money so fast they couldn't count it."

But Congress passed the excess profits tax, so that the mills couldn't keep what Michaels called "blood money." According to him, their solution was to go on a spending spree; buying new machinery, building mill additions and new mill housing and installing in water systems and electricity. Rather than raising wages, they offered bonuses. "A man might earn as little as $10 a week yet draw $25. However, they kept a string tied to the bonus, and if a man got sick and lost a day, it might cost him $15, notwithstanding he only made $2 a day."

When the war was over, the excess profits law was repealed. "They cut wages in many mills more than half, and they got some of their money back by charging the hands high prices for water and lights."

Joseph Michaels moved his family once again to Chesnee and made a good crop on shares: 24 bales from 20 acres. "But 1920 was a bad year on the cotton farmer," he lamented. "I got 32 cents a pound for the first bale, but the price went down faster than the cotton could be picked." His last bale brought 10 cents a pound.

After paying all his debts, there was "little left to count," so he went to Ranlo, North Carolina to work in the mills. Wages were so low that, by January of '21, he and his boys took a job in Saluda County, South Carolina, clearing and breaking in a big cotton plantation. This time, the work was partly on shares, partly day wages. He put in 200 acres of cotton in 1921. Boll weevils moved in before the crop was ten inches high. He settled with the landowner and took off for the mills of Spindale.

"For the next ten years, times were kind of up and down. The Depression hit the textile industry and everybody connected with it. I have always thought that it was the Lord showing his disapproval of our evil ways. During that time, me and the boys worked around wherever we could find anything to do. In 1930, I moved to Belmont, North Carolina and there I lost my wife," Michaels told John Abner, who was a relative by marriage.

"In 1933, I moved here to Burlington and have lived here ever since. And I wouldn't be sitting here telling this story if I had a job to work at."

HOW WE PLAYED

Will this generation—or future ones—ever realize that they can have fun without spending money? That is, they can "make their own fun," like the children of the Depression did. But then, life was not so different in some ways then as compared with now. As poor as they were, people were attracted to the hope of gambling and the exhilaration of sports.

NORTH CAROLINA

Tomboy by Necessity
by
Virginia Olive Hartzog

Growing up on West Third Avenue in the town of Lexington in Davidson County, I found my playmates in the neighborhood. They were all boys.

Alvin Philpott was my age; his brother Hubert, a year older. Carroll Wall, a year younger, joined in our made-up games. The Philpotts lived behind us, and Carroll was next door. Hubert was the one that always got us in trouble but looked so innocent afterwards.

We often climbed the apple tree in our backyard and jumped down into the sandpile below. We got so daring that my mother would say, "I'm not going to watch," and retreat to the kitchen. Sometimes, we just made sand pies with the apples.

Like most children we knew, we were unaware of the Depression or great poverty, although I do recall the day Mother gave a meal to a man who knocked on our door asking for food. When Daddy found out she had fed him at the kitchen table, he really got upset. After that, she would hand a plate out the back door and let him or her eat on the back porch. (There were women hungry, too, you know.)

My favorite fun in the early '30s was digging a hole in the back alley and building a fire. When it died down to the hot coals, we would go into one of our families' vegetable gardens and get turnips or potatoes and roast them. Cooking may have been

Four friends: Carroll Wall, Alvin Philpott, Virginia Olive and
Hubert Philpott in Virginia's yard Circa 1931

considered "sissy" for a boy to do, but not on an outdoor campfire.

When we played football, I was one team; they were the other. I was bigger than they were. Clothes also set me apart: the dresses and Mary Jane shoes we girls were expected to wear. Mother made all my dresses with matching bloomers for obvious reasons.

A big day was when Hubert got a bicycle. We soon figured out how two could ride one. The person on the handlebars would guide it, while the one on the seat would pump. Of course, I wanted a bicycle, too.

I finally got one: A boy's! I didn't want one for girls. I'd have never heard the end of it!

Lard Buckets, Cotton Ties and Sardine Cans
by
Harvey Michael

"What are y'all doing?" I asked Warren and Dick, two of my older brothers. "I'm going to tell on you if you don't tell me what you're doing right now."

As a little brother, I knew I was treading on dangerous ground, approaching them this way. But I had been drawn immediately to their activity when I saw the box of matches. Before them on the ground, wedged between rocks, was a lard bucket. The lid was crammed down tight. There was a small hole in the bottom, an ominous noise coming from inside and a strong unfamiliar chemical smell all about.

"Shut up and get out of the way!" one of them yelled, as the other lit a splinter of pine and inserted it into the hole. POP! the bucket jumped; the lid blew off and sailed across the yard.

I was caught up in the excitement. "How did it do that? Make it do it again!"

Thus I was introduced to one of my first lessons in chemistry, as I discovered a new way to have fun.

Somewhere over near the Southern Railway tracks was a storage place for carbide—calcium carbide, to be specific. When the gray crystals were mixed with water, acetylene gas was formed. Acetylene is volatile. Kids with time on their hands could invent many exciting uses for that stuff!

We may have been short on cash at the Eagle Mill village in

Harvey Michael, 10, and his brother Fred, 7, show off their home-made "weapons." They salvaged discarded metal cotton ties from behind the Eagle Mill bale-breaker room and beat them into swords like the one Harvey is pointing at Fred. The "rubber gun" Fred is using to threaten Harvey was cut from wood with a hand-saw. A clothespin triggered the projectile, a piece of inner tube. Harvey adds, "I never felt fully dressed without a slingshot hanging around my neck. " Apparently, Harvey is underdressed. 1938.

Belmont, but we had our toys. Fortunately, not all of them were as dangerous as home-generated acetylene, but all were obtained by some unabashed spirit of acquisitiveness and innovation.

My tricycle had wooden wheels (made by my dad) on the back axle of a discarded frame he had found somewhere. A steel hoop made from the rim of a small wheel made a ringing noise as I rolled it ahead of me with a heavy wire bent into a "U" on the end. Before "cool" meant anything other than the absence of heat, it was cool to stop abruptly while rolling the hoop, catch it on the "U" and let it spin on its own momentum while others looked on with admiration.

Creativity flourished in the world of my childhood.

Harvey Michael with his wooden-wheel tricycle

My brothers, Fred and Jack, and I played with realistic-looking swords made from cotton ties. We made a wagon from old wheels, recycled boards and nails and a broomstick (as axles).

A large sardine can, licked clean by a dog, presented interesting possibilities: make a lid and it was a box for valuables like favorite marbles, an Indian head penny or a glittering piece of mica; attach a mast and a sail to make a boat or put wheels on it and it's a car.

A cedar shingle became a Mississippi paddle boat driven by a strip of rubber inner tube. Or it became material for the wing of an hand-carved airplane.

A lard bucket lid would sail like those plastic discs kids throw today—especially if it were propelled by an acetylene explosion!

Store-bought toys were rare and were cared for as treasures. My cousin James (we called him "Junior") had a brightly painted toy car made of steel. He kept it in a box under his bed. It was taken out often to be admired, and on rare occasions it was pushed gently across the linoleum. It's probably still under his bed.

Recently, I bought a scale-model replica of an airplane used by Texaco Oil Company in the 1930s. For some reason, I appreciate its metallic solidness, its rakish lines, its bright red paint more than a man my age should. But I still whittle toys from wood, and I like them just as well.

Equal in God's Sight
by
Betty M. Hinson
Author of From This Red Clay Hillside
The Eagle 1924 - 1950

Cotton mill people have often been the objects of scorn and ridicule by their peers. Class distinction in those early years was prevalent in the schools, the workplace, and even in some Southern churches that claimed we were all equal in God's sight.

Betty Miller with
her dog Bozo

One bright spring Sunday in April 1939, when I was 10 years old, we girls in the Sunday school class of our up-town church in Belmont began to plan an Easter egg hunt. I promptly invited everyone to come to my house for the hunt. In the Eagle Mill village, we had large walnut trees, oaks, lush green grass and purple irises bordering the yard — perfect places to hide eggs.

A classmate spoke up and invited us to hers.

Wanting to be fair, our teacher had us to draw straws.

I drew the smallest and lost. Showing my disappointment, I said, "Oh, I wish the class could come to my house."

One of the girls who lived in town said, "We wouldn't have gone to yours anyway."

197

The "Butter and Egg"
by
William S. McClelland

My African American friend, John Camp introduced me to a new kind of entertainment, the "Butter and Egg."

This was an unlawful gambling scheme based on the numbers in the butter and egg quotations in the local paper. For instance, if I picked 694: the last two numbers in the Chicago Mercantile butter quotation would have to be 6 and 9; the last number in the egg quotation must be 4.

I don't know what the top limit of a bet was, since John and I had to stretch to get a two-cent bet down each day.

There were hundreds of people taking the bets, but John had to place mine. Nobody took bets from a white kid from Myers Park.

If you hit, the return was pretty good—600 to 1—or $6 on a one cent bet! People bet on their hunches, on their dreams or on unusual occurrences. John told me of old women who made a living interpreting in people's dreams to indicate the winning number. The whole thing was practically an industry.

Neither of us ever won. And since I was bank-rolling John, I reluctantly came to the conclusion that it was a "sucker's game."

Playing for Food or Marbles
by
Furman Bridges

As the ninth child of the fifteen of Joseph and Senora Bridges, tenant farmers in Cleveland County, I was not aware that we were in the Great Depression. But many of our play hours were spent catching food.

By the time I was 6, in 1929, I would carry water to those laboring in the fields of whatever farm our family was working. But until I turned 13, I did not have to do much farm work. So, when we weren't in school (which was open only six or seven months a year), my young brothers and I were often running rabbits or fishing.

Sure, we had rabbit boxes, but it was more fun chasing them with dogs. And, in the snow, rabbits can't run fast. Our dogs would run them until they got real stiff. That night, Mama would take some lard (made after the hog-killing in the fall) and fry them for supper.

There were plenty of small branches in every area we lived in around Shelby and Boiling Springs. And, though the fish were small, they were really delicious. Mama fried those, too, for some *good* eating.

Like most kids of that time, we made our own equipment, like sling shots. It was difficult to hit a bird in flight, but that was just a sport. We did not eat birds. Well, on second thought, we *did* eat the bantam chickens we shot out near the barn. Our marble-sized rocks were big enough to kill that small breed of fowl, but we got our bottoms burned for doing it.

Once we found some wheels, so we made a wagon. We rolled used rubber tires with our hands and had races.

Our most popular game was shooting marbles in a hand-drawn ring. To get them, we sometimes traded eggs. The best way, of course, was to win them from each other.

Steel marbles were special. We found them in old farm equipment. I now know that they were not marbles at all. They were ball bearings.

The Yodeling Rangers
and The Trail Riders
by
Marvin R. Sechler

Dad used to play an autoharp, fiddle and mouth harp before he died in '29, when I was 14. My mother played an organ and guitar. She was the one who showed me the chords on her guitar. I was soon playing it with the Happy Trexler Band, and we were on WBT radio late at night for a couple of months. Later, I bought my own guitar, a Gibson, and then another, a flat-top Gibson, in 1935. Of Dad's 11 children who grew up on a Rowan County farm, four of us boys played about every schoolhouse in North and South Carolina during the '30s as The Yodeling Rangers.

George was our announcer and played fiddle. John Ray, whom we called "Curly," was on the tenor banjo. Duard ("Lucky") played guitar like me. They called me "Slim" because I never put weight on. Mike Belk traveled with us as a comedian. A neighbor, Mike played a washboard and blew a jug. For our opening theme song, we all yodeled.

We could fill a schoolhouse, but at 15 to 25 cents a head (and that divided by five), we didn't make much. I was working at

Cannon Mills off and on. The Yodeling Rangers did best when we were appearing at night in theaters or schools and on radio in the daytime. We'd broadcast in the studio at WSTP in Salisbury and, through a special hook-up, we were simulcasting on WSJS in Winston-Salem, WBIG, Greensboro and WPTF, Raleigh. Most of that period, we were advertising Robinson's Proven Fertilizer. Another time, Ruston's Furniture Store in Salisbury. Uncle Dave Macon and his son, Dorris, played on our show once. They were on the Grand Ole Opry for years.

The Yodeling Rangers, who sometimes included a Johnson family (Happy Gad, Smiley and their sister Jolly), changed its name in 1937 to The Trail Riders. Just the original five were in that group. We bought new hats and usually dressed in Western style.

One day, we found Charlie Monroe waiting after we got off the air. He was wanting Curly to go with him and gave an offer. He and his brother, Bill, a tenor, had split up and Charlie thought Curly sounded a lot like Bill. It took a couple of months to decide, but we figured that Curly could get us a lead to go to Nashville.

Curly and Charlie ended up on WWVA's Barn Dance in Wheeling, West Virginia, along with String Bean, who later was on the popular TV show HeeHaw.

Lucky played with Mack Wiseman (who is one of the old-timers on the Grand Ole Opry) and Curly, who was still with Charlie Monroe (another legend in the bluegrass field), changed over to a mandolin and then turned to picking guitar and singing tenor.

The Trail Riders were set up for an audition to go Nashville, when George got drafted into the Army. Lucky soon joined the Merchant Marines. I got married in December, 1941 and went to work at a shipyard in Newport News. I was rejected from the Army because of my bum leg. Curly had asthma real bad, so he didn't serve in the Armed Forces, either.

Curly was the one who hit the "big time" in bluegrass. He played for twenty-some years with Lester Flatt and Earl Scruggs and the Foggy Mountain Boys for Martha White flour. They also made the music for the movie "Bonnie and Clyde."

For nine years after Flatt died, Curly took the group over as the Nashville Grass. Marty Stuart was with him then. Johnny Cash was a guest star on one of their records, "Take a Little Time."

Lucky died just recently, but before he did, he and I and Bill Price played around in most of the retirement homes in Union County, where I live now.

I still like to play. Just ask me.

The Yodeling Rangers - Back row: George Sechler, Marvin (Slim) Sechler, Jolly Johnson, John (Curly) Sechler, Duard (Shorty, later known as Lucky); 2nd row: Happy Johnson, Smiley Johnson. Floor: Mike (Shy) Belk. The Trail Riders - Marvin, Duard, John and George Sechler. Floor: Mike Belk.

The Senior Prom
by
James Robert Clark

The 1935 school year was coming to an end slowly but surely. I had always loved to study and was looking forward to the day when I could step up and receive my high school diploma, but the dating game at Charlotte's Tech High was agony.

I never made a move on any of the girls in our class for a date. In my mind, I assumed no one would care to go out with a boy with pimples. The senior prom was looming high on the horizon, but I decided not to play the game. A serious character, I was shy to say the least. I kept telling myself that I could have a good time without a date. Also, I could take off when I wanted and not have to take anyone home.

Time was getting short. I kept asking myself, "Are you going to change your mind?"

Out of the blue came the answer. I was cornered by one of the best-looking girls in our class. Mary could have been a movie star. As she walked toward me, I noticed she seemed sad. She said, "Robert, I don't have an escort to the prom. I would love to go with you."

I made many excuses why I couldn't take her. Mary cut me off at the pass and moved very close to me. She had me in a trap. I heard myself saying, "Yes, I will be very happy to be your date."

When I went home, I had another problem to face. I had to talk to Dad about using the car.

He said "No."

Not giving up, I promised to be very careful. I knew I had to, because he was a policeman, and I knew all the rules.

He finally said, "OK, but do be careful."

On the Big Night, I picked up my date, drove uptown and parked in front of Efird's Department Store on North Tryon Street. The party was held on the second floor, and we were lucky that this was the only store in town with an escalator. As we stepped off into the bright room, the beauty of Mary's dress almost knocked me flat.

The food was good, but I don't remember a thing I ate. After stuffing ourselves, we found the dance floor and danced to dreamy music until midnight. We were so tired, we hardly had any conversation on the way home.

The graduating class of Tech High School met May 7 in our homeroom. I was taken by surprise when all 60 of our class gathered around me and yelled, "We gotcha!" They had pulled off their little side show, and my girl friend of last night was the ringleader.

I had passed the word around that I would not be going to the prom, and Mary informed her friends that she could get me to give in and attend. She announced that she would be my date.

When everything had settled down, I told her that I thought I was the winner, because she had given me so much pleasure the night before.

We left our homeroom for the last time, and made our way to the auditorium, walking in a single line. Mayor Arthur Wearn gave us our diplomas. I decided not to hang around—I had gotten what I had come for. I didn't go out the front door but chose the steps in back of the school. Halfway down, I met my prom companion. Our eyes made contact, and Mary and I floated into each other's arms.

Believe it or not, I never asked her for another date!

John, Chat and Hippo
by
Anonymous

I never felt the Depression.

I had a lot of advantages and a wonderful childhood. When I went to college in 1943, someone asked me if I lived in a mill town.

"I don't think so," I said. But my town really was. We had quite a number of textile mills, some with nationally-advertised products.

In my graded school in Rockingham County, I didn't notice any children poorly dressed or fed. We girls all wore cotton dresses with thin sashes. We were divided into A, B and C sections, and all my friends and I were in the A section. We gave each other silly names. I was Penny and there were Pie Face, Fifi and Hippo. Hippo, whose father was president of one of the mills and later a high-ranking government official, was my best friend.

After school, my playmates and I—we were all tomboys —played tag and hung upside down in trees, but then I would go upstairs, take a bath and change for dinner. I would sit on the front porch in my pretty dress and taffeta hair ribbon, waiting for John to come home and the cook to finish fixing dinner.

John and Chat, my aunt and uncle, were my surrogate

parents. I never really knew my father. When I was very young, Dad, who was a lawyer, had a stroke. He died when I was 5 and my brother Bill was 9. My mother, a school teacher, rented our home to another family, and we moved in with my grandfather and with John and Chat, who lived a block away and had no children of their own. I really lived both places, but my uncle and aunt's sleeping porch was my room.

Our New England style house, built in 1840, was in the middle of town and a mecca. When people would come to shop at my grandfather's general merchandise store or to get a soda at the drug store, they would stop in to visit. My tall slender aunt, Chat, was a "people person," who kept everyone entertained. She and John had lots of dinner parties and bridge games. My job was to carry the coats upstairs. Chat had gorgeous clothes, but I thought she looked best in the Herbert Sondheim long black crepe gown with a V neck and jet epaulets.

Whenever Jeff Penn of ChinquaPenn came to dinner, Chat always had a bowl of white beans at his place. He grew up in the country, you know, and married a wealthy lady from the North. I enjoyed his visits, because he'd let me sit in his lap and was very talkative.

Hippo and I had birthdays close together, and when we turned 12, they gave a party for us with twelve or fourteen boys and girls dressed as formally as 12-year-olds could. My long dress was of aqua taffeta. We had a great time—and no one threw food!

Every summer, we packed up the Packard and headed for the beach for a month. Sometimes, we rented a house at Nags Head. Other years, we stayed at the Ocean Forest Hotel or The Patricia at Myrtle Beach. Of course, John could not go because he was the town's beloved family doctor. He never even played golf; he loved to practice medicine.

I adored John and would ride with him sometimes to make house calls. One day, I was standing on the front seat next to him when I asked, "Where do babies come from?" His only answer was that he would tell me when I was older. That's all I needed to know.

I do know that he charged $10 to deliver a baby. When his home became mine, I found his old ledgers. He never sent bills. People just paid cash at the office or gave him hams, produce, etc. On some evenings, he would come home and hand me a pocketful of crumpled paper money and say, "Here, Honey, straighten this out."

In the ninth grade, Hippo moved to New York, where she

attended Friends private school. I missed her. We could no longer roller skate together or go camping or jitterbug in our basement playroom. But that did not stop our friendship. She was just a train ride away. Once she invited me to a dance at Friends. I rode the streamliner to New York and stayed in her home in Gramercy Park. With our evening dresses, we wore wedge-heel shoes and white socks. All the Big City girls wore stockings. Later, her father planned wonderful trips for us, even to Canada.

By then, my brother was well on his way to following in John's footsteps as a doctor. I wanted to do the same. John was so loved in our community. He was a charter member of a savings and loan and chairman of the board of many organizations and businesses, but most important, he helped people get well.

After graduating from high school at 16, I went to college to become a physician. I was determined—until I hit chemistry class.

Maybe I was really more like Chat, a "people person."

OVER THE EDGE - NORTH CAROLINA

Leisure? What's That?
by
Paul Jernigan

Growing up during the Great Depression in a puritanical family and neighborhood in rural Eastern North Carolina, where the work ethic was honored, I experienced very little of what is today called leisure.

Vacations, holidays and long weekends as we know and observe them today were unheard of. Christmas and Thanksgiving Days were the only two holidays on which we did not work.

Our work week was from early Monday morning until late Saturday afternoon. Sunday was a day for rest and observation of the Sabbath. We were to keep it holy. We all went to Sunday school and preaching services each week.

Several times a year, we socialized there and ate dinner on the ground. Those dinners were great occasions for us boys. We usually gorged ourselves with fried chicken, country ham, pies and cakes until our bellies were as tight as full ticks.

As young boys, we rambled and explored the woods on Sunday afternoons. Sometimes, our whole family visited my grandparents or other relatives and friends, usually within a few miles' radius of our home.

Common everyday means of amusements, such as card-playing, dancing and movie-going, were considered sinful and were forbidden. Sermons were preached from the church pulpits denouncing them. As we grew older, we indulged in some of these sins on the sly.

In summer, we hunted, found and ate wild plums, huckleberries and blackberries. In the fall, it was crab apples, persimmons and wild grapes.

For excitement, my friends and I would hide and smoke rabbit tobacco. Our mothers would smell it on our breaths and switch us for it.

In the winter, we made crude rabbit boxes, which we set out around the edges of the woods and caught rabbits and an occasional opossum or cat. It gave us a thrill and provided a goodly amount of meat for our family.

Most boys had a sling shot, which we made with two strips of rubber from an old automobile tire inner tube, a leather tongue from a discarded shoe and a forked prong cut from the branches of a dogwood tree. Assiduously, we scoured the woods for that perfect prong.

We became fairly accurate with these weapons, depending upon the smoothness of the small pebbles we used as ammunition. We hit an occasional sparrow or robin, never a quail, crow or blackbird. I don't recall anyone bagging a rabbit or squirrel.

Old automobile tires were used to entertain young children. A tire suspended by a rope from the branch of a tree made an excellent swing. Young boys rolled tires up and down dirt roads and paths, keeping them rolling and guided by a regular pat or slap of the hand. Boys enjoyed racing each other with their tires.

The rims or steel tires off abandoned wagon or buggy wheels were another favorite. About five feet in diameter, they kept an energetic kid happy just rolling them by hand or stroking them with a short stick. The metal rims, about 12 inches in diameter, off the hub of a wagon wheel were propelled and guided by a three-foot long stick with a cross stick nailed to one end. It took a good amount of practice and skill, but it kept us from being bored.

Sometimes, we would slip off to a shallow creek deep in the woods to play in the water. This was a whipping offense from our mother, as she had a morbid fear of water and drowning. Too, it was desecrating the Sabbath. I got several switchings as the result of coming home with damp or wet clothes.

Marbles were prized toys. We got them for Christmas. There were three types of marbles. The cheapest were made from clay and broke easily. The next in value were made of glass and called "glassies." The top of the line, rare and highly valued, were ball bearings from an old automobile transmission. They were made of steel and called "steelies." If shot hard and accurately enough, a steelie could chip and break glass and clay marbles.

Playing marbles for keeps was outlawed by our parents as being unfair and gambling. But the more skillful shooters had most of the marbles. Once I was heartbroken and bereft because I had lost my marbles.

In my mid-teen years, my parents relented and let us play baseball on Sunday afternoons. There was no money to buy equipment. We made our own. For bats, we used straight saplings of ash or hickory. We selected those of the needed size, sawed them into correct lengths, then whittled and shaped them with a drawing knife. To obtain a smooth finish, we scraped the shaped bat with the sharp edge of a piece of broken glass.

Baseballs also were improvised from scraps we had. We began with a piece of tightly wadded scrap of rubber inner tube, around which we firmly wound discarded pieces of string or twine until it was almost the size of a regular baseball. Then we bound and secured it with what we then called "tar tape," which was a sticky black tape and has been superseded by plastic electrician's tape. Sometimes, we used them without tape, as a roll cost 10 cents.

Never having enough boys in the neighborhood to form two full teams at our impromptu games, we elected captains who took turns choosing the players (the poorest player being the last one chosen).

We played in cow pastures and had to be careful when running bases, as the pastures usually contained mules and cows. Stepping on the wrong base could be disconcerting.

Home-Style Sports
by
Selby A. Daniels

Nobody ever bought me a baseball, a bat, swimsuit or football, but I enjoyed all those sports. Our fun was mostly of the "homemade" variety.

Baseball was the primary sport that my two younger brothers, Kline and Chick, and our neighbors played in our cow pasture on Sundays. (We worked on our Wayne County farm the other six days.)

We made our own bats and balls, because our parents had no money to buy these items in a store. To make a bat, I went to our woods and selected a young ash tree the right size. I then used my father's drawing knife to pare down and shape the hand-grip area. After shaping it, I finished it with a piece of broken glass, preferably from a Pepsi or Coca Cola bottle. Mother made our field gloves and more-fully-stuffed catcher's mitts from our worn-out overalls.

To make a baseball, I used an old cut-up golf ball as the

208

centerpiece, Then I would wind some three-ply tobacco twine on the ball to the desired size. Sometimes, I had to substitute a large black walnut. We all preferred a golf ball, as we could hit it farther than a walnut-center ball.

One day, my cousin Albert Aycock was playing baseball with us, He was running to catch a fly ball, brushed up against a pine tree in the outfield and stepped into a cow pie. Albert was so upset—so mad—that he broke up the game.

Summertime swims were special treats. Usually, either my father or my Uncle Jasper Aycock took us to Contentnea Creek in Wilson County, as it was free. We could not afford the nominal cost of the only swimming place in Goldsboro, Crescent Lake. We didn't have bathing trunks anyway, not at that time, so Contentnea Creek was the only place we could go "skinny dipping." Obviously, our sisters and female cousins were never invited. How I survived the rocks in Contentnea Creek, the leeches or the water moccasin snakes is another story. Yet, it was there that I learned to swim. Self-taught, I first mastered the "dog paddle" and finally the "Australian sweep."

Our winter farm sport always started after hog-killing time. This usually occurred the very first day of a hard freeze. My parents would give me hog bladders, which I cleaned well. I blew them up and tied a string to hold in the air. For what? Hog bladders made excellent footballs!

Ever wondered why football is a fall sport? Or why another name for a football is "pigskin"? Now you know.

SOUTH CAROLINA

Let's Play Make Believe
by
Jerri Gibson McCloud

"Wow! It's huge," I thought to myself. There was scarcely enough space to sit in the living room of our small mill house located in the sleepy little town of Winnsboro in Fairfield County, South Carolina. However, quite a few of Winnsboro's finest sat around, pushing and pulling their needles with tiny stitches of perfection, the ultimate goal being completion of a beautiful quilt of many colors representing our "America the Beautiful." This is where

I learned to create my own.

Norma, my one-year-older sister, and I would sit for hours playing under this "tent" stretched over a gigantic frame while the local women quilted. A small child of 5, I found this lots of fun. You could take a scrap of fabric, stuff more scraps under the center, tie thread around the stuffing for a head— voilà! You had a doll! We created a whole family, playing until the ladies were ready to go home.

Sometimes their children came with them and my, my, did our doll family ever grow! If there were an old newspaper around, which was not often, we cut out paper dolls, frequently leaving them strung together forming a continuous row of dolls. Of course, they did not look great, nevertheless, that did not matter to us. We had busy little hands.

Still under this huge "tent," Norma and I would sing and sing and sing. She had a powerful voice whereas mine was always mediocre. Fortunately, we both could carry a tune and as we aged we learned to harmonize everything we sang. If it was not harmonizable, we did not sing it.

You could hear me whenever I had a doll in my arms singing to her "Rock-a-bye baby, in the tree top," etc. You know, it didn't have to be a doll. This is where the poor kittens came in. Lucky for me they were gentle no matter what I did to them. I dressed them in the smallest things I could find. One time, I put a tiny sweater on one whereas, all of a sudden, he disappeared somewhere in the sweater! I took a square of fabric, another time, placing him in the middle like a sling hanging it from a tree branch. All the time I was still singing "Rock-a-bye Baby." Remember the part "When the bough breaks..."? Occasionally it did!

Every Saturday when Norma and I walked to town to see a movie, we always passed a store window with dolls. Behind the glass was the most beautiful doll I had ever seen, crying out to me as if to say "take me home." On a good day, Almer, our adoptive father, probably full of guilt, would take us to town, and I'd show him the doll. That Christmas, to my surprise, I got her!

Our play became very messy at times. We pretended one of our dolls had a devastating case of the measles or chicken pox, requiring red paint. Aunt Willie Mae's lipstick worked great for paint! It never occurred to us how to remove the red spots. Water! We scrubbed and we scrubbed, but the water caused the composition to crack or craze. Do you really believe this stopped us? Not on your life! We thought the doll's *life* was much more important.

210

Playing doctors or nurses was a fun pastime for us. We had so many dolls with bandages made out of scrap fabrics or strips of torn clothing, one could fill a hospital. After the dolls were all bandaged, then there were the kittens. You could hear the giggles as the kittens tried to get up and walk. The giggles quickly turned to sympathy and the bandages were removed.

Many a rainy day, we gathered grownup clothes, hats, necklaces, and shoes to play dress-up. Ladies' dresses were too long, so we hitched them up with a belt and off we went to a pretend dance. This was fun until Norma got mad chasing me in shoes too large, and I fell, putting a gash in my head from the door frame.

" 'Magine if..." you were a queen, Snow White, Cinderella, the Fairy God Mother, a cowboy hero, or a mommy. "'Magine if..." you were riding a flying horse all over the world which seemed to stop at the southern edge of Winnsboro. This was the game we played, the game of pretend, of make believe. Always creating new ideas, we were seldom bored.

When I was in the second half of the second grade we moved to the Blackstock community near Great Falls, South Carolina. Living with my Grandmother Gibson was even more fun, as there were cousins upon cousins to play with and more animals than you could count. I had a name for all the animals and fell in love with the horses, though some were just mules. Farm animals were great fun and entertainment.

A favorite thing was to go to the hill beside a little branch, where we sometimes got water, to create a playhouse. We looked for a flat spot under a shade tree. Each of us had our own little house, big enough for our pretend furniture. Old limbs with leaves were perfect for sweeping the area clear. Those same limbs, once stripped, made terrific walls for the house as well as room dividers. Sometimes we just drew the house in the dirt if the ground was clear enough. You guessed it! My house always had a "baby's room" with a drawn-in bed for my doll.

The horse buggies sitting under the shed were used to take our favorite dolls for a ride to town, racing another family's buggy and anything else imaginable.

Pretend and make believe could put me anywhere I wanted to be. It took away the tears of sorrow and put a happy smile on my face. Perhaps that is why I carried my love for dolls into adulthood, creating Dolls by Jerri, a manufacturer of dolls. I can still pretend and play make believe and help thousands of others do the same.

Even Prisons Have Recreation
by
Mary Mooneyham Dixon

Fun for us at the South Carolina School for the Deaf and Blind in Cedar Spring meant "freedom," albeit limited.

Members of the basketball team could leave campus to play against schools in outlying areas around Spartanburg. I was a guard on the girls team. When we had the games at our school, the students could see them by paying a nickel. We won some and we lost some, but they brought a touch of the outside to us.

I will never forget the Spartanburg Lions Club. When I was in the fifth through the seventh grade, these nice men took groups of us to the movies and to a dairy creamery afterwards for a nickel cup of ice cream, which we ate with a wooden spoon. They could only take small numbers of us at a time, because they used their own cars.

Just before Christmas, we were told to write letters to Santa Claus. The Lions Club brought each of us one thing on our list plus a bag of fruit, nuts and candy. They even put a tree up on the auditorium stage for us. We would all sing Christmas hymns, both the deaf and the blind. The Lions never once complained that we sounded awful. One year, all the girls found a pair of cotton bloomers in their bags, while all the boys on the other side of the aisle received flashlights. We heard a lot of giggles coming from the boys' side about the girls' gifts. Some of the girls didn't want those bloomers and said their mothers would not wear them, so I had five or six pairs to take home to my mother for the holidays.

At Halloween, we always had a party, and on May 1st, we had a May Court with a May Pole. After the dance around the pole, we got cake, cheese sandwiches and punch.

Birthdays were not celebrated, but most of us got packages from home. One girl from Florence got a package filled with fried chicken. It must have been up to three days old, but she didn't get sick. I asked for the bone when she got through and savored every little morsel I could suck from it. We never had chicken of any kind at the school, so even that was a treat.

Dating was unheard of on our campus. During all my years there (1931-1943), the boys and girls were strictly separated. In chapel, the boys sat on one side, the girls on the other. Likewise, in the dining room.

Our intermediate caretakers would let the boys and girls play together outside under their watchful eyes. The girls' dorms were upstairs; the boys' on the ground floor—with outer entrances only. But we found a unique way to communicate. As the windows had no screens, we would tie notes to a long string and dangle it down to them. One of the girls had a flashlight, and we would have fun passing our early bedtime hours exchanging notes with the guys.

When I first moved to the older girls' dorm at age 15, the caretaker would open our packages to look for notes or letters from boys. That was stopped about a month after I got there. But the practice of the principal reading our mail and correcting our mistakes continued.

When I signed one of my letters "With love" to a boyfriend in Columbia, my hometown, she forced me to write it over and sign off "Sincerely." After that, I asked my friend, Evelyn Taylor, and her sister, Sadie, who was also deaf, to mail my letters to him. They went home to Laurens every Friday until the war started, and gas rationing reduced their trips to every other Friday. The principal stopped censoring letters about a year after I moved up.

If word reached the superintendent of two opposite-sex students falling in love, he ordered that everything be done to discourage it, even to facing them away from each other in the dining room or making sure that they never saw each other.

Until my last year there, we could only talk with one another in class, at parties, basketball games or slyly in the dining room.

Cedar Spring girls on a picnic in Spartanburg with their middle school "manual" deaf teacher, Mr. Braunagel. Circa 1940.

If we could find a chaperone to take a group of us to the movies on a Saturday, we could sit together in the theater and on the school bus that took us. Many times, I didn't have the money to see a movie, but I relished that little opening to the door of freedom.

In my last years on campus, the boys were allowed to come over to the girls' side outdoors to talk. Sometimes we took walks together. One of our favorite places was down the hillside past the colored peoples' building to a spring, from which the school's water was pumped. Growing beside it was a cedar tree, hence the name "Cedar Spring." We would sit around the nearby gazebo talking and enjoying the scenery. There was a large pipe with delicious water flowing through it. We'd put our mouths to it and drink.

Enjoyable as this was, it was all done under strict supervision.

The Best Toys Were Homemade
by
Thelma Percival Kube

Beautiful dolls that said "Mama" and closed their eyes sat on our dresser, while my sisters Mary Alice, Elsie and I let our imaginations run rampant with more creative entertainment.

In the spring, small sticks dressed in jasmine, honeysuckle and woodbine became beautiful ladies. Large maypops with toothpick legs were the ladies' horses. In the summer, we robed corncobs in clothing made from old sheets dyed with poke berries.

By fall, dolls were forgotten. Our brothers Frank and Doug made scooters by nailing straight boards onto barrel staves. Then they sanded the staves and polished them on green pine needles. We had fun all winter, climbing to the top of a huge sawdust pile, carefully sitting on the scooters and shoving off. The exhilarating speed built up momentum that took us across broom sage fields beyond the bottom of the sawdust pile.

We had no television, telephone or radio, but we never lacked for entertainment in Edgefield County.

One summer, Frank and Doug made a waterwheel from tin Coca Cola signs. With various items they found on the farm, they made a little saw mill. They dammed the creek, placed the waterwheel under the spill, connected the wheel and mill with pulleys and belts. We called it a "flutter mill," and everyone had fun sawing sticks and pine bark—even Irving Eubanks, a married man with a child, had fun playing with our toys.

My favorite toy was a most unusual one made by Frank. He carved a mule, then made a wagon and hitched it to the mule. He whittled a man and placed him standing at the front of the cart, holding the reins. He then carved a goat, placed it standing behind the man. Each time the wheels turned, the goat would butt the man's rump. One day I caught Mother playing with it.

My First Taste of Politics: A Chicken in Every Pot
by
Thelma Percival Kube

I was a skinny little sun-baked kid growing up in the wilds of Edgefield County in South Carolina. (That corner of the county is now a part of Sumter National Forest.) During the entire 12 years of my life, I had been as sheltered as a silk worm in a cocoon.

The year was 1932 and I was a bit confused, to say the least, when my blue chambray homemade romper was taken off me, and I was dressed up in my only Sunday dress and my hair tied back with a ribbon.

I was put in a panel truck with all the other children who attended Red Hill School and transported to the city of Edgefield. Placed in a line of children from all over the town and county, I was given a small flag to wave and told to chant, "A chicken in every pot! Hooray for Roosevelt!"

The older children carried placards that read "Vote for Roosevelt!" Caught up in the excitement, I paraded as lively as the rest. Around the square, up streets and down streets, we chanted, "A chicken in every pot! Hooray for Roosevelt!"

One little girl caused a stir when she called out, "Hooray for Hoover! Hoover made fatback taste like chicken!" But her words didn't rain on our parade. And Roosevelt won by a landslide.

A Family Fish Game
by
Daisy Butler Gibbs

On Sunday mornings at our home in Newberry County, our favorite breakfast was grits and fried fish.

215

The day before, our parents would go to town to sell their vegetables and molasses and stop by the fish market on the way home.

Much to Mother's dismay, our older sisters liked to play a little game at the breakfast table. They'd take a vote on which of their boyfriends the rest of us liked best. Each of them had two, so Josephine would hold out her open right hand and say "Ozie." Then she'd extend her left hand and name the other boyfriend of that week. Jessie Mae did likewise, naming "David" and "Governor." Then we younger children would slap a fish into the hand named for our preference.

Who won? Josephine and Jessie Mae. They got extra helpings of fish!

Dream Date?
by
Irene LaGrone Thomas

In 1930, I went to my first dance with Strom Thurmond.

So did several other Edgefield County teenagers. When a girl got to the age to attend a dance, Strom would ask two or three to the same affair. He never took just one.

When he got us on the floor at the Pavilion in Edgefield, he would bring other boys over to introduce us and we had a wonderful time.

He liked to call it "safety in numbers."

I thought it was a political move, myself.

NORTH CAROLINA/SOUTH CAROLINA

Childplay
A
Compilation

Most people who were children during the Depression reported playing jacks or marbles, jumping rope or bouncing on a spring board. Girls played with dolls, homemade or store-bought. Boys preferred target practice with a sling shot or pocket knife. Both enjoyed tire swings and see-saws. And even girls played baseball.

Like the boys from Wayne County, children from the South

Point area of Belmont, North Carolina, made balls and bats out of whatever was handy. According to Julia Neal Sykes, they stuffed rags in an old stocking, wrapping it with strings, to make a softball. The bat might be a stout stick or a board. A tennis ball substituted for a basketball to be thrown through a wire hoop nailed to a tree.

Jump ropes were usually made from vines. Julia also tells of children tying a string to one leg of a June bug and watching it fly like a jet plane—round and round.

She noted that her family did not do much outside their own community "because of the Jim Crow situation."

"When friends came over, we played Annie Over with two teams, one on each side of the house," said Lexie Little Hill of Union County. "To alert the other team that we were ready to throw the ball, we shouted, "Annie Over!" Then we threw it over the house. If someone over there caught the ball before it hit the ground, they tried to tag a member of our team. There was an element of surprise here."

For some, music was a source of great pleasure.

"My father bought a Victrola in 1928, and we danced the jitterbug. I was pretty good," said Daisy Butler Gibbs, one of 11 children from a Newberry, South Carolina, family. She laughed. "Our family could have a dance party all by ourselves."

Cato Coleman, also of Newberry, played a harmonica. "For 25 cents, I could get a good harmonica. For 50 cents, I could get a better one." He would play hymns in churches and get together with other harmonica players just for fun.

Card games were popular, too, except among certain groups like Methodists, who equated cards with gambling and deemed them evil. Families played board games together, though, especially checkers and Monopoly. At least *someone* at the table could be "rich" for a little while.

Those who could afford a radio allowed friends and family to gather around to hear favorite programs like Fibber McGee and Molly, Amos n' Andy or Edgar Bergen and Charlie McCarthy.

Anyone in town with a dime could get into a movie. "We went to the movies on Saturday morning," said Charlottean Betty Houser Ford. "They were all cowboys, like Hoot Gibson. I never saw him packing a gun."

Almost everyone mentioned church activities when telling of family fun.

Lois Moore Yandle of Mecklenburg County told of trips to the woods with her daddy to play in the creek. "He told us stories of his childhood and made whistles for us."

Perhaps most astounding to the "TV generation" is the old childhood pastime enjoyed by city and country folk alike: reading!

Depression Dating and Teenage Fun
A
Compilation

No money, no fun? Not at all. Teenagers during Depression days show us that dates didn't have to be expensive to be fun. Sometimes the free ones were best.

And holding hands and kissing were quite special.

"You did not kiss on the first date," Connie Conley Flynt from Wilson quickly said. "You were wild, if you did." She recalled her first date, "He came to me on a bicycle and took me to the movies, then bought me a nickel Coke at the drugstore. It was such a simple time."

"That was real companionship," said Dan Knee of Charlotte.

"You did a lot of porch-sitting, watching people go by and talking to them on the street," remembered Elizabeth Barkalow Shuman, also of Charlotte.

"I was 16 before they got me out of the trees." Connie commented. "I loved to hang in trees. I wanted to be a boy worse than anything in the world. Mother said 'You gotta be a girl,' but I liked to play kick-the-can and hide-and-go-seek at night with everybody in the neighborhood."

"We used to have parties, where we'd all get together at one person's house. And then we'd break up and have five-minute dates," said Elizabeth.

"We used to do that!" said Mary Huffman from Catawba County.

Connie's laughter rose above the squeals of delight from everyone within hearing distance. "We were retarded. We didn't know about that."

"We had time to walk around the block," explained Elizabeth. "Then you'd go back and you'd get another date."

"Was this orchestrated by the parents, or did you all do it?" asked a much-younger Mary Davis Smart from the Museum of the New South.

"Oh, you always had parents there," everyone agreed. "Always." "You never had a party without parents." "They were

218

there." "Very much so."

"Even at church socials you did that," said Mary.

"Spin the bottle!" Connie reminded the group.

Mary enthusiastically remembered, "Oh yeah!"

"Wasn't that risqué?!" Connie made an admission with a smile, "The first time I got got kissed. I thought this is the greatest thing—or maybe there's something wrong with me. I liked it too much."

"Dating was riding uptown on the streetcar (for seven cents) and going to a ten-cent matinee," said Lalla Marshall Gribble, "or just gathering at one friend's house, playing records and dancing."

Ann Mauldin Elliot agreed. "In my dating days, 1936 to '42, we were accustomed to fellows not having much money."

On weekend nights, teenage boys in Charlotte liked to go "checking around." According to Ann Elliot, "Boys would pile into a car and visit a girl, staying about 45 minutes, and head to the next house." Sometimes, they would take a girl along, but Ann and her friends made excuses to stay home to see who else might drop by. "It was a gauge of our popularity."

"We were a dancing crowd," Ann added. "At Christmastime, we sometimes had three dances in one day—a breakfast dance, a tea dance and a dinner dance, all private parties."

Generally, at a dance, there would be five "no break" sessions. Girls were expected to be with their date for the first "no break," but dance with other boys during the next four. Ann carried a red book to keep track of who had requested which "no break."

From the male point of view, the best dating plan was to get to a movie theater early to take advantage of the reduced rate.

Boys really liked to take their girls to a ball game. Sportsman Jack Wood of Charlotte took his to amateur baseball games at Independence Park. They were free.

"Many dates were spent in the parlor with the whole family," reminded John Williams from Yadkin County. "Unless the weather was warm and the swing was free on the front porch—or you took a walk."

He also recalled that many attractive girls from out-of-town lived in Winston-Salem's YWCA, where parlor dates were common.

"Once I had a date with a good-looking young lady, Jackie Stinson," recalled Jack. "I told her I had no car and she said, 'Come any way you can.' And so I took the streetcar to Queens College and walked way out Sharon Road almost to Morrocroft, about two miles, to get to her house. Then I had to leave early to catch the last streetcar."

"The streetcars ran until midnight," John Gill, also of Charlotte, interjected.

"That's what time they got back to the barn. They left the neighborhoods earlier than that," said Jack.

All three men told about the three famous musicians from Charlotte: Hal Kemp and Johnny Long, who had nationally known bands, and John Scott Trotter who arranged the music for Long before he went to Hollywood's MGM.

"Johnny Long was a left-handed violinist," said Jack. The others knew that. "You know why? He was feeding pigs and one bit his right hand."

All during the Depression, no matter how bad things got, the Myers Park Country Club in Charlotte held Christmas and spring dances attended by many teenagers, most from Central High School.

"We'd pile six in a car and go," said Jack.

Central High School also had a number of dance clubs organized by the males. The Navajos are still meeting (to eat, not to dance.)

"And there were Friday night dances at the Woman's Club on East Morehead," said Jack.

Dan H. Wolfe was in the class of 1939 at Central High. "Our class was the first one to be able to have dances in the school gym."

When teens got together, they liked to play practical jokes.

John Gill told of the time some boys picked up an Austin Healy (a small car) and placed it crosswise in an alley between the Latta Arcade and the YMCA on South Tryon. It belonged to Jake Houston, the Golden Gloves photographer.

It might have been envy, but in Yadkinville, boys did something similar. According to John Williams, they would pick up a car belonging to a "rich kid," and put it between two trees. He couldn't back up or go forward. The only way to get it out was find other guys to lift and turn it.

He changed the subject. "You know what was Charlotte's fast food outlet? Little Canary near the bus station on West Trade. You could get a hamburger for ten cents, a hot dog for five cents and a Coke for a nickel."

"There was another Little Canary across from the *Charlotte News* on Church Street," recalled John Gill.

Thelma Percival and friend, Edgefield County, SC 1938

"The hot spot in town that stayed open until 1 a.m. was the Tavern at the Hotel Charlotte. I used to go after I got through at the *Observer*," said Jack Wood, who became a young adult during the Depression. "They had live music that was broadcast on WBT."

No one else seemed familiar with that.

"You know where the ladies of the night were?" (silence) "Near the post office on Mint Street," informed their worldly elder.

Thelma Percival Kube noted that, by the end of the 1930s, there was more purchasing power in her part of South Carolina. "Bowling alleys, dance halls and pool halls sprang up around Edgefield County like mushrooms, and there was a jukebox in every establishment."

Thelma's "gang" (that's what teenagers called a group of friends back then) didn't bowl much. They frequented the Quarry Tavern in the town of Edgefield, Kid's Place in Plum Branch and Edmonds' Place in McCormick, where they'd play a record for a nickel or three for a dime. Glenn Miller's "In the Mood" was her favorite for dancing the jitterbug.

She chuckled, "I think the men who hung out at the pool hall could play a better game to the tune of Clyde McCoy's 'Sugar Blues.' You could hear that song all over town coming out of the pool hall."

Julia Neal Sykes and her group hung out at Bill Foxx's Cafe (and dance hall) in Belmont to socialize."It was rather peaceful," she said, "most of the time."

Bill Foxx's Cafe, Belmont NC

HOW OTHERS PLAYED

Mill owners, town leaders, laborers, farmers and children knew the value of sports, get-togethers or even the silliness of just passing time could help people forget their troubles.

NORTH CAROLINA

My Grandfather, Baseball Outlaw
by
Scott Verner
Co-Author (with Hank Utley) of
*The Independent Carolina Baseball League
1936-1938: Baseball Outlaws*

Growing up, I always knew my grandfather as a man of irreproachable integrity, friendly but stern, deeply religious, high-principled and quite strict. So I was astonished to learn, years after his death, that he had been a team owner in an outlaw baseball league.

Carl H. Verner—I call him Pop—grew up in Martin, Georgia, and pitched for a town team there. He was a young man coming of age when the National League and the new American League played their first World Series in 1903, and like almost everyone else in America, he was a big baseball fan.

A 1912 graduate of Atlanta Medical College (now the Emory School of Medicine), he moved to Forest City in Rutherford County with his wife, Flora, in 1927 to set up a private medical practice.

The next year, Forest City played Whiteville for the state high school baseball championship. Pop took his family to the game in Statesville—some 80 miles away and about a half day's drive. The way my father tells it, the Forest City team did something spectacular at some point during the game, and Pop got so excited that he climbed eight or ten feet up the chicken-wire grandstand screen.

The excitement must have stuck with him. He soon owned Alexander Park, the local baseball field. For the next eight years, he

223

was always an official or owner of Rutherford County's semi-pro team.

During the Depression, Pop was better off than most in Forest City. Under the Roosevelt administration, doctors began to get some government pay for office visits and house calls. Patients rarely paid in cash but would bring him whatever they had: a couple of chickens, a mess of rabbits, a sheep, even a bedstead with a mattress. One fellow brought an old mule with an arthritic knee. It wasn't any good for plowing, so Pop gave it to my father, Hugh, who rode it. Every now and then, that front leg would give way and young Hugh would fall off over its head.

In 1932, Pop acquired a set of ballpark lights from Branch Rickey's St. Louis Cardinals organization and installed them at Alexander Park, so that his team could play night games — the newest money-making idea in baseball. More fans could attend night games, after they got off work. My grandmother reasoned that since the team was going to play nocturnally, they should be called the Owls. That summer, the Rutherford County Owls became the first team in North Carolina to play night baseball.

Dad, a young teenager then, and his friend Jim Hemphill were batboys for the team. The incandescent bulbs for the light standards cost about $5 each — a lot of money in those days — and if it rained while they were burning, the cold water would hit the hot bulbs and burst them. So Pop told the boys, "You keep a sharp eye out, and you know where the main switch is... If it looks like it's going to start raining, you run and pull it. I don't care if it's in the middle of the pitch or what — pull the switch."

In the 1920s and '30s, textile mill teams were made up largely of millhands and local country boys. Some had had careers in the minor leagues before settling down to mill work, sometimes drawing extra pay for baseball. (That's what made the teams "semi-pro.") As rivalries budded and blossomed, mill executives looked for ways to build stronger teams and beat the mill across the county.

It was common practice to hire a player or two — often a pitcher — for a game against a rival. The team would find a player who wasn't playing for his minor league team that day and pay him $5 or $10 to pitch.

In doing so, the minor leaguer was violating his contract with organized baseball — the monopoly of the major and minor leagues. The reserve clause of the standard minor league contract gave the signing team complete control over a ballplayer, until it either traded or released him. He was forbidden to play for any other organization, even if the team that owned his contract wasn't using him.

The Depression devastated organized baseball, which opened the 1929 season with 26 leagues operating at all levels and had only 13 by 1932. Hundreds of high-quality professional ballplayers were out of work. Many heard about a couple of textile leagues in the North Carolina Piedmont that played well and ignored organized baseball's contracts. Textile league rosters began to swell with these professional players.

Organized baseball was classified and paid its players according to the population of the town where the team was based. Had it been invited, Forest City would have been at best a Class D town—at the bottom rung of the hierarchy. Class D players earned about $16 to $18 a week. By comparison, Southern mill workers were making 25 cents an hour, or $10 a week, if the mill was running enough to get in a whole 40-hour week.

As rivalries among the mill towns grew, these "outlaw" teams in Class D-size towns began paying salaries that players otherwise could earn only in Class A or AA cities. To raise the money, civic leaders conducted "subscription" campaigns, community-supported charity drives. Admission to games generally was 25 cents.

The local owners also usually offered players off-season jobs—some in the mill, others as teachers or car salesmen. All the players were local heroes. They lived with local families, ate at their tables and were idolized by their children.

During that golden age of baseball, the ballpark became a popular social venue. Prominent women wore their good dresses and spread picnics in the grandstands. For big games, the downtown businesses closed. Along with radio programs and the occasional movie, baseball was one of the few pastimes available to millhands. It wasn't unheard-of for as many as 6,200 people to attend a ball game in Concord, a town of only 10,000.

In 1935, Forest City was part of the Western Carolina Textile League, playing three to four games per week with a team made up of several experienced professional players, some ambitious college players and local millhands. By the end of the season, leaders of the Western Carolina Textile League and several teams in the Carolina Textile League agreed to form their own full-time professional league, playing six days a week. (It was full-time baseball; in the South, there were no games on Sundays.)

Although invited to join organized baseball in Class C, the

new league resolved to remain independent. Its leaders were convinced they could attract better players and put on a better quality of baseball on their own.

So when the Carolina League was formed in 1936, it was a grand civic enterprise. In its three years, no one but the players made a penny. Its leaders wanted to give townspeople a share of the national pastime, a way of forgetting their economic troubles for a couple of hours, and a group of local heroes to bind the town together.

Within a month of the league's opening games, the National Association of Professional Baseball Leagues declared it outlaw. Many of the players who were under binding contracts to organized baseball were blacklisted. Some subsequently played under assumed names to escape detection.

Pop was undoubtedly excited at the outset of the 1936 season. He was an owner in a professional baseball league with a strong team, featuring home run champion Ray Brannon. But like all the teams, his lost money, making the subscription campaigns and the behind-the-scenes support from the local mills necessary.

On July 3, Forest City played its biggest rival, Shelby. There was always a fight or two among the fans when those two teams played. Fans continually gambled at the games, and they were likely to take things seriously when they believed a call had been botched. That particular night, the Owls had lost 9-7, and the fans took out their frustrations on umpire C.T. Skidmore. "After that ball game, they got old Skidmore," Jim Hemphill said. "They really worked him over good."

It fell to Pop to treat Skidmore's injuries. The next day, Carl Verner turned in his Carolina League franchise.

The independent Carolina League ended in 1939, as organized baseball recovered from the Depression. Never again did baseball in the Piedmont draw such huge crowds and intense fan interest as it had between 1936 and 1938, when outlaws ruled the diamond.

Just Pickin'
by
Lexie Little Hill

One of our favorite pastimes was to pick on our siblings. That wasn't just confined to our family.

Several brothers in a family we knew got so exasperated with their youngest brother's constant quoting of Scripture, that they devised a joke on him.

One early morning, as their brother was plowing, they slipped to the edge of the field and talked through a guano horn, "Zeb Caudle, I want you to preach my Gospel. Zeb Caudle, I want you to preach my Gospel."

A guano horn, used to distribute fertilizer, has a four-foot spout, and when Zeb's brothers spoke through the horn, their words were greatly distorted.

Zeb threw down the plow and ran to tell his mother, "God called me to preach!"

The joke turned, however, when Zeb spent his life as a faithful preacher of the Gospel.

The Lure of the Corn Shucking
by
Lexie Little Hill

Corn shuckings, so common on the Southern farm in the '30s, disappeared when prosperity ushered in machinery—an advancement, no doubt, But, sadly, a special bond among neighbors vanished.

Every fall, after all the crops were harvested, corn shuckings provided a way for farmers to unwind, to laugh and be sociable, while providing a much needed service for their neighbors.

There were corn shuckings all around, but everyone knew that Edmond Hill had the "corn shucking of all corn shuckings" around that part of Union County, so named because he seemed to have the largest pile of corn to be shucked and because he went the extra mile in preparation.

A mountain of corn was piled in a semicircle in the barnyard in front of the corn crib. Barrels of apple cider, made with Polk Mountain apples had been working off seven days, and men who never let a drop of whiskey pass their lips couldn't seem to resist the temptation to imbibe a little, so they could count on 75 to 100 men being there.

The gigantic responsibility of feeding those hungry men fell to Edmond Hill's wife and older daughters. In the Home Comfort wood cook stove with its massive oven performing double duty, they cooked 25 or 30 pies, cakes of all kinds, one pan after another of biscuits. They prepared beef stew, chicken dumplings, ham and vegetables too numerous to mention.

Men with their unique personalities began arriving at sundown. The first was their nearest neighbor Billie Buck Griffin, spit can in hand. He was the best tobacco spitter around, landing a spit just where he wanted it. Billie Buck, perhaps, felt he was returning the favor of getting enough persimmon and locust early in the summer to make his persimmon and locust beer.

Claude Little came early with his hymnal tucked under his arm and positioned himself under one of the possum hunting lanterns circling the corn pile, intending to lead the men in singing when they shucked the corn.

The best corn shucker in the area was Newgene Newsome, a huge heavy man ("fat as a fatnin' hawg"), his bib overalls stretched over his belly. Some said they had seen him eat a whole pie at one sitting. He had big hands, strong, too. He could shuck four ears of corn to any man's one, and everyone desired his presence at their corn shucking.

Monroe McBride, Joe McBride's boy, was a jack-leg mechanic. Some referred to him as "that young whippersnapper without a grain of common sense," but he was all the community had for fixing things, and somehow he managed to leave every corn shucking with a list of broken farm machinery that needed repair.

A skinny, quiet man, Bradford Davis was the best worker around, steady and dependable. He was generous in trading work with his neighbors, and when he worked for them, Bradford carried his end of the load and some of theirs. Everyone knew he was a little off center. His elevator didn't go all the way to the top, but he was well respected in the neighborhood.

Good-ole-boy Clarence Mayhew was a little short on motivation, "too sorry to hit a lick at a snake," some said, but he sure knew how to liven up a corn shucking. When he got wound up, the men whooped and hollered at his jokes, and the laughter could be heard for miles.

A regular at all corn shuckings was Mr. Charlie, who had a reputation for being tight. You might say that every farmer in the '30s was tight (they had to be), but Mr. Charlie was tight as the rubber band around a little girl's pigtail.

Around 9:30 p.m., the men began to unwind. Their singing stopped, their risquè jokes weren't so funny, and they were getting tired. Most were listening for the cider call. Their reaction to the call is best exemplified by Mr. Luther Mullis, who never talked nor smiled because, he said, he was deaf.

Edmond's son Kemp whispered to his dad, "Is it time to bring out the cider and make the cider call?"

Mr. Luther jumped up so fast he turned his stool over, lifted his hands above his head, clapped three or four times and yelled, "Yippee! Believe I will, believe I will!"

Courthouse Entertainment
by
Lexie Little Hill

The week of Civil Court brought farmers from all around to Monroe, North Carolina, and the streets surrounding the courthouse were crowded with Model Ts and horse-drawn wagons.

Farmers in the '30s chose one day that week to bring their wagons filled with wheat to be ground into flour at the mill. They brought along a packed lunch, and, if they were lucky, they might be at the courthouse by the time it opened. That early, they could find a shady spot on the lawn near an open window so they could hear the goings on inside.

All day, farmers sat in little groups talking to each other, listening to the trials inside and watching traffic on the streets. Occasionally, the Clerk of Court appeared on the front steps and shouted a name of someone to serve on jury duty.

Streets around the courthouse became so congested that policemen were assigned to direct traffic.

WHEN PROHIBITION AND THE DEPRESSION COINCIDED

The Volstead Act had been in effect since 1920, so by the time the Depression was devastating families, the means of obtaining liquor had been "perfected."

Although national prohibition ended December 5, 1933 with the ratification of the 21st Amendment, many states had already enacted their own laws curtailing or outlawing the sale of alcoholic beverages. That did not stop citizens from thirsting for a little "pick-me-up" during such a "down" time.

North Carolina was first to adopt statewide prohibition by direct vote. It, however, was the only state to put that control at the county level and devised an Alcoholic Beverage Control Board which allowed quasi-autonomous local boards to operate ABC stores for selling bottled liquor. The first county board was organized in '35; the state board, in '37. In its first year, state ABC agents destroyed 1054 illegal stills, and arrested 2,900 people.

Mountain counties were known for their "stills in the hills," and it is common knowledge that early stock car race drivers got their training outrunning revenuers. Wilkes County, labeled "bootleg capital of the world," was conveniently accessible to the Carolinas' Piedmont.

NORTH CAROLINA

MA PAXTON
A Collaboration*
From *Prohibition Didn't End in '33*

Ask Charlotteans to tell about Prohibition days, and they'll get to talking about Ma Paxton every time. Ask them to write about Ma, and they'll suddenly get forgetful.

But members of the Navajo Club, about 100 male Charlotteans, ages 70-90, don't mind telling. They say Ma's reign as Bootleg Queen of Charlotte spanned over three decades.

230

Joe Paxton, Ma's policeman husband, and his cousin Jim were motorcycle riding along The Plaza on Sunday, July 30, 1922, when they had a horrendous accident. Jim was killed instantly when he was thrown over the handlebars and hit his head on a light pole; Joe, who was riding in the sidecar, was seriously injured. "You could still see the imprint of Jim's head on that steel pole," said Lewis Diggle, who came along ahead of the ambulance. "From what was left of Joe when they picked him up, he must've been a cripple the rest of his life."

Legend says that Joe's police buddies told his wife, Lula, who had four young children to feed, "Now, we know you'll need to make a living somehow. Whatever you do, we'll support you." Guess what she decided to do!

No one recalls seeing Joe after that. Some speculated that he was institutionalized. But the city directory shows that, after a period of "no occupation," he worked for and even owned a service station before moving to the country. Lula was not listed as a widow until 1934, although she was shown as the head of household beginning in 1930 (city directory information, however, is about a year old). That year, she was running a boarding house on East 9th. But Lula and her son and three daughters moved frequently.

Diggle, who left Charlotte in 1930, remembers Ma, whom he called "Aunt Lou," and the house on North Brevard Street, where she served corn liquor. "She had it in a coffeepot on the stove. You could get a small glass for 15 cents or two for a quarter." Generally, a customer would drink at her kitchen table or take out a pint. "A screwtop pint bottle was $1," Diggle recalled. "Then they started having 13 oz. bottles. We called those B-flats." He smiled. "Sometimes the phone would ring, and she'd say, 'You gotta go, boys.'"

Everyone insists that Ma ran a respectable, pleasant place with no prostitutes. "She was on the up and up," said Lewis Diggle. "The only females there were her daughters and you'd better keep your hands off them."

Like other local bootleggers, Ma got her booze from Wilkes County. Later, she offered "bottled in bond," too. Joe's nephew, Clyde Paxton emphasized that "she sold it; she didn't make it." He alluded to her tragic life and how she had raised her fine children and worked while suffering from rheumatoid arthritis. A distant relative told of her kindness. If someone could not pay, she would hold a piece of jewelry as collateral. He said she never sold the ones that were unclaimed. When she died, her descendants found a box full of assorted watches, rings and more.

Ma's most famous place was the Flat Iron Building at the intersection of South Tryon and Camden Road, which had businesses on the main floor and her apartment upstairs. Clients would open a side door and simply walk up the steps. Besides the family quarters, there were three rooms with tables and chairs. Her supply was kept in a secret false room with a dumb waiter. By this time, she had home-delivery drivers, the Grier brothers, Joe and Tom. They and her son, Jay, by then a young man, sometimes were bouncers. P.K. Kirkpatrick worked as a drink-fetcher.

Carlos Kumpe and some of his friends stopped by Ma's about 9 p.m. one Sunday. Jay, who had obviously been sampling his mother's products, was in charge. "Okay, you can have a 10-cent, a 15-cent or 25-cent shot," he told them.

Kumpe said, "I'll have a 10-cent."

Jay filled a water glass half full of whiskey. Kumpe's big-spender friend ordered the 25-cent pour. He got the same size glass filled to an inch below the brim. And with what? Whatever brand they had on hand. There was no choice except between corn liquor and commercially distilled bottled whiskey.

The liquor supply was never kept in sight. Drinks were served openly, unless "the heat was on."

About a half dozen men including Thad Adams were there on the night of a raid. "I had a pint of liquor in my pocket. I put it in the window. I should have kept it." Everyone got sent home, but Ma was not taken to jail that night.

Navajo members knew about her other locations on West 5th Street, Seigle Avenue and especially Ma's upstairs apartment across the street from Central High School (probably in the late '30s). At lunchtime, boys would sneak over to Ma's to "get a little knock." Elmer Garinger, the school principal, and a teacher flushed out some of their students one day and chased them up the street. Lula didn't stay there long.

But she was forever popular with Central High grads. On the day of her graduation, Charlotte Hawthorne, who had never had a drink, was riding in a car with a group of friends, when one of the guys said, "Get down on the floor girls." They obeyed and Dickie Lisk pulled up at Ma Paxton's Wilmore address. He ran in to get a bottle, which they passed among them. "I didn't know where we were. I was still hiding," she said grinning.

By the late '30s or early '40s, Lula's liquor was selling at $1.50 a pint, and her drivers were getting craftier. One had brackets for bottles under the hood of his Ford. Approximately 80-90% of her business then was carryout.

Relatives say that Lula Paxton was beautiful. Customers remember Ma after she had some age on her: stringy hair, dumpy, rather ordinary.

On the other hand, her daughters were world-class beauties. Frances graduated from Central High in the class with John Gill in 1933. Virginia, who was two years younger, left Central early to join Frances to seek a show business career. Having trained at Charlotte's Henderson Dancing School, they were, as Gill puts it, "well known in dancing circles."

Joe Grier (Ma's driver, not the prominent lawyer) and Marion Diehl, a local amateur boxer, gave the girls a ride to New York when they made the 17-hour drive to see the Max Baer-Primo Carnera world championship boxing match in June, 1934.

They soon became known as the Paxton Sisters. But Hollywood's lights seemed brighter than Broadway's, so they moved west to break into pictures as dancers.

By 1937, Frances had been crowned Miss California and competed in the Miss America Pageant. *Life* magazine said she should have won more than the talent contest, but officials had disqualified her when they discovered that she had been married.

Meanwhile, Virginia Dare Paxton had changed her name to Virginia Dale and was appearing regularly in the movies (about 50 in all).

Navajo Club member Tom Lane could attest that he danced with her first, for he took Virginia to a Panhellenic dance at David-son College, but her most prestigious dancing partner was no less than Fred Astaire. Yes, Virginia Dale played her finest role as the second female lead in "Holiday Inn" with Bing Crosby and Fred Astaire in 1942.

Those who knew all three Paxton girls believe that Joey, the youngest, was the most gorgeous of all. Her only claim to fame was the title Miss North Carolina, 1941.

Legend has it that Ma Paxton was convicted only once. Her sentence supposedly was to be deported from the state as an "undesirable." The officers assigned to get her out of town drove her across the South Carolina line and then delivered her to her home with the statement "Sentence completed."

* John Gill and Thelma Kube contributed to this story

Movie star Virginia Dale (Virginia Dare Paxton, daughter of "Ma" and Joe Paxton) with Emery Wister, *Charlotte News* Movie Editor, on the set of "Death of a Champion," June 21, 1939.
Photo courtesy of Paramount Studios.

Ma's Competition
A Collaboration
From *Prohibition Didn't End in '33*

Charlotte's population was 82,675 in 1930. A majority of those adults must have been thirsty, for there were plenty of entrepreneurs willing to break the law to supply them.

The "ultimate" bootlegger, according to Charlotte's Navajo Club, was Zeb Hargett. "He sold only the best stuff, and he had a very select clientele," said one member, who recalled the delivery vehicle as an old Ford. But another remembered Hargett's Chrysler-77 roadster, which had a secret compartment in the rumble seat. Hargett called that car My Blue Heaven.

Where did the country club get their booze? "Zeb Hargett," said someone in the know. Club employees also sold it to members.

If this is a folk tale, it's a sweet one: the story goes that, when Hargett's daughter was at Piedmont Junior High, someone insulted her because her father was a bootlegger. She ran home crying. After Zeb heard the reason for her distress, he stopped selling liquor and became a legitimate businessman.

Ma Paxton may have been the bootleg queen, but Dick Smith, who lived near the Catawba River, was the reputed kingpin. He supplied the suppliers and ran numbers, too. His key associates were Carl Lippard, Sr. and Carl Vann. The numbers business was called "butter and eggs" because the winning numbers came from the Chicago Mercantile listings for butter (the last two digits) and eggs (the last digit).

Bootlegger brothers, Joe and Mike Davis were Italian. Several Navajos had bought their wares, but one recalled the cops chasing Joe, who was speeding his Packard near Central High. The sedan flipped. Corn liquor spilled all over Cecil Street.

Most Charlotte speakeasies were private homes, like Ma Paxton's. Some of the others were located on Graham Street and "somewhere from 24th to 30th Street" off of North Tryon.

Folks say that when the police wanted information about blacks, they'd ask Jim Massey, whose bootleg business moved from 7th Street to Long Street. In the Cherry area, people of both races would stop in a particular road and honk. Someone would ask what they wanted and then fetch it. A Navajo Club member was on that street one night to buy a pint. A woman met the car, took his order and pulled the bottle from her bosom.

Thirsty travelers had to rely on bellhops to refer them to a speakeasy or to provide a surreptitious room service—liquor and women—for a tip. A black bellhop who had worked at the Mecklenburg Hotel near the railroad station during Prohibition went to a lawyer some years later to draw up his will. The 70-year-old wanted to divide his sizeable estate and real estate equally among his children. To the attorney's astonishment, he had three wives, three families—and three names. But there would be plenty of assets to go around.

The Great Depression did not seem to affect Charlotte's bootleggers. It is said that two products sold even better during the Depression. Even the poor could somehow find money for chewing gum and liquor.

An Unusual Evening
by
Elizabeth Barkalow Shuman

Hugh McManaway was different—odd, mentally deficient but musically gifted. He played the piano and violin well and often spoke in rhyme. "My name is Hugh. How do you do?" he would say. Later, he changed it to: "My name is Hugh. I am cuc-koo."

At Charlotte's Central High School, which I attended in the early 1930s, Hugh stood out among the 1200 students.

One night, a group of us girls and boys were invited to his home on Queens Road. Originally built on West Trade Street uptown, the house was moved when Myers Park was developed. We were intrigued by the mysterious house with its distinctive Italian Renaissance architecture and rather gloomy interior. His mother fit the setting. Her hair was dark and piled on top of her head; her old-fashioned dress, black and long.

The high spot of the evening occurred when we went outside, and Hugh flagged down the streetcar on the rail line that ran right in front of his house.

The motorman let us all on board, and we rode the couple of blocks to the end of the line. Then Hugh helped the motorman release the connecting rod at one end of the car and hook the rod at the other end to the overhead electric line for the return trip uptown. Inside, the rest of us were switching the backs of the seats so that the passengers could face forward. Soon, we were hopping off the streetcar at Hugh's house, thanking the motorman for the unusual treat.

That evening was unique in two other ways. Hugh's mother served us fruitcake and homemade blackberry wine from her cellar.

Now, my sisters and I used to help our father make home brew. When it got strong enough to lift the top on the crock, he would stick one end of a red rubber hose in the liquid and sucked the other to start the flow, like siphoning, then quickly fill each bottle. That's when we pitched in, using a hand-operated capper. Although we assisted in this process, we were never allowed to drink the brew.

Hugh's mother had different ideas about alcoholic beverages for teenagers. Hugh's father had been a physician, so we entertained ourselves by sipping wine and looking through some medical manuals, showing drawings of parts of the human anatomy. This caused blushes and giggles, because we knew we were not supposed to see things like that.

As I said, it was an unusual evening.

The Fountain (UGH!) of Youth
by
John Gill
From *Prohibition Didn't End in '33*

In the mid '30s, when the Charlotte police would catch bootleggers, they would transfer their loads into police department storage rooms for evidence at the trials in court.

I was told that some of the good stuff could be had out the back door, if you had good connections (this, of course, would be for medical purposes, the only legal use in North Carolina).

When the storage space filled up, the evidence became a problem. What to do with it all? Dump it down the drain seemed to be the logical answer. The "bottled in bond" could be sold to states that permitted legal sales. The "rotgut" was disposed of. There were pictures in the paper of the dumping: police pouring out the fruit jars into the floor drains.

Those drains at the station fed into the storm drains, not the sanitary sewers. The police department was located a few blocks west of Sugaw Creek on East Fourth Street. The storm drains emptied into that creek under the bridge at the corner of the old Thompson Orphanage property.

The smell of corn whiskey filled the air around the bridge, as it flowed from the large concrete drain pipe. Passing motorists noticed it. Some stopped to see what was going on.

It didn't take long for some of the whiskey lovers to locate the source of the aroma and collect some of the liquid, as it spilled out of the pipe along with street trash and whatever else was traveling with it.

Police arrived much too soon to suit some of the collectors.

The "fountain of youth" was closed.

Now You See Them, Now You Don't
by
John Gill
From *Prohibition Didn't End in '33*

My brothers, Bob, about 20, and Ike, 16, were returning home from a picture show in downtown Charlotte on a nice summer night just after midnight in 1933.

Bob, always considered the best driver of the Gill boys, was headed out Elizabeth Avenue and was about to make a left turn on Hawthorne Lane. He noticed an automobile approaching from his left that had disregarded a stop sign.

Bob quickly darted straight through the Presbyterian Hospital gates to dodge the oncoming black Ford coupe. He almost made it, just getting the rear bumper clipped. The coupe ran into the heavy brick structure at the gate.

A few seconds after the impact, the smell of moonshine filled the air. The Ford's driver was running down Hawthorne Lane toward St. John's Baptist Church. Brother Ike, a 200-pound high school football player started the chase. He caught up with the man, who whirled in his direction with a pistol in his hand. "I'll blow your head off" was all it took to turn Ike around.

But the joke was really on the bootlegger, for as onlookers gathered, some lovers of spirits began to hide jars in the thick hedge along the street—that is, until the police arrived.

He Did WHAT?
by
Joseph C. Grogan

Our entire family used to regularly travel from Winston-Salem to Henry County, Virginia, to visit our grandfather. My great

238

uncle Bob Grogan lived with his family at my grandfather's house. He was my hero. I thought he was a cowboy. A tall man, he wore a pistol at his side, pants tucked into boots, a Stetson hat and a badge. To me, he was Tom Mix and Hoot Gibson all rolled into one.

After one visit, I asked Mother why he wasn't a cowboy anymore. "He no longer wears a badge or a gun," I noted.

My father got a bang out of that. He knew the answer.

She told me that my uncle was a "revenuer," and his job was to break up stills in Virginia and to capture "rum runners" transporting whiskey from North Carolina. When Prohibition ended, he lost his job.

My North Carolina mother explained it another way: "He had to give up his job, because it was slowly killing him to see so much booze being poured out."

The Moonshine Search
by
Lexie Little Hill

Most farmers in Union County raised chickens and eggs to sell. Some, especially those with 10 to 12 children, made and sold moonshine under cover.

Many chicken houses were built on the side of a hill with an access door to the basement. Others raised the floor of the chicken houses several feet and dug basements. The fire in the basement, with its smokestack going through the chicken house, often had a dual purpose: to keep the chickens warm and make moonshine.

My husband's father Edmond Hill had hen houses and brooder houses, enough to accommodate 500 or more chickens and a smokehouse to store eggs.

Few farmers knew a revenuer when they saw one, but Lee Traywick, the community's alcoholic, did. So the day a stranger with a large truck stopped at his store, he knew who this inquisitive man was.

"Anybody in this area raise chickens?" the stranger asked.

"Yes," said Mr. Traywick, "Edmond Hill."

The revenuer paused, then asked, "How does he heat his houses?"

"With a furnace underneath."

"Ummmm. Tell me how to get there."

239

"Turn left at the next road, then right at the first road past the church. 'Bout a half mile on your right."

Mr. Hill heard the truck's horn blasting before it reached his farm. When the stranger saw him, he stopped his truck and stuck his head out the window. "Got any chickens for sale?"

"Sure do. About 500."

The stranger looked around, pausing when he saw the chicken houses. "I'll take 'em all." After they weighed the chickens and put them in the truck, he asked, "Got any eggs?"

"In the smokehouse. About 25 dozen."

"Take all you got," the stranger said.

When he insisted on loading the eggs himself, Mr. Hill knew this man was a revenuer. And the revenuer knew that, if Mr. Hill made and sold liquor, he would find a half-gallon jug of whiskey in the corners of the egg crates. Since the crates were divided in the middle, that meant four gallons of whiskey and about six dozen eggs in each crate.

Mr. Hill watched in amusement as the revenuer searched and loaded the crates, then asked, "Mind if I look around and see how you raise these chickens?"

"Go right ahead."

Mr. Hill chuckled while watching the revenuer snoop around, then leave, his truck loaded with chickens and eggs.

Lee Traywick recognized the revenuer when he stopped at Traywick's store for gas. "You catch the man making whiskey?"

"NO!"

Laughing, Mr. Traywick admitted, "I could have told you, but you didn't ask. Besides, the man needed the money." He continued to laugh. "What you take for the chickens you bought?"

"GO TO HELL!"

One might say the government made a dry run.

A Corny Tale
by
Margaret G. Bigger
Co-Author (with J. Carter Goldsborough) of
Only Forty Miles of Pavement

Some people thought liquor was a leisure-time necessity, Many considered it a business necessity. Apparently, my father, John Carter Goldsborough, was one of them.

He tells a Depression-years story of trying to get business in his United States Gypsum Company's North Carolina territory. His headquarters was Raleigh, but he traveled to sell building materials from the Pamlico Sound to the Roxboro-Durham area.

Because of the government jobs at Fort Bragg in the mid-'30s, he headed for Fayetteville's Prince Charles Hotel almost every Sunday evening to see contractors who would bid on jobs the next day.

On one of those Sunday nights, he and Clyde Lamkin, a Lehigh Portland Cement salesman, were bringing in liquid refreshments for entertaining.

Daddy told how they sneaked the contraband into the hotel. "Clyde carried two fruit jars of corn whiskey just like a baby, with his topcoat draped over them. I handled one jar inside my overcoat."

The Prince Charles lobby was brimming with mostly elderly tourists on their way to Florida. Two paces ahead of my father, Clyde was almost in front of the desk when one of his fruit jars dropped and smashed between them.

"My God, Goldy. Be careful. See what you've done!" innocent-faced Lamkin said in a loud voice. Corn whiskey was spreading out across the tile floor.

Daddy's face turned red just as it must have done that night. "Little old ladies seated on a leather sofa were lifting their open-toed shoes to avoid the smelly mess and frowning at ME!"

241

What Mr. Hicks Did for a Living
by
Selby A. Daniels
From *Prohibition Didn't End in '33*

One summer weekend during the year of 1931, a Mr. Hicks came to visit us. He was a tall, slender man with suspenders and a handlebar moustache turned gray. His broad-brimmed hat had a half-executed crease at the front top, much in the manner of a Texas rancher. In spite of his big hat, he had a good suntan. He was about the age of my grandfather.

We lived on my mother's Aycock ancestral farm three miles north of Fremont, North Carolina. Nearly all of our neighbors were also our relatives. Mr. Hicks had no close kin, so he adopted us. Every day, people outside the family ate meals with us: hired hands, visiting relatives who spent the night and others. Mr. Hicks was different from us. We were farmers. Mr. Hicks was a guard for the Wayne County Chain Gang Camp, then located just outside of Goldsboro, the county seat.

As a young boy, I used to listen to him with awe, as he told us about his work. He would give brief sketches of the men he guarded, even many who had already been released.

Chain gangs, as a part of the penal system, were maintained exclusively in the American South at that time. In North Carolina, the counties operated separate systems. About one-half of all convicted prisoners were sent by superior court judges to a chain gang, as an economic means of maintaining roads. Of course, they had to be able-bodied, for they were compelled to do hard labor under the gun in all kinds of weather. Usually, they had to wear shackles, chains, and stripes, although some county convicts wore faded uniforms.

Chain gang prison camps were on wheels. Mini-boxcars of steel or wood could be moved from one location to another. These cages with cross-hatched bars on both sides, which truly resembled circus wagons for ferocious animals, were generally 18'x 8'x 8', built to sleep 18 men. The three-decker bunks were stacked too tight for convicts to sit up in bed, and the 2' passage was too small for everyone to stand. Prisoners were padlocked inside every night and on weekends and bad-weather days. Their only amenities were a night bucket (toilet), drinking water pail, kerosene lantern and a small stove for heat. Tarpaulins could be dropped over the sides to shield occupants from rain or snow, but as there were no windows, they cut off all ventilation.

The county superintendent of each respective system in the state was a virtual dictator who totally controlled prisoner discipline with his own personal rules. These varied camp to camp. They worked 12-hour days, beginning at 4:30 a.m. with time out for lunch. Any infraction or breaking a camp rule was noted by armed guards, and punishment came after work or during the weekend. Most guards had instructions to shoot to kill an escapee. White prisoners, supposedly, were treated the same as segregated black ones, although statistics show otherwise.

One Sunday afternoon, my father asked me to go with him to take Mr. Hicks back to camp. As we rode along, I wondered about those prisoners and how they would look in their confinement. I wanted to make the trip so as not to miss out on any camp story Mr. Hicks had to tell.

The camp was in a grove of oak trees off the main dirt road. As we approached the caged trailers, we saw a white convict standing "spread eagle" (arms stretched and tied side to side), receiving a flogging on his bare back administered by a guard. The convict's back was literally covered with huge red welts and blood. The convict would cry out piteously with each stroke of the lash. Already so weak that his words were incoherent, he appeared to be trying to say, "Oh Lord, have mercy on me."

Typical chain gang "cage." Photo from *The North Carolina Chain Gang* by Jesse F. Steiner and Roy M. Brown ©1927 by the University of North Carolina Press. Used by permission of the publisher.

The guard would grunt heavily with each delivery, indicating he was using all his strength with each blow. I was absolutely horrified. I could feel my own body cringe and convulse with uncontrollable tremors as I watched. I had never before witnessed such cruelty from one human to another.

My father turned to Mr. Hicks and asked, "Why is that man being whipped?"

Mr. Hicks replied, "Probably because he didn't tip his hat to his guard one workday last week when he had a nature call."

About that time, the flogged convict was cut down. He dropped to the ground in a crumpled heap and did not move.

Daddy let his answer pass, then asked, "What did the convict do to get on the chain gang?"

The old fellow with the mustache frowned. "He was a boot-legger."

Buying Time—Of Convicts
by
Selby A. Daniels
From *Prohibition Didn't End in '33*

In the spring of 1933, my father brought two white chain gang prisoners home to help us work on the farm. Daddy had purchased their remaining "time" from Pender County, North Carolina, from whence they came.

A common practice in most poor counties at that time was to sell the service of their convicted prisoners to another county or to farmers. Only those who had earned the status of "trusty" were considered for this contract service. This practice helped poor counties meet payroll obligations during the early years of the Great Depression.

Both the men who came to us had exactly 91 days of their sentence left to serve, just enough time to help plant our crops and harvest them, too. My father was responsible for those men and honor bound to return them to their home county for their release at the conclusion of the contract period. Their surnames were Chavis and Glass. Chavis was a small, red-haired, freckled-face man and the most talkative. He spoke freely about how he was caught with a neighbor at a whiskey still, which was co-owned by both men, near his home community of Atkinson, North Carolina. He explained that the only reason he had the still was to supplement his meager income. Times were hard then. At his trial, a man whom he recognized as a long-time well-known bootlegger testified that Chavis tried to sell him some whiskey. Chavis declared this was an outright lie, that the man used this ploy only because he wanted to eliminate Chavis as a competitor.

Mr. Chavis was sent to the chain gang, where he had been flogged for some rule infraction. He pulled off his shirt, revealing the scars. Then he lifted his pants legs to show me where he had been shackled with leg irons. He had tried to escape after he was whipped, so he was then clapped in irons. His lower legs looked terrible. They were still raw.

I had been selling Cloverine, a pink salve that was supposed to be good for burns and cuts, so I gave him a can. Generally, I sold Cloverine for 25¢ a can, remitting 15¢ to the manufacturer. Cloverine healed Mr. Chavis's wounds. I was pleased that the product worked. But, unfortunately, he still had red and purple colors around his legs at the end of his service on our farm.

Mr. Chavis had said his only reason for co-owning the still was to supplement his farm income. Before my father took him back to Pender County, Chavis asked me to give him the name and address of the Cloverine salve manufacturer. It was my fervent hope that he would sell it instead of whiskey. After all, he could personally attest to its healing powers.

SOUTH CAROLINA

Stepping High
by
Thelma Percival Kube
From *Prohibition Didn't End in '33*

In the rural community of Red Hill, South Carolina, where I lived in the 1930s, obtaining liquor before and after Prohibition was no problem. Moonshine, a homemade liquor, and a collage of other intoxicants were readily available. Some of the popular drinks were raisin and persimmon wines and a home brew from locust pods. Another favorite, "pummin juice," was a seasonal drink made in the fall when the sorghum cane was harvested.

Will Brunson, a respected man in the community, owned a syrup mill. He extracted the juice for syrup, then tossed aside the cane stalks, which were known locally as pummins. His son, Frank, retrieved the pummins, put them in barrels with water and other ingredients, let them ferment and then made a very potent drink he called pummin juice. One day, when Will's wife Emma was going to the mill to take lunch to her husband, Frank asked her to bring home a lard bucket of pummin juice. In those days, lard was bought in five-pound buckets.

Returning home, which was about a mile from the mill, Emma's curiosity overcame her contempt for fermented beverages. She really wanted to know why the young men from Edgefield and McCormick Counties were drinking this concoction. Emma took a sip from the bucket. "It tasted real good and made me feel warm inside," Emma told my mother. "So I stopped and sipped about every hundred yards. By the time I got home, I was stepping high, reaching up for the ground."

There must have been *many* people stepping high back then, since there was so much pummin juice sold in those parts.

Buried Treasure
by
Nancy Artemus Gough

"No matter how hot it is, you may not play in the ditch," our parents told us children who lived on Columbia's Calhoun Street. They were referring to the big drainage ditch (four-to-five feet wide) in front of the house where I was born. Cool clear water ran across clean sand, but it was a forbidden "beach."

Early one morning, when I was out on our front porch, I understood the reason why we were denied so inviting a play spot.

Actually, my brothers, sisters or neighbors would see them two or three times a week: two white men (not always the same guys) came to "plant" flat whiskey bottles just beneath the clean sand. Or they were there to dig up what they would sell, or drink, that day.

In that time of our history, they knew that, even during Prohibition, no one in our neighborhood would call the police to report them. They saw us watching them but ignored us. Those dangerous men did not have to answer to our parents or anyone else in the black community.

Once Prohibition ended, the whiskey-burying intruders stopped coming to our ditch. But I have to chuckle about it now.

Calhoun Street lies four blocks due north from Benedict College and Allen University.

They were just lucky the college kids didn't find their treasure!

NORTH CAROLINA/SOUTH CAROLINA

The Dorothy Lee
by
Joy S. Burton
From *Prohibition Didn't End in '33*

The Catawba River is just about the same as it has always been since 1927 when Duke Power dammed it to make a large, snaky lake. We now call "the river" Lake Wylie.

This is a story about a lady who lived on the lake for 57 years, all through the '20s, '30s, '40s and into the 1950s. She was built by Tom Owens, a carpenter and all-round handyman working for the legendary Dick Smith. Dorothy Lee started life as a barge, built only to haul whiskey across the river to Pine Harbor, Dick Smith's restaurant pavilion. She was quite a girl in her day and time. The boat had a definite personality split: she was truly a *lady* of the afternoon and a *working woman* of the night.

In the daytime, she toured folks up and down the water on sightseeing forays and great drinking parties. Sometimes, I've been told, the bashes almost became orgies. Dickie Smith, Jr. and his younger brother, Todd, used to hide out in the bow and watch some of the couples exchange partners! The skipper, Tom Owens, would turn his back and pretend not to see. When Tom would begin to head the excursion boat into dock, he would yell to everyone to straighten up and get their act together.

One oldtimer out in the lower Steele Creek community told me that he drank 16 bottles of beer one party afternoon on the decadent Dorothy Lee. He swears he has not had a drink since.

The river is the boundary line between North and South Carolina. The states have forever had different personalities. For many years, North Carolina stayed dry and South Carolina, wet. The Charlotteans who wanted something wet had to drive to Fort Mill, South Carolina, to buy liquor, or they visited Dick Smith's Pine Harbor, a "wild and woolly" place.

247

The tour vessel was a two-story wooden contraption big enough for 30 people or more. She was motor-driven by a 1930 water-cooled Packard engine. It was a sight to see her running up and down that large stream in all her glory with partying revelers.

At night, the Dorothy Lee ran whiskey from the South Carolina side to the pavilion in North Carolina. The alcohol was usually brought down to South Carolina from Tennessee. Dick Smith had a special boat access into the center of the three-level pavilion, where the numerous bottles could be unloaded. They were stored in a hidden warehouse. Only a very few people knew where that secret place was.

How many trips did she make over and back each night? That varied. At the slightest hint of trouble of being spotted running "booze," she would turn into a regular excursion boat.

How do I know this? I spent all of my childhood summers at our river cabin at the Island Point Club across the back cove from the log house owned by the Dick Smith family.

Oh what parties people had on that old wooden craft —especially on full moon evenings! I can still sometimes hear the ghostly sounds of laughter and partying drifting up and down from the Dorothy Lee.

Your Nose Knows
by
John Gill
From *Prohibition Didn't End in '33*

From my experience on Duke Power construction crews (building substations and generating plants), I made an interesting observation: many hard-working people became hard-drinking people at night.

In 1939, our crew was doing mostly electrical control work at the Cliffside Steam Plant in Cleveland County. We were connecting up the controls to the many motors, switches and relays for the plant. The summertime heat multiplied several times, when we had to work in a closed place with little air movement. Each night, the men I worked with had a few drinks—some more, some less. If they went to the liquor store across the South Carolina line at Chesnee, they would get bourbon, applejack or a blend whiskey. If they bought locally, it would be "rotgut."

It was sickening to work near those men in some of those

tight spots. You could tell by the aroma what kind of liquor they had had the night before. The applejack had a sweet smell; the bourbon and blend would smell rather harsh; the "rotgut": whooo! You couldn't stay near without vomiting!

I often wondered just how bad those men must have felt and why they would go through that situation day after day, night after night.

Bootleggers Funeral
by
Joy S. Burton
From *Prohibition Didn't End in '33*

This tale was told to me by a bootlegger's son:

In the 1930s, when a large order of whiskey had to be delivered by a certain time (usually around festive seasons like Christmas) the bootlegger kings had to come up with a very clever way of transporting the bottles from Wilkes County across North and South Carolina into the Piedmont and beyond.

The bootleggers would put on a grand funeral. A modified black sedan was purchased and kept for just such occasions. A large casket would be loaded with whiskey bottles. The driver would be attired in a somber black suit, tie and hat and wore a "terrible" long face. Even an elaborate spray of florist flowers would be laid across the bier.

Down the highways and byways, often quite a long trip, the alcohol procession made its way through small towns and villages. The police and citizens and all traffic would come to a complete halt. Cars would pull over to the road shoulders, as everyone held their hands over their hearts. Gentlemen removed hats and gazed down at the ground.

The "leggers" didn't like to resort to this expensive form of delivery, but oh, they surely could put on a good funeral.

WHAT WAS *REALLY* IMPORTANT

Here are a few more glimpses into the past, emphasizing critical times, suffered collectively and individually. Following a summary of the causes of the Great Depression and the steps to recovery, we point out some lessons to pass on to future generations.

NORTH CAROLINA

Unspent Savings Lost Forever
A
Compilation

Although President Roosevelt declared a "bank holiday" closing all banks in March, 1933, many small town banks were already shut tight. When withdrawals outnumbered deposits, what else could be expected?

Some families took all their money out because they had lost confidence in the banking system. Others, by showing confidence, ended up losing all their savings when their neighbors' predictions came true. People already strapped were devastated. Even some bankers were in the same dire straits as people on the other side of the counter.

Charlotte residents knew of a local bank president who lost his home and was seen downtown selling apples on the street. He had lost his house and cars, and his daughter had to drop out of prep school. The talk of the town, he moved his family away from the area.

Lalla Marshall Gribble was in the fourth or fifth grade when one of her good friends had a father who had lost everything. "He went down to Latta Park and shot himself," she said, shuddering at the memory. "His five children and their mother moved back to be with her parents in Georgia."

"Someone else jumped out of the Commercial Bank building onto American Trust," said another Charlottean, who prefers to remain anonymous. Another recalled a prominent attorney's suicide.

When First National closed, a man came beating on the door with a shotgun, according to Jack Wood. "All my money is in this bank," the irate customer had yelled. "I'm going to kill that bastard!"

"That was probably my granddaddy!" said Joy Smith Burton. "He had only gone to the fifth grade but he had become a millionaire." On second thought, she realized it was a different Charlotte bank that had closed with her granddaddy's money inside. But it was shocking to hear that her mild-mannered grandfather, who never took the Lord's name in vain, let out a blast of curse words at the bank officials.

Some people got so emotional they couldn't take the strain. "A good friend of ours had a mental breakdown and never recovered," Ann Mauldin Elliot said, indicating that he believed other people blamed him for their troubles. "He needed custodial care until he died in the '60s. The family with five kids lost everything. They went to live in the mother's brother's house in the country."

When farmers and small businessmen could not repay loans, the banks didn't have enough cash to sustain a "run" by depositors. Small town banks were particularly vulnerable. Many folded, never to re-open. Not the one in Belmont, North Carolina. W.B. Puett and the Stowe family get credit for keeping the confidence of their customers.

Even children in Charlotte were affected. Elizabeth School children were encouraged to put their savings into a local bank, Independence Trust. Dan H.Wolfe put in ten cents at a time. That was one of the three or four in Charlotte that failed and never reopened. Eventually—several years later, the children got some of their money back, a few cents on the dollar.

John Williams of Yadkin County pointed out that once Roosevelt had closed the banks, it took time to examine them. They re-opened on a staggered schedule. Banks of various sizes were interdependent. "Prior to the holiday, small town banks made deposits in larger banks, and the big banks would pool their money to get 7 1/2% to 8% interest and give back 7% to the small banks, who, in turn, could pay 6% to their depositors. When one bank folded, it pyramided, and panic set in."

Was cash crucial to life? Those who thought so had to learn to "live off the land" and barter, like farmers had done for generations.

Even so, for Southerners, "Black Thursday," October 24, 1929 was not the most memorable day of the Depression. For many, it was March 6, 1933, the first day of the bank holiday.

As John A. Rainey of Vance County says, "The stock market, to us, was a place to sell cows and hogs."

NORTH CAROLINA/SOUTH CAROLINA

Those Who Really Suffered
A
Compilation

Basic to human life are food and shelter. Only a few of our authors truly went hungry or lost their homes, but several knew of people who did. Death from starvation was not unheard of.

Sharecroppers seemed to suffer the most, as Furman Bridges, Annie Belle Wright Chappelle, Lilla Childs Durham, Alberta Black Harris, Paul Jernigan, Julia Neal Sykes, and Fred Whitten can attest. Most of them will tell you, though, that they were poor *before* the Depression as well.

Eloise Shavitz, who spent her early years in what she terms "a shack with cracks in the floor you could see through," in Nash County, North Carolina, blames her biological dad. "My father was an alcoholic. He worked when he wanted to," Eloise explained. "There were times when I was very hungry and would eat the rich red clay, which would allay my hunger."

Her favorite food was a gift from a relative. "My uncle from up North brought peanut butter one year. I had never tasted it. Pure ambrosia! I couldn't get enough, as we had to share. I still eat it from a jar with a spoon."

At her family's lowest point, Elizabeth Barkalow Shuman says that their family was down to "15 cents and a box of grits." Her father's business in Charlotte folded due to a bank failure. He had to take jobs he was unsuited for to keep food on the table. When they had only grits, Elizabeth's mother had to pawn her diamond engagement ring.

David G. Kelly, who grew up in Charlotte, lived in fear part of the time. "We did not have food, proper clothing, fuel for the stoves or fireplace."

And yet, when people came to their door asking for food, his mother never turned anyone, black or white, away. "She would give them something to eat," he said, "such as it was."

He remarked, "There was no money for school lunches, but we were too proud to let anyone know how desperate our situation was."

Many times, neighbor would help neighbor.

A small family with two children who lived across from Jim

252

Clark in North Charlotte were obviously hungry after the father lost his job, so Jim's mother gave them eggs, buttermilk and milk to help sustain them.

Sometimes, the bond of helping one another took an interesting configuration. A Charlotte attorney who lived in a fine home "uptown," Zeke Henderson had purchased in 1926 what his son described as "a hundred acres of worn out red clay south of the city."

David H. Henderson remembers that, with the stock market bust, went his father's prosperous law practice. "This proud man was forced, hat in hand, to ask the note-holder for delay in paying the interest on the home mortgage."

The major-domo of the farm he called "Scalybark," was Walter Mitchell, whom David describes as "big, black and with a boisterous laugh." The Hendersons and Mitchells soon became intertwined. "With wife Viola and a handful of 'chirren,' we made two families into one. With no cash money, the farm became a way of sustenance."

David had to sacrifice, too. "My saddle horse was pressed into harness to pull a plow for the garden. Everybody: boy, girl, white, black, big or little spent time in the summer chopping weeds, planting, picking, slicing and helping with the canning."

Eventually, the government stepped in with commodity foods.

Thelma Percival Kube of Edgefield County, South Carolina, knew that people from her community could get commodities from the government at the Red Hill schoolhouse: mostly cheese, butter, flour, peanut butter and sugar.

Julia Neal Sykes of Gaston County was aware of government commodities coming through the schools. Through the NYA program, she was paid to prepare food in the cafeteria for school children who qualified. She recalls opening large cans of pinto beans and giving out cereal and bread during the late '30s.

During the strikes, mill workers were told that the union would feed them. Sometimes they got flour, sugar, molasses and other commodities, but, according to Betty Miller Hinson, whose family worked at the Eagle Mill in Belmont, occasionally the people would go only to find out that the food hadn't arrived—or it would have run out.

In the cities, the Salvation Army or another charitable organization would have soup kitchens or bread lines. In Charlotte, say Jack Wood and John Gill, the Salvation Army worked out of

O'Donohue School across from the the Court House. Men would be asked to split wood out front before they came in to eat.

People had pride back then, they didn't want handouts, the group from Charlotte agreed. "But some waited until dark so they wouldn't have to cut wood," said John Gill. "So they put up lights out there."

"Sometimes we'd go down to the train yards and sit and watch the trains come in and the hobos hop off," Jack Wood recalled.

"They'd go to homes and beg around the railroad tracks of Belmont," said Betty Hinson.

"They'd come to your back door, ask for the lady of the house and say, 'For a meal, I'll do anything for you. Split wood, whatever,'" remembered John Williams, who was from Yadkin County. "One time, my mother did the wash by hand in our backyard for a family of four."

John Gill of Charlotte saw the men hopping off trains, too. "Every boxcar had people on top or inside. After a while, the police wouldn't let them get off. But people who'd ride those trains were good, honest people looking for a job."

He and Jack Wood spoke of the "hobo jungle" near the tracks that crossed Pecan Avenue, where men lived in the woods and empty boxcars on the side tracks.

"They had an ethical community," said Joy Smith Burton, who grew up in Charlotte, too.

Lewis Diggle, who was 20 years old when the Depression hit, had another image of the Seaboard railroad line which ran behind Pecan and Central Avenues. "Firemen threw coal out of the tender," he said. "It cost 50 cents a bag for your furnace, but you could get it a piece at a time there."

Among the many who left town to make a living, Lewis joined the Navy. "I got $30 a month and three meals a day."

Cleo Templeton Gullick recalls the situation in Iredell County: "Many lost their homes in the towns and cities. They had to move back to farms and live in rental shacks or with their families."

Susan ("Susie") Stevenson Griffin's family were living in a rented apartment in Charlotte, but when her father's fortunes changed, she had to leave town.

"Daddy worked for the Ford plant, and the plant closed, so he didn't have a job. My sister and I went to live with our grandparents in Blackstock, South Carolina. She was in the sixth grade and I was in the third. There were two grades in each room.

We had a lot of fun and moved back to Charlotte after Daddy got another job."

A few people made money unscrupulously during the Depression. For every dollar they made, someone lost an equal amount—or much more.

Several North Carolinians reported the story of the prominent politician who married a millionaire widow. He lent money to farmers, foreclosed on their lands and, thus, put huge properties together.

Medical Insurance: Stay Well
A
Compilation

From Marshville, a North Carolina town of 2,500, one physician served the entire community, according to Lexie Little Hill. But the lack of money forced most people to suffer through their illnesses. "Since children received their smallpox and diphtheria shots at school, I was 15 before I saw a doctor."

Lexie's family got their medical care from "Dr. Mom." "Mama had home remedies to take care of most illnesses. For coughs and colds, Mama rubbed my chest with Musterole or Vick's salve, covered it with a warm flannel cloth and sent me to bed. If the coughs were accompanied with a fever, she spread foul-smelling mustard on the flannel cloth. For infections, she placed fatback over whatever was infected and wrapped it with a cloth. Potato, scraped into a pulp over a burn, soon eliminated the pain."

As Lexie got off the school bus one afternoon, she saw the bright red and black sign on her front door with the words "Quarantine-Scarlet Fever" in bold letters.

Diphtheria, scarlet fever and tuberculosis were so feared that victims were kept isolated and quarantined until the doctor verified the recovery. Those with TB were sent to a hospital near Asheville (Oteen) and forced to stay until they were cured or died.

Lexie's brother Norris, fortunately, was the only one in their home with scarlet fever, but everyone in the family was put under what Lexie termed "house arrest."

According to Joseph Grogan of Winston-Salem, "Any nerve or mental problem was kept secret. People didn't discuss their problems." He was aware that both men and women committed suicide because of huge debts and that there were many crippled children. "Health care was way down the list, and people couldn't take care of themselves."

"I'm almost sure some of the children's illnesses and deaths were due to malnutrition," attests Helen McDade Linder who lived in the Erlanger mill village in Davidson County.

"Dr. Moms" everywhere had their own remedies.

"We stayed in bed if we had fever and gargled with salt and soda," said Margaret Ashburn McInvaill of Forsyth County. "Sometimes they'd cook onions, wrap them in a cloth and put them on the feet to get rid of a fever. They did that to my little brother, and he got well."

Tunk Ancrum from Spartanburg, who had both rickets and worms as a child, says that drugstore medicines weren't easily affordable, and sassafras tea was often used as a laxative. He eventually realized that "Eat this; it's good for you" meant that it would make you go to the bathroom.

Eloise Bogen Shavitz of Nash and Wake Counties recalls the use of baking soda, vinegar and water for heartburn, talcum powder for cuts.

Carter Goldsborough, who lived in Raleigh, regularly drank a mixture of vinegar and honey for a variety of maladies and sometimes because it was "good for what ails you." As soon as he left home, he never touched another drop of castor oil for a "spring clean-out," but whenever he felt a sty coming on, he rubbed the back of his gold watch on the sty, and it would disappear.

From Darlington County, Cleo Alford Yongue remembered midwives and doctors coming to homes when a mother went into labor. "The doctor bill was $5 to deliver my babies," she added.

A farmer's daughter from Iredell County, Cleo Templeton Gullick knew of only one family doctor—a local boy who had managed to get through school and set up an office in his father's living room.

As for health care from the medical community, Lucille Michaels Nash of Belmont still wonders why her mother, who died of bladder and uterine cancer in 1932, went all the way to Rutherford to get radium treatments, when a Charlotte hospital was closer.

Julia Neal Sykes, also from Gaston County, told of a nurse, Bertha Davidson, who worked at Charlotte's Good Samaritan Hospital, treating the minor ailments of a lot of people in her home. "Several black doctors from Charlotte made weekly visits to Belmont," she added. As children, she and her friends were vaccinated for smallpox only. "You went through measles, mumps and whooping cough."

Students from Reid High School in Gastonia were sent to the clinic downtown to be tested for a venereal disease when Julia was in the seventh grade. Hers came back positive! She and her parents were devastated. Scared and confused, she had no idea how she got it. The test results were erroneous and future tests came back negative, but the doctor accused her of taking some kind of medication to "foul up" all the rest of the tests.

"I cried, when he talked so ugly to me," Julia said. "I told my daddy and he ordered me not to go back."

Lois Moore Yandle, who grew up near Highland Park Mills in Mecklenburg County, recalls a social worker/nurse, who would come around to check on children and put up quarantine signs when necessary.

Edna Garibaldi Soldati was glad that Charlotte's Nalle Clinic had doctors who would make house calls. She had 29 diseases, including two surgeries, as a child.

Charlottean Elizabeth Barkalow Shuman says that dental care was provided in the schools and points out that the Health Department had doctors and nurses available.

The first county health care in Edgefield, South Carolina, began in 1934, when there was an epidemic of typhoid fever, says Thelma Percival Kube. "Doctors and nurses traveled around the county immunizing people."

Daniel "Clyde" Lisk, Jr. tells of another side of Charlotte's health system: "My father ran a pharmacy on Belmont Avenue and another on Hoskins Road. He could not afford a druggist's salary to relieve him, so he would ride the streetcar back and forth to fill all the doctors' prescriptions himself. So many of his customers fell behind on their bills that he sent out a letter to notify them that he would forgive their past-due bills if they would continue to use his pharmacy and pay cash. Many did this—and some, in years later, would come pay those past-due bills."

When asked about medical care in his rural South Carolina county, Bob Edmonds of McCormick said, "You are joking! We had none. The first time I went to a doctor was for a military physical."

Like many Carolinians, Jack Wood had a family physician who was a friend. Like other doctors, he probably got food or various valuables instead of much cash. "He even made house calls," said Jack. "He hoped to get paid."

257

Roosevelt and the Rainbow
by
Margaret G. Bigger

Everyone who has spoken to me about that day mentioned the rainbow.

Franklin Delano Roosevelt was, to most Southerners, the savior of America's economy, the deliverer from degradation. Even his detractors had to admit that the President's New Deal had changed the course of history (and many people's way of life) for the better. And so, when it was announced that President Roosevelt would come to Charlotte, the hero worshippers rejoiced—and WPA workers hurried to finish Memorial Stadium in time for his visit on September 10, 1936 at the Green Pastures Rally.

Attorney H. Haywood Robbins, the organizer of the event, wrote in the program that it was for the "people of the new and progressive South." He praised the residents of the seven sponsoring states (Alabama, Florida, Georgia, North Carolina, South Carolina, Tennessee and Virginia) for their "new spirit of progress and mutual helpfulness" and for cooperating in the "magnificent struggle out of the Depression." He noted the progressiveness of this section of the country. According to another local leader, Cameron Shipp, "The idea was born in admiration and faith and gratitude for Franklin D. Roosevelt and his New Dealings."

Not touted as a campaign speech or a Democratic rally, it was, indeed, conveniently scheduled as a 1936 election kick-off.

Why "Green Pastures" Rally? The day after Robbins made the initial announcement in early March, J.E. Dowd wrote an editorial in *The Charlotte News* that, to be a success, the meeting must have a name. "Robbins makes us think of Spring. Spring makes of think of Green Grass; green grass makes us think of-Eureka! There it is! The Green Pastures...It's a natural!"

According to *The Charlotte Observer*, 100,000 people welcomed the President to the city. The day had been dark. The President's motorcade from Asheville had been delayed, so he was an hour late. Despite being soaked by rain, his admirers waited to cheer for him.

Before he proclaimed how the South and the nation were seeing prosperity restored and purchasing power increased without the infringement of states' rights or individual liberties, Roosevelt exclaimed, "There's a rainbow in the sky!"

Indeed, the symbol of hope and a sunny future shone above.

The President's platform and crowd at the Green Pastures Rally in Charlotte's Memorial Stadium on September 10, 1936. Photo by Jerre Caldwell Whitsett. From the H. Haywood Robbins Papers, Special Collections, UNC Charlotte Library.

Reasons/Recovery
A
Summary *

For readers who did not live through the Great Depression and those who have read only selected stories by the ones who did, we offer a brief overview of the reasons why it occurred and how it ended. Keep in mind that the Great Depression was nationwide, and even worldwide, but we are concentrating on the Carolinas' Piedmont.

Farmers and their families in this region remember being poor long before the stock market crashed in 1929. They had good and bad years, but weather—and, in cotton country, the boll weevil—caused their debts to go unpaid. Even landowners generally borrowed to buy seed, fertilizer and equipment and paid with interest after harvest. Store owners often sold on credit. If their customers couldn't pay, they, too, were in trouble. So were the banks.

Meanwhile, mill owners were making more profits and producing more goods, but not passing along their good fortunes in higher pay. People with low-paying jobs were unable to buy the excess products available.

Because the stock market had been soaring (the average price doubled from 1925-29), ordinary wage-earners were buying on margin, expecting huge profits. Instead, after the crash, they owed huge debts. Banks and business owners had also invested in stocks.

The trickle-down effect magnified the problem, as businesses called in their debts or shut down. Mortgages were forfeited and farm prices dropped even lower. Jobs were lost. Many of the "lucky ones" who still were employed took pay-cuts. When families lost their homes, they doubled up with others or took to the roads. Some teenagers and men seeking work took to the rails.

Banks were failing at an alarming rate. In a panic, depositors were withdrawing their savings, causing more banks to become unstable.

President Herbert Hoover expected state governments to take care of their own people, but they, too, had financial problems. In the Carolinas, state salaries had been cut and South Carolina began paying in scrip. Hoover's one major effort, the Reconstruction Finance Corporation (RFC), helped by lending money to banks, railroads and large institutions.

When Franklin Delano Roosevelt accepted the Democratic presidential nomination in 1932, he pledged "a new deal for the

American people." He was inaugurated on Saturday, March 4, 1933. On Sunday, he called Congress into an emergency session. Among other things, they gave him the power to call a bank holiday, which was announced in the Monday newspapers. Auditors were sent into all national banks to determine solvency. North Carolina and South Carolina declared a holiday for state banks as well. By mid-March the holidays were lifted, and the solvent banks re-opened. The others had to restructure or remain closed.

FDR's New Deal, designed during a special session of Congress called the Hundred Days in 1933, started the turnaround. Three federal programs put unemployed Americans to work creating what we now call "infrastructure."

Older teenagers and young men could enlist in the Civilian Conservation Corps (CCC). They were issued uniforms, fed in mess halls and housed in barracks. In addition to food and lodging, they earned $30 a month, most of which was sent to their families.

Generally, the CCC was assigned to conservation and refor-estation projects in state or national parks. They would clean creeks, fill gullies to stop erosion, do minor repairs on bridges, build paths and campsites, construct dams, plant trees and put out forest fires.

The Public Works Administration (PWA) gave jobs to construct bridges, dams and schools. In 1935, the Works Progress Administration (WPA), which was later known as the Work Projects Administration, allowed local authorities to decide what projects should be done by WPA workers. Women who were designated as "economic family heads" were included in the workforce. Ideally, the workers would learn new skills, preparing them for private employment.

The majority of the men worked on highways (farm-to-market roads), construction jobs or sanitation projects. Eliminating the need for outhouses, according to health officials, would dramatically decrease the spread of infectious diseases.

Women were given "more suitable" tasks, like distributing surplus commodities, making garments to be given out by local welfare departments or assisting with school lunches. Some did clerical or cleaning jobs.

In North Carolina, there was an emphasis on recreation. According to George W. Coan, Jr., the state administrator, recreation brings people together and gives a sense of community. The WPA funded theater, music, arts and writing programs. The NC and SC Writers' Projects are best known for the legacy of cata-loguing county archives, historical records and the demographics of counties and cities as well as doing oral history interviews.

As of 1937, North Carolina had 206 recreational programs underway and completed (or in progress) the construction of 304 tennis courts, 9 golf courses, 19 gymnasium, 37 school athletic fields, 23 armories (to also be used for community events), a stadium and athletic field for NC State College, as well as swimming pools for African Americans in Raleigh, High Point, Durham, Winston-Salem and Greensboro.

In Charlotte, WPA laborers built the first runway of what became Douglas International Airport (the original hangar is still in use as the Carolinas Aviation Museum). A PWA grant created Charlotte Memorial Hospital, now Carolinas Medical Center. New Deal workers built Memorial Stadium and took down the old US Branch Mint in downtown Charlotte and re-assembled it in suburban Eastover as the Mint Museum of Art.

In South Carolina's Piedmont, WPA workers built Spartanburg's Duncan Park and a football stadium at Pine Street School. Civil Works Administration (CWA) laborers helped build the Municipal Stadium in Greenville, the American Legion Club House in Spartanburg and the Laurens Airport. The CCC developed Table Rock State Park, Paris Mountain and other parks in the Piedmont.

The National Youth Administration (NYA) gave part-time jobs to needy high school and college students, with the purpose of keeping them in school and out of the main labor market. Money was given to the school administrators, who would assign tasks to the students. In some Piedmont communities, the NYA established training programs to teach boys no longer in school certain marketable skills such as carpentry (including how to construct a house).

Meanwhile, the Federal Emergency Relief Administration (FERA) gave states money to help the needy. FERA distributed surplus foods, assessed needs, assisted the poor and gave jobs through the short-lived CWA.

The South Carolina Emergency Relief Administration (SCERA) is credited with saving thousands from starvation. A fourth of that state's citizens went on relief.

Another cluster of federal programs aimed to cut overproduction on the farm and in the factory.

The Agricultural Adjustment Administration (AAA) was the most effective. By paying farmers to take land out of production, the AAA succeeded in boosting farm prices. The "allotment" system doubled tobacco and cotton farmers' income its first year and remained in effect for over six decades.

In 1933, the National Recovery Administration (NRA) set up a code of a 40-hour workweek at 30 cents an hour. But it was not a guarantee, and the textile code did not outlaw speed-ups or stretch-outs.

Despite mill owners' promises, textile workers found pay envelopes even emptier than before, and during the Strike of 1934, mill hands walked out across the South in America's largest job action ever.

The National Guard was called out in both Carolinas, and there were many violent incidents, some resulting in serious injury or death. In Anderson County, South Carolina, seven strikers died.

The strike was quickly broken by mill owners, but it helped push Congress to pass the 1938 Fair Labor Standards Act, which mandated the first US minimum wage (25 cents an hour) and established first the 44-hour and, by 1940, the 40-hour workweek, allowing longer hours at "time-and-a-half."

Some say that, after strikes during the early '30s in the two Carolinas turned violent with the help of outsiders, both the mill owners and the workers were more determined to work out their differences without the help of unions.

Rural Carolinians point out other programs particularly beneficial to them: the Rural Electrification Administration, Federal Housing Administration, and the Farmers Home Administration.

The REA brought electricity to areas where it was not feasible for power companies to serve. Farmers banded together to form co-ops, which could get low-interest loans after turning in an engineer's plan, survey and cost study. Successful co-ops expanded, and small towns picked up on the idea.

Electricity not only improved the quality of life but also the efficiency of farming. With power came refrigeration, water pumps, and lights for chicken houses (to fool the hens into laying more eggs during "daylight"). And electrical power brought small factories and new jobs into rural areas.

Some communities expanded the concept to form telephone co-ops, but REA funding dried up during World War II.

The Federal Housing Administration insured mortgages for private homes and rental housing and insured loans to improve property. If the property owner could get a 4 3/4% loan, he would pay 5% interest. The remainder went into a reserve pool to pay off forfeited loans.

The Farmers Home Administration was a boon to former sharecroppers and other small farmers, who could get credit and practical assistance. This agency of the Department of Agriculture set up offices in Piedmont counties for a rural development program with a college-trained agent to teach agriculture and management skills, a clerk to keep detailed records on each family's expenses, production and inventory, and a home economist to show how to preserve meats, can garden vegetables and dry fruits and even how to dig a milk well or build a milk house to retard spoilage of dairy products. The main purpose of the agent was to help families to learn how to manage their farm as a business.

The capstone of the New Deal, in the eyes of Roosevelt and many historians, was the 1935 Social Security Act. It granted pensions to the elderly and the disabled.

As confidence in the federal government grew, business and industry geared up, and more jobs became available. But just as life in the United States was improving, a recession began in 1937 and went into 1938. Roosevelt's programs were being criticized as wasteful and costly, putting the country into debt. Many of the make-work jobs were termed "trivial" and expenditures "boondoggling."

Without enough taxes to cover expenses, the federal government sold bonds. By 1939, the federal debt was more than $40 million. As late as 1940, eight million Americans still had no jobs.

Although the Democratic Party was stronger than it had been since the Civil War, with the new support of African Americans, unions and reformers, President Roosevelt was losing popularity.

The recession showed that the New Deal was not the total solution to the multi-faceted problem.

Simultaneously, the country was facing another danger. Could it be that a new fear would hasten an upturn in the economy?

With war raging in Europe and rumors of war circulating in the United States, the WPA and other agencies designed more projects involving war preparations even before December 7, 1941.

Camp Jackson was being transformed into Fort Jackson near Columbia, South Carolina. Construction was also underway for air bases in Lexington and Sumter Counties in South Carolina and at Fort Bragg, North Carolina.

A selective service act was passed in 1940, putting more young men on the government payroll and in the military.

While many national leaders were isolationists, the government was taking precautions and making plans for the inevitable.

After the Day of Infamy, both government and industry shifted into high gear to build resources for the war effort. Employment opportunities—and pay—increased dramatically. And as the men joined the military, women took their places in the job market.

By 1942, the Great Depression was over.

* Dr. Tom Hanchett and John Williams contributed to this summary.

Edgar, Walter. *South Carolina, A History*. Columbia: University of South Carolina Press, 1998. pp. 499-510.

So, What Was *Really* Important?
A
Compilation

What if there is another Depression? Heaven forbid, but this is not beyond the realm of possibility. The big question is: What lessons can we pass on to future generations?

The answer: Probably the ones passed along by our own parents, which we took to heart only half-heartedly, our children rejected, and our grandchildren have never even heard!

These common adages should be memorized and followed:

Waste not, want not.

Don't put all your eggs in one basket.

If you really want something, save for it.

A penny saved is a penny earned.

Save something for a rainy day.

Make do with what you have.

These "saving" lessons can be taken to extremes, however. A woman who grew up in Gaston County is a typical example of compulsive saving, so prevalent when money was scarce. She never threw anything away that was not garbage, assuming she would find uses for them. And, like Abraham Lincoln, she wrote notes on the backs of old envelopes.

Fortunately, as she grew older, she got a larger home.

Her son laughed at his mother's obsession until his wife was in charge of decorations for a dance. When she stopped by her mother-in-law's house to get some roses, she asked what to use to keep the roses fresh in 30 dainty baskets. The elderly woman stepped down into her basement and brought up 30 little tin cans exactly the right size.

When it came time to help her break up housekeeping, her family realized that she really had carried saving to the point of absurdity. In the attic, among other odd collections of what we would call trash, were suit box after suit box full of florists' tinfoil, flattened out and stored. In the basement were multiple cans of used rusty nails and numerous containers of burned-out light bulbs. Her son secretly carted ten van loads to a Dumpster.

Then they found a box full of train schedules from long-defunct railroads all over the country, dating from the 1920s. Paper memorabilia, they discovered, is very valuable, especially if the company is now out-of-business. So are really old appliances and the brochures that came with them. Flea market buyers were delighted.

Since then, her family members have become "selective savers."

We should hope that our grandchildren will discover that you don't have to have a Nintendo, a TV, the internet or the latest commercially-hyped battery-operated toy to have fun. Perhaps they will learn to play some of the games described by our authors, for even the poorest of children during the Depression found ways to "make" fun!

The one dominant theme throughout this collection of life-experience history, however, is the importance of three "f-words" — family, friends and faith.

Family members and close friends stood by you, fed and took care of you, cheered you through failures and successes and, at times, let you live with them.

Visiting relatives and friends were major pastimes.

When asked what her family did for leisure and recreation, Lucille Michaels Nash, who was raised in Belmont, wrote in large capital letters: "CHURCH."

And as Helen McDade Linder of North Carolina's Davidson County put it, "The church played an important part in our lives—provided some of our social activities, too!"

At Nancy Artemus Gough's Baptist church in Columbia, South Carolina, education and high-class music were emphasized. "Our pastor came from Morehouse College and was a professor at Benedict College," she explained and then added, "Everyone in the neighborhood was white except at our church, Second Calvary. The people were very nice to us, though."

She particularly enjoyed hearing the fine music during the services and attending weekly Baptist Training Union meeting, where they got Christian education.

"At Hammond School, we got a Sunday school lesson from our teacher every Friday after big recess," said Fred Whitten of Anderson County, South Carolina. "Then on Sunday, we'd hear it again at our Presbyterian church."

He explained that, because people didn't have cars, they attended the nearest church. He and his neighbors, thus, were Presbyterian.

"Country churches didn't have money to pay a preacher, so one would come from town on Sunday afternoons, a couple of Sundays a month."

He then told how some families paid their pledge. "They'd

set aside a plot of land—'God's little acre' and give the church the proceeds."

"Our church was usually full, even though people didn't have cars," remembered Cato Coleman from Newberry, South Carolina. "Church always had its impact, as imperfect as it is," he said. "If there were no church in a town, I wouldn't want to live there."

"My dad helped build our church (Mount Zion Reformed Church near China Grove)," said Marvin Sechler of Rowan County, North Carolina. "As large as our family was, we all went every Sunday—filled up a whole pew. Sometimes we had dinner on the grounds." He also told of a summer children's program at which they taught music. "I never did learn to read music," he admitted, even though he spent much of his young adult years picking and singing country music.

Thelma Percival Kube writes, "People of Edgefield County had a great reverence for the Lord and accepted whatever was God's will. They also feared His wrath and considered the Depression punishment. There came about community awareness, camaraderie and neighbor helping neighbor."

"A family in our church came down with scarlet fever. No one would go near them, terrified of getting the disease. My mother, Maude Percival, went and cared for them. My dad, Milton, met her at the barn with Lysol for her to bathe herself and her clothes, so she wouldn't give the disease to us. She was a real Christian. Two women in our neighborhood died in her arms."

In Charlotte's Greenville neighborhood, where Thereasea Clark Elder lived, church bells rang when someone needed help. "We took care of each other like Hospice," she said. "Church members would gather around like caring friends, even sitting up all night with someone who was dying. Children would see that the fire was kept going. When the person passed away, someone would ring the bells at that family's church (one of 13 in our community), so others would come to clean the house and bring food."

How did her family (a widow with ten children) cope? "'With the help of God,' my mother always said," recalled Margaret Homesley Marrash from Cherryville, North Carolina.

David G. Kelly of Mecklenburg County summarized what most of his contemporaries alluded to: "We had our church and faith in God that strengthened us and brought us through those terrible times."

Index

About the Editor

Since 1989, Margaret Bigger, the author of *Recalling Your Memories on Paper, Tape or Videotape,* has taught senior citizens how to get their memories on paper in courses and seminars sponsored by Queens College, Central Piedmont Community College, Shepherd's Center and Elderhostel as well as libraries, senior centers and retirement centers in three states.

Under her guidance, her students have written the trade paperbacks,*World War II: It Changed Us Forever, Prohibition Didn't End in '33 , Gray-Haired Grins & Giggles* and *Kitties & All That Litter.* The first two were commissioned by the J. Murrey Atkins Library of UNC at Charlotte.

She is best known, however, for her wedding humor books, *There's No Such Thing as a Perfect Wedding* and *You've GOT to Have a Sense of Humor to Have a Wedding.* These earned her appearances on 11 national TV shows (including Sally Jesse Raphael, Maury Povich and EXTRA—The Entertainment Magazine), more than 450 radio shows and at least 60 TV interviews throughout the U.S.

All of her books are collections of true stories or funny lines. For this book, Bigger departed from her humor collections to return to life-experience history. This is her 18th title. Her others are: *Only Forty Miles of Pavement* (with J. Carter Goldsborough), *Equaling Excellence,* the Biography of Oliver Reagan Rowe, *Small Church with a BIG Mission* (with Katherine M. Dunlap), *You Can Tell You're a Charlottean If..*(with Betsy Webb), *You Know You're in Charlotte If.., MEN! Cry Flustered, Frustrated Females Everywhere, Churchgoers' Chuckles, MotherHoot - The Lighter Side of Motherhood* and *DaddyHoot - The Lighter Side of Fatherhood.*

She is currently seeking more humorous anecdotes for *ParentHoot,* a wedding "threquel," *TeacherHoot, Churchgoers' Chuckles, Vol. II, Kitties & All That Litter, Vol. II, Puppies & All That Waggin'* and *But Not for Lunch* (about retirement years).

A popular speaker, Margaret Bigger has been featured at numerous conventions, writers' workshops, author luncheons and business seminars. This '61 UNC-Chapel Hill graduate has lectured to classes at UNC-CH and six college in Virgina. She is currently available to do "Recalling Memories for Posterity" seminars and humor talks. Bigger can be contacted through A. Borough Books.

About the Illustrator

"There *is* life after 50," attests Lexie Little Hill.

Her years of raising children were filled with responsibilities of such magnitude that she had little time for thoughts of "frivolous" activities. Later, when the children left home, she found loneliness from an empty house. "I realized I must change my focus," says Hill. "My decision to learn oil painting changed my life and became my focus."

Consumed with a passion, she learned everything she could, studying and attending classes on drawing and oil painting.

Although, according to Hill, her sister was the artist in the family, she had displayed her own artistic talent with basket weaving: the egg basket, hearth basket and square baskets with elaborate designs. She taught basket weaving and sold her handiwork in stores near her 150-year-old log home in Cabarrus County.

After her husband, Kemp, retired, she stumbled on a rather unique idea of using thin strips from pine boards that Kemp had cut on his table saw. She glued them on the canvas to form structures such as barns, sheds, or a mill or old covered bridge. By painting the background and sometimes the structures as well, she created images of the past, reminiscent of her youth on a Union County farm. Kemp Hill used his woodworking skills to frame her art.

Another favorite art form, according to fan letters, is her manner of painting farm scenes on antique saws.

From 1982-1989, she exhibited her work two or three times a year at the Spring and Christmas shows at Charlotte's Civic Center and others in Myrtle Beach, Burnsville, Raleigh and Augusta.

Then she took up poetry and writing, discovering more new talents. She wrote and illustrated *My Journey, A Backward Search Down a Long Road*, a book of memoirs for her family. Five of her humor stories (two of which appear in this volume) were published in the trade paperback, *Gray-Haired Grins & Giggles* by A. Borough Books in 1995. Her Great Depression story about WPA standing for "We Piddle Around" appeared in a *McCormick Messenger* article by Bob Edmonds, another of the authors in this book. Now in fourth printing, *Gray-Haired Grins & Giggles* came out in a Large Print Edition in 1998. Two years later, her story about Kemp's "driving attitude" was in A. Borough Book's *MEN! Cry Flustered Frustrated Females Everywhere*.

At 77, Hill continues to paint. As she says, "Life is good."

Pen and Ink Drawings by Lexie Little Hill

Other Illustrations

Vintage Photos

Miscellaneous

True-experience stories and anecdotes:

___copies *The Great Depression: How We Coped, Worked and Played* Life-experience stories from the Carolina's Piedmont
65 authors Illustrated by Lexie Little Hill
2001. 131 stories. 288 pp. ISBN:1-893597-04-0
Vintage photos and Index   Paperback @ $15.95 $_____

___copies *Gray-Haired Grins & Giggles*
Guess what - Grandy & Grammy have a sense of humor, too!
True tales from 45 authors. Cartoons by Loyd Dillon
1995. 160 tales. 128 pp. ISBN:0-9640606-3-9
4th printing 1996.   Paperback @ $12.95 $_____

___copies *Gray-Haired Grins & Giggles* LARGE PRINT
With the seal of approval of N.A.V.H.:
1998. ISBN:0-9640606-7-1   Paperback @ $13.95 $_____

___copies *World War II: It Changed Us Forever*
From the battlefront to the homefront and places in between
33 authors tell it like it was! Vintage photos and Index
1994. 93 stories. 140 pp. ISBN:0-9640606-0-4
3rd printing 2001.   Paperback @ $12.95 $_____

Bigger's guide to recording memoirs:

___copies *Recalling Your Memories on Paper, Tape or Videotape*
Self-help guide to preserving memoirs & photos. Also, how
to assist relatives. Excerpts from seniors' family booklets.
1996. 160 pp. ISBN:0-9640606-4-7
Vintage photos   Paperback @ $13.95 $_____

Bigger's humor books of regional one-liners:

___copies *You Can Tell You're a Charlottean If...*
244 ways that people from Charlotte, NC differ from the
rest of the world. Margaret Bigger & Betsy Webb
1998. 96 pp. ISBN:0-9640606-6-3
Cartoons by Loyd Dillon   Paperback @ $7.95 $_____

___copies *You Know You're In Charlotte If...*
90 contributors show the uniqueness of Charlotte
+ cute & clever business names & license plates
Charlotte celebrities & Local Sports History Quiz.
2000. 96 pp. ISBN 1-893597-03-2
Cartoons by Loyd Dillon   Paperback @ $7.95 $_____

Please complete the other side of this order form.

Bigger's collections of humorous anecdotes:
Humor makes great gifts - autographed & personalized!!!

___copies *MotherHoot - The Lighter Side of Motherhood*
True anecdotes about moms from pregnancy through grandmotherhood
+ MotherHoot Tips for Sanity Cartoons by Loyd Dillon
1999. 128 pp. ISBN 0-9640606-8-X Paperback @ $9.95 $_____

___copies *DaddyHoot - The Lighter Side of Fatherhood*
True anecdotes about dads from expectancy through grandfatherhood
+ DaddyrHoot Tips for Sanity   Cartoons by Loyd Dillon
2000. 112 pp. ISBN 0-9640606-9-8 Paperback @ $9.95 $_____

___copies *MEN! Cry Flustered Frustrated Females Everywhere*
True MALETALES, Givens & How Comes from 44 FFFs proving that
males don't think/act/talk like females. Cartoons by Loyd Dillon
2000. 96 pp. ISBN 1-893597-01-6 Paperback @ $7.50 $_____

___copies *Churchgoers' Chuckles*
True Tales - You Can't Make This Stuff Up! From 16
denominations and 30 states. Cartoons by Loyd Dillon
2000. 96 pp. ISBN 1-893597-02-4 Paperback @ $7.50 $_____

___copies *Kitties & All That Litter*
Mewsings, GRRRoaners, true cat tales and kitty limericks
by 26 cat-loving curmudgeons. Cat-tooned by Loyd Dillon
1999. 96 pp. ISBN 1-893597-00-8 Paperback @ $7.50 $_____

___copies *You've GOT to Have a Sense of Humor to*
Have a Wedding Humorous, outrageous & disastrous true tales
+ advice not found in wedding guides. Cartoons by Loyd Dillon
1997. 128 pp. ISBN 0-9640606-5-5 Paperback @ $9.95 $_____

Subtotal $_____
Discount   (20% for 10 or more)
NC residents must add 6.5% tax $_____
Postage & handling $3 for 1st 2 books
              +$1 more for each multiple of 5 $_____

               TOTAL $_____

Name_____ **Phone #**_____

Address_____

City, State, Zip_____

Mail check or money order to:
   A. Borough Books P.O. Box 15391, Charlotte, NC 28211

   Specify here how you want your books to be personalized: